For my wife Lisa and my children Maisie and Miles,
I am truly blessed to share my life with you.

AUTHOR'S NOTE

I have used soldiers' real names in this book when they have been published in the press, or whenever individual soldiers have indicated to me that they were happy for me to do so. I have been asked to use pseudonyms for some of the Special Forces and other elite operators still involved in sensitive operations, and have done so where appropriate. Otherwise, all aspects of this story remain as they took place on the ground.

I have done my utmost to ensure the accuracy of all the events portrayed herein. Few written records exist covering the events described in this book. Accordingly, I have recreated conversations from how I remember them and in discussions with the others who were involved. If anyone has a different recollection, I am happy to discuss and to amend in future editions if necessary.

I have been asked by the Ministry of Defence to include the following statement in this book: 'The views and opinions expressed herein are those of the author alone and should not be taken to represent those of Her Majesty's Government, MOD, HM Armed Forces or any government agency.'

Seems pretty obvious to me.

Still, ours not to reason why.

STEVE HEANEY MC
WITH DAMIEN LEWIS

X PLATOON

THE TRUE STORY OF AN ELITE BRITISH UNIT

An Orion paperback

First published in Great Britain in 2015
by Orion Books
This paperback edition published in 2016
by Orion Books Ltd,
Carmelite House, 50 Victoria Embankment,
London EC4Y 0DZ

An Hachette UK company

3 5 7 9 10 8 6 4 2

A CIP catalogue record for this book is available from the British Library.

ISBN 978 1 4091 4850 0

Typeset by Input Data Services Ltd, Bridgwater, Somerset

Printed and bound in Great Britain by
CPI Group (UK) Ltd, Croydon, CR0 4YY

The Orion Publishing Group's policy is to use papers that are natural, renewable and recyclable products and made from wood grown in sustainable forests. The logging and manufacturing processes are expected to conform to the environmental regulations of the country of origin.

www.orionbooks.co.uk

ACKNOWLEDGEMENT

I'm indebted to those people who have helped me with the detail for this book and to those who have encouraged me over the past twelve months to write it. In the course of doing so I have experienced a raft of emotions as I transported myself back through my early childhood and then to my life in the military, encompassing great laughter and sadness as I reflected on the good times in my life and then the heart-wrenching moments I felt at the loss or injury of fellow operators. I look back at my time in the military with tremendous affection and feel immensely honoured to have served alongside some of the finest men I have had the great privilege to know. I take nothing for granted and appreciate every opportunity the army has given me. I understand fully that it was this organization above all others that helped to shape and define the values I hold so strongly today, and for that I will be eternally grateful.

My family has been incredibly supportive during the development of the book and they will forever have my love and gratitude. Damien Lewis, my co-author and good friend, helped me piece together my memories and get them down on paper, whilst we blew the froth off a few beers. A special thanks to the team at Orion publishing in particular Alan Samson and Lucinda McNeile for their support and tireless efforts in making this book a success, and to my literary agent Annabel Merullo and her assistant Laura Williams for their advice and guidance. Thanks to film agent Luke Speed for representing this and my first book, *Operation Mayhem*.

A special thanks to General Sir Peter Wall GCB CBE for the Foreword to this book. I feel incredibly humbled at this tribute from an outstanding commander for whom I have nothing but the greatest of respect.

My greatest debt goes to my wife Lisa who has been steadfast in her support of me during the long days and nights I was sat behind my desk, and to my children Maisie and Miles who are now more than ever extremely interested in my life in the military and are asking very searching and often amusing questions.

Find out more about Steve Heaney at:
www.steveheaneymc.com

From this day to the ending of the world,
But we in it shall be remembered—
We few, we happy few, we band of brothers;
For he to-day that sheds his blood with me
Shall be my brother;

—William Shakespeare, *Henry V*

Success is not final, failure is not fatal:
it is the courage to continue that counts.

—Winston Churchill

I don't know what effect these men will have upon the enemy,
but, by God, they terrify me.

—The Duke of Wellington

FOREWORD

by General Sir Peter Wall GCB CBE
Chief of the General Staff, 2010-2014

Sergeant Steve Heaney, MC, late of the Parachute Regiment, treats us to his fascinating insights into life inside the Pathfinders – the leading element of our airborne and air assault forces.

The Pathfinders, in their modern guise, started as a 'Cinderella' organisation on the Army's 'black economy' in the mid-1980s. Their covert role was greatly enhanced by the fact that they didn't officially exist.

Having demonstrated the essential nature of their function, the Pathfinders are now clearly established in the Army's order of battle as a vital part of 16 Air Assault Brigade.

Still, very little is known about them and this book sheds some light on their evolution, and the way their reputation for excellence in the most exacting of situations has been earned.

It charts the selection procedures, the rigorous and exciting training regime, and their early operational experiences in Belize, Kosovo and Sierra Leone, where they came of age. The importance of their highly skilled contribution was recognised, and they became an essential part of any future deployment of the Brigade.

Ultimately the Army is all about its people. Heaney explains the characters that make the Platoon so special, and its appeal to young soldiers. He reveals the very high degree of personal ambition, self-belief and commitment needed to join their ranks. This is a story of mutual trust and how that is inculcated.

The book also recounts Steve Heaney's personal journey from mischievous, headstrong schoolboy in Middlesbrough to Pathfinder Platoon Sergeant, surely the most demanding platoon sergeant's job in the Army.

The story is told from the vantage point of a consummate professional, who took the fullest advantage of the challenge and opportunity offered by the Army, and in so doing shaped the future of the Pathfinders, as we know them today.

It's a great story told by a very special bloke with typical humility. I hope it inspires lots of young soldiers to follow in the author's footsteps – however daunting that may seem. Go for it! You will surprise yourselves. . . .

1

'Heaney – Red Route One!'

The voice belongs to one of the DS – Directing Staff – and I've just been given my marching orders.

I head for the truck marked 'Red One' – my allotted route for today, otherwise known as 'hell on earth'. Throwing my Bergen and weapon in ahead of me, I choose a space on the hard bench amongst the dozen-odd blokes likewise allotted to Red One.

The others will be setting out in separate trucks for 'Green One' and 'Blue One' – alternative launch-points for pretty much the same murderous circuit.

A few weeks back Selection had started with a hundred fit young guys from across the three services, each chasing the dream of joining this elite, mystery-enshrouded unit. We're into the 'Hills' stage now, and we're down to less than a fifth of that number.

Nineteen of us are left chasing our dream – the eighty-plus that we've lost falling victim to injury, or extreme physical and mental exhaustion.

Their dream has died.

Mine is still alive and kicking – but only just; like most of those around me, I'm hanging on by my fingernails.

The routine this morning was identical to those that went before: reveille at 0430; washed, shaved and breakfasted by 0445; armoury to collect your weapon at 0500; on parade on the square by 0515 to get your day's route and running order.

Those of us who remained had squatted on our haunches, resting our weight on our Bergens, as we were given the day's instructions. Each massive rucksack is fitted with a fluorescent orange safety panel. It's there to provide a visible marker for those who might be sent to find you if you get lost or injured on the unforgiving rain- and wind-blasted hills.

By the looks of the dark and evil clouds that are scudding across the sky, there is every chance of that kind of thing happening today. A thick halo of mist and rain is already swirling around the higher peaks of the Brecon Beacons.

Today's torture is known as the 'Point-to-Point' – a gruelling forced march 28 kilometres across the most unforgiving terrain of the British Isles. We have seven hours to complete it – the golden rule on Selection being that you have to average four kilometres an hour to pass, whether going uphill, downhill or on the flat, and regardless of the weather.

I must have done this route half a dozen times before. Practice, practice, practice is the secret. But contrary to popular belief this kind of thing never gets any easier the more you do it.

As I rest my aching, torn limbs on the hard bench of the truck – savouring the few moments' respite before it all begins again – I reflect on how this is the last day before the Big One, *Endurance*. Endurance is the final event of the Hills Phase, and the greatest single test of physical and mental robustness in the entire British military.

It's a sixty-four-kilometre forced march across the highest and most brutal terrain the Brecons have to offer. In theory, all I have to do is get through today and Endurance tomorrow, and I'll pretty much have done it – *I'll have passed Selection; I'll have won my dream.*

Because of the sheer length of the Endurance march and the incredible pressures placed upon the human body, the speed required to pass it is dropped to three kilometres an hour – which is about as close to a dollop of compassion as you'll ever get when attempting Selection.

I have a phrase that comes to mind for things that don't exactly compute, things that don't add up: 'things that make you go – *hmmm*'. Sitting here in this swaying truck as we approach the start of the Point-to-Point is definitely one of those moments.

We pull to a halt. The silence hangs suffocating and heavy in the semi-darkness. I stare out at the curtain of grey drizzle that has descended across the mountains. Whatever time of year, the Brecons are more or less permanently shrouded in the shittiest weather imaginable.

The conditions can switch in an instant. A wide patch of blue sky can rapidly transform itself into a glowering mass of sleet or snow, seemingly without warning. It's hardly surprising that civvies often get into serious trouble when walking these hills, and even guys attempting Selection have got injured or died up here.

We pile out, stiff limbs aching and groaning from the weeks of punishment.

The DS calls me forward and gives me the grid reference of my first checkpoint, seven kilometres away. I study my map, locate the grid, set the bearing on my compass and indicate with my gloved hand the direction I intend to take. The DS gives me a nod, issues the obligatory warning not to use any tracks or roads navigable by vehicle, then waves me on my way.

This first leg will take me to Spot Height 619, an isolated jumble of rocks marking a high-point in the terrain. It's seven klicks (kilometres) as the crow flies, but I'll need to allow for at least a further two as I traverse a huge re-entrant – an impassable V-shaped incline – that slashes across my route.

I allow one hour forty-five to get me to Spot Height 619, including time to complete the horrendous ups and downs.

By the time I'm approaching the checkpoint my gloves are wet through, my unfeeling fingers clamped to the cold metal of my weapon as if they're frozen solid. On Selection you have to keep your assault rifle gripped in your hands at all times, as if you are on a mission for real; as if you're poised to unleash hell at the slightest sign of the enemy.

I can feel the sores on my back smarting and weeping, from where the protective zinc oxide tape that I'd applied that morning has peeled away. The shoulder straps of my rucksack – my Bergen – have long ago rubbed me raw, leaving the flesh blistered, red and bloody.

But no matter how much you strap the lesions up with zinc oxide – medical – tape, each new murderous beasting under a crushing load rips them wide open again. That's just how it is. Better get used to it.

I get a much-needed morale boost as I locate the tiny fluorescent orange tent that houses the DS. They're camped out right beside Spot Height 619, and are snug in their maggots – military sleeping bags – despite the thin canvas of the tent flapping wildly in the wind. As long as it doesn't get blown away it'll keep them warm and dry – which is far from how I'm feeling right now.

I kneel before them, looking and feeling like a sodden mess, and check in: 'Heaney, Staff!'

The DS glances up from some semi-pornographic magazine he's been reading. *NUTS* or *FHM* – I'm too knackered and cold to register which. The expression on his face makes it crystal clear he'd far rather be ogling some pin-up's arse than speaking to the likes of me.

He indicates my map. 'Show me where you are, Heaney.'

'Here, Staff.'

He flicks a page on his glossy boys' mag. 'You certain?'

For the briefest of moments I wonder if I've screwed up. I double-check the map. 'Yes, Staff.'

He doesn't take his eyes off Cheryl. 'You absolutely sure?'

'Yes, Staff.'

He shrugs. There's the hint of a smile creasing his eyes. I know I'm in the right place. I know this is Spot Height 619. The guy is just trying to mess with my head. He eyes the desolate terrain, the wind whipping across the bog grass like a tsunami beating the ocean into a bloodied pulp.

His eyes fix on some distant point. 'Next grid – two nine zero four four three.'

I repeat it back to him: 'two nine zero four four three, Staff!'

It's the next checkpoint – Triangulation Point 642. I point it out to him on the map.

'Get going,' he tells me, as his fingers turn to his next favourite girl in the mag.

Triangulation Point 642 is a place that has been immortalised in elite forces' legend. It is a lonely concrete pillar, sitting atop a savage, sheer-sided chasm known as 'VW Valley'. VW stands for 'Voluntary Withdrawal' – the process via which any bloke has the right to pull off Selection at any time. Of those that we've lost a good number have 'VW'd' – VW Valley marking the breaking point for many a man's spirit and resolve.

I start out, shoulders hunched, face into the stinging, wind-whipped rain.

My route to VW Valley leads across a massive, high plateau of 'babies' heads' – clumps of gorse and bog grass about the size of a baby's head, hence the name. It's exhausting, ankle-twisting, backbreaking work, but somehow I make it to the point via which I plan to make my descent into the abyss – into VW Valley itself.

As I gaze into Mordor, rain sheets in thick curtains across the dark and desolate emptiness, blocking out all view of the valley floor far below. I half expect to see a horde of orcs and cave trolls swarming out of the swirling mists, looking to feast on my bones.

As none appear, I figure I'd better start my descent.

There are only two possible routes into VW Valley: this one, which is extremely steep but doable, or a lesser gradient a further two kilometres along. I don't have the time to leg it to the easier descent, so it's this way or no way.

As I study the route ahead, one thing is clear to me: the slope is slick with run-off. It casts a dull, slithering skein of silver across everything. The terrain is so waterlogged that excess liquid is seeping up from below, pooling like a river, and flowing in sheets across the surface of the hillside.

This run-off is a far greater danger than the Dark Lord and his orcs and cave trolls. It will make for doubly treacherous going. I'll be climbing down a near-vertical wall of grass that is slick with freezing-cold water. But right now if I want to finish Point-to-Point this is my only option.

I take the first step; step one of a massive descent, heading for the Old Roman Road that snakes along the valley floor far, far below.

As I start to crab my way downwards, I use my upper leg like an anchor as the lower one feels for the next foothold. Because I have to carry my weapon at all times in a way that makes me ready to open fire, I can't use it as a makeshift walking stick. Plus I can't use my hands to aid my descent, for they're gripping my weapon.

To be seen doing either by the ever-watchful DS would mean an instant fail.

As I slip and slither downwards, my 45lb Bergen twists around agonisingly. Each step threatens to unseat me, as my boots fight to keep a grip on the slick, oily grass. I dig in my heels and my side-grip, trying to cut steps into the sodden earth, as inch by inch I lower myself towards the relative safety of the valley floor.

And then I make the fatal mistake: I try to shift my weight onto my upper leg, so as to be able to lift the lower one, and a split second later my feet shoot out from under me. It all happens in the barest instant, and my balance is totally gone before I even realise what's happened.

The weight of my Bergen slams me into the wet grass. It's like a sheet of ice, and my legs go flying up in front of my face. Stunned and winded by the force of the fall, I find myself sliding downhill like an upended tortoise . . . and rapidly gaining momentum.

With my rifle gripped in one hand the other claws at the grass, desperately. I try to anchor myself, but all that happens is that water mixed with torn vegetation sprays up from my gloved fingers.

Frantically, I try to dig the talon in deeper, but it just rips away the sodden moss and mud, shit spraying all over me. It does nothing much to slow my fall.

For a good fifty yards I plummet. I'm falling faster and faster towards the valley floor, and there's nothing I can do to halt my progress.

It's then that I fly into the open air.

I shoot off the end of a steep slope and suddenly I'm in freefall.

It feels like I'm tumbling earthwards for a lifetime, but in reality it can only be a matter of seconds.

I land with a sickening, jarring crunch.

My back takes the brunt of the impact. I come to a halt wedged into a fold in the ground, daggers of pain shooting up my spine and into my brain. Worse still, I can't seem to feel my legs or my arms any more.

I lie there for what seems like an age, water cascading onto me from the slope above, and my breath coming in short, sharp, agonising gasps. I'm in a world of hurt right now, but from all my medical training I know that I should stay absolutely still. Any movement could worsen a spinal injury – and I don't doubt that my back is badly hurt.

As the seconds become minutes, I realise that the feeling is gradually coming back into my legs and my arms, and that I still have movement in them. The more I concentrate on the pain, the more it seems to be localised in my lower back region.

I decide to risk rolling onto my side, so I can loosen the straps of my Bergen, get out of it and attempt to stand.

It takes me ten minutes of sheer agony to do so – which just goes to show how bad my injury is. I struggle to my feet, waves of pain and nausea sweeping over me, and try to take stock of my situation.

I've lost a good fifteen minutes already. Any chance of passing Selection is rapidly eluding me. More to the point, this is fast becoming a survival situation: how the hell am I going to get myself off this mountain, semi-crippled as I now am?

Blasts of agony burn through me. I try to block them out. Now is decision time. Has the fall pushed me to the limit, the injury bringing me to my breaking point? Or can I somehow carry on with Selection; can I somehow keep the dream alive?

The pain in my back is worsening, and the whole area is stiffening up. I decide to break the cardinal rule of Selection, by pushing my Bergen ahead of me and using my weapon as a walking stick, as I try to press on down the treacherous slope.

Gritting my teeth I inch forwards, but each step is sheer bloody torture.

2

We had to make our own entertainment where I grew up as a kid, in the industrial heartland of North East England. From my earliest memories that meant doing the opposite of what I was told.

I was the kind of toddler who'd climb into the washing machine, or hang upside down behind the door to give Mum a fright. If she thought school would knock some sense into me, she was bitterly disappointed. You know those kids who sit at the back of the class, lobbing missiles at the teacher?

That was me.

I grew up in Middlesbrough, the first town in Britain to have the shit bombed out of it in the Second World War, when the Luftwaffe attacked the local steelworks. By the time I came along, in 1969, the steel was still being churned out, plus chemical works dotted the skyline. An acrid haze hung over the place, the local football team being branded the 'Smoggies' by rival fans.

I hadn't been at primary school long before one of my first teachers, Mrs Witkins, decided I was not 'academically inclined'. Mrs Witkins was a kindly, sixty-year-old woman with grey hair and glasses. But the most striking thing about her was that at 4' 8" tall, she wasn't much bigger than most of my classmates.

And that made her an easy target for pranks and wind-ups.

I would sit at the back of the class with my best buddy, Sam 'Simmo' Simpson, tearing up bits of paper and smothering them with spittle, to make chewed-paper cannonballs. Whenever Mrs Witkins' back was turned we'd launch them at her with little flicks of our rulers.

After a while our aim got really good and we started scoring direct hits. We covered ourselves in glory in the eyes of our classmates, an ill-disciplined bunch who thought it was the funniest thing ever.

But one day Mrs Witkins turned round just as the two of us were doing a pincer movement and firing simultaneously. She not only dodged the missiles, but she wiped the grins off our faces by sending us to the headmaster's office. But the head was away on some training scheme, and so we got Mr Byrne, the temporary stand-in, instead – a guy with a fearsome appearance.

Mr Byrne summoned the entire school to the assembly hall. The other kids sat on the floor with slack-jawed anticipation – *what horrors might Mr Byrne serve up?* – while I was marched to the front with Simmo. We stood there, heads bowed, awaiting our punishment like condemned men.

'Take a long look at these two,' Mr Byrne declared, evilly. Hundreds of children gawped. 'They thought it was clever to disrupt their class. It wasn't. It was very, very stupid.'

A long pause for effect. 'Now, in case any of you are tempted to treat a member of staff with anything less than the utmost respect, I'm going to show you what happens.'

'These two,' he glared down at us, 'are worse than naughty. They are disgusting individuals with filthy habits. I will not tolerate such behaviour – so be warned.'

For some reason I was singled out to go first. Mr Byrne made me turn around and face the wall.

'Bend over,' he instructed, with quiet menace.

I did as ordered. Out of the corner of my eye I could see what he had in his hand: an old rubber plimsoll with a black sole. I braced myself, my heart thudding so loud I figured it could be heard at the back of the hall.

It seemed like he raised his arm in January and brought it down in December, and he did so with such force that I ended up in a heap on the floor.

'Up!' he roared. 'Up!'

Three times I stood and got knocked down. My arse was on fire and it was all I could do not to yelp. But I would not give him the satisfaction of seeing me crying. Then Simmo got done too, just the same as I had.

We were ordered out of Mr Byrne's sight. I was only just able to walk back to the classroom, and no way could I sit down. Byrne by name, burn by nature. It would have been like squatting in the flames of hell. I stood at the back, staring straight ahead. Sensing all the other kids staring at me, I put on my brave-and-defiant face.

The only pleasure I took that afternoon was from the guilt on the gentle Mrs Witkins' face. Sure, we'd deserved a good dose of punishment, but she hadn't quite banked on the stand-in headmaster's sadism or his brute ferocity.

I still couldn't sit down when I got home.

'What's wrong with you?' Mum asked.

'The new bloke, Mr Byrne – hit me at school.'

She stopped whatever she was doing. 'He hit you? What for?'

I shrugged. 'Dunno, Mam.'

Her reaction took me by complete surprise. She grabbed me by the arm and dragged me down the road, ignoring all the other mums and kids coming the other way. She was mentally rehearsing the speech she was about to give, although I had no idea at the time.

Marching me up the steps of the school, she swung a sharp right towards the head's office and burst through the door. Mr Byrne recoiled in shock. Sat behind the desk and faced by my Mum in full fury, he suddenly didn't seem so scary.

'Did you hit my son?' she demanded.

'Now, now,' he said, rising to his feet, as if his secure little world had just been stormed by a hostile enemy . . . which as a matter of fact it had.

'Don't you now-now me! Did – you – hit – my son?'

I was starting to enjoy this. But then events took an unexpected turn.

'Pull down your trousers and show your bum,' Mum commanded.

'Mam, Mam, Mam,' I tried objecting, but I could see she was in no mood for any arguments.

I did as I'd been told and can only assume my nether regions were not a pretty sight, because Mum puffed herself up into an even greater rage.

'If you hit my son again, I will come down here and wrap that chair around your backside. D'you hear me?'

She didn't wait for a reply. She stormed out, dragging me behind her.

My mum, Kathleen, had worked behind the bar at the Jack and Jill pub, in Berwick Hills, in the east of the town. My dad, Joseph, had been a regular there, and one thing had led to another. They'd ended up getting married and moving in with Mum's parents. It can't have been easy, the two families crammed into the one council house.

By the time I was born my parents were desperate to get their own place. Dad was an electrician working for British Steel, but still there was no way they could scrape together enough money to buy their own place.

All that changed when Dad suffered an accident at work. The steelworks was like a massive industrial hangar five stories high. One day someone erected some scaffolding, leaving a hole in the floor. Dad didn't see it, fell through and dropped thirty feet, breaking several vertebrae.

British Steel knew they were liable. They somehow found out that my parents' dream was to move to a new housing development on the edge of town, so they offered my dad the deposit as compensation. That's how he got the money together to buy the house that I grew up in. It cost £4,500 at the time.

My brother, Neil, arrived just after we moved in, so when I was still a toddler. He and I had the run of the local fields, at least until the estate expanded all across them. Neil loved nothing more than kicking a football around, perfecting his lobs and volleys and spending interminable hours on keepy-uppy.

But it looked as boring as hell to me.

I preferred to run around the local farms and fields, with the north wind whistling in my ears. When I moved to St George's Roman Catholic Secondary School I carried on running. I did well enough at 800m and 1500m to get chosen to run for the county. It almost made up for being crap at football. Generally, I was reduced to yelling out: 'Pass it to me – my brother's a footballer!'

My speed saved me in other ways too – most notably from the regular bouts of Catholic-bashing that St George's boys were subjected to. St George's was situated near a local landmark, called the Avenue of Trees, a wide corridor of grass running between two rows of giant oaks.

At the far end of the Avenue were two Protestant schools. At lunchtime the boys that went there would gather together and come looking for us. There were far more of them than there were of us.

But I soon learned not to run whenever we sighted the enemy. I realised I could use my speed in other ways. And once I'd got a taste for fighting I simply got ready with my mates for a pitched battle.

The oldest boys on our side were sixteen. Then came a few fifteen-year-olds, followed by the youngest – Simmo and me. Simmo was big and strong, and he played up to his gorilla-like appearance, dragging his knuckles along the ground to display the brute force he was about to unleash.

If you were seven stone of skin and bone like me, Simmo was a reassuring presence to have at your side. Lining up with him against the Protestant boys gave me my first taste of camaraderie, and of going to 'war'. We were always outnumbered, but we were the better fighters and we gave as good as we got.

Claret was spilled on both sides, on a regular basis. Teeth were lost and knees were scraped and twisted. But the black eyes, bruised jaws and ripped jumpers were worth it. They were the marks of a fighter – and with that came a certain sense of pride back then.

Our teachers took a different view. One lunchtime they came up with a new tactic to try to stop us. A dozen of us were about to head out to the Avenue when we found the school gate blocked by a phalanx of adults – arms folded, stares unblinking.

Enough is enough, the teachers told us. No more muddy trousers and nose bleeds. But we were too fired up to think of trooping back to the playground. One of the older lads came up with an alternative plan.

'Listen, how about we sneak through the back gate and double back to the Avenue? They'll never see us. We'll ambush the Proddy boys, then peg it back and school won't be any the wiser.'

Plan sorted, we slunk through the back gate in groups of two or three at a time. We mustered out of sight, crept forward using the thick foliage as cover and broke into a run only when the leaves thinned out.

We were the Spartans – we few, we happy few – advancing undetected to glorious battle. As St George's receded behind us, the enemy – the kids from the rival schools – came into view. There were thirty of them, but they were looking the wrong way. Every one of them was glaring up the Avenue in the direction of our school, wondering what had kept us.

They never even saw us coming. We smacked into them so hard we knocked some clean off their feet. The bigger ones did their best to recover, of course, and they thumped us back. But it wasn't long before some of the smaller Boynton boys broke and ran. Cowardice is contagious. When one or two turned and fled we knew we had a rout on our hands.

And that was it – battle most decidedly won.

We headed back to school somewhat the worse for wear. A couple of us had had our ties ripped off. One lad had torn his shirt and another was holding his head back and pinching the top of his nose.

We were hoping to sneak back in the rear gate and go for a quiet clean-up in the toilets. Instead, we were intercepted by a group of vengeful teachers. We were ordered to back up against the school fence. They made us stand in the sun facing inwards, as the kids in the classrooms stared back at us. We stayed there for the whole afternoon looking wrecked and bloodied, but not exactly bowed.

If the teachers had thought this would humiliate us, they couldn't have been more wrong. Parading us in front of our mates only made our stock soar higher.

At the end of the day we were summoned to the head's office and given a letter to take home. This was the hard part. We may have become legends at school, but it was going to be very different when I got home.

Mum and Neil were out, but the garage door was open – a sure sign that Dad would be in his overalls, working on our Ford Cortina Crusader. Since the accident at British Steel Dad had found work on the North Sea oil-rigs, but he had the mortgage to pay and two growing boys to keep in football boots and running shoes, so money was tight.

From necessity he was his own mechanic.

'Dad, I've got this letter,' I said, as innocently as I could. 'From school.'

He was covered in oil and didn't so much as glance up. 'Oh, right, yeah, what is it?'

'You have to read it.'

'Okay, put it on the kitchen table. I'll read it later.'

I did as asked and went to the front room to watch TV. It was 4.30 p.m. on a still summer's afternoon, and nothing on the box could distract me from the shit storm that was brewing.

Dad must have realised there was something unsavoury awaiting him in that envelope. When he came in from the garage he put off dealing with it. First he made a cup of tea. Then he fetched some Rich Tea biscuits. Then he read his paper, and indulged in a good dose of dunking.

But eventually he brought the envelope into the front room, sat on the sofa opposite and opened it. I couldn't look at him as he read the letter. He folded it up in total silence and I knew what was coming.

Finally he glanced at me, a dark look in his eyes. 'You are an absolute bloody disgrace. And you know something – I am ashamed of you.'

Somehow, that was the last thing I had been expecting. I was steeling myself for a good clip round the ear, but to be told by my dad that he was *ashamed of me* – that really hurt.

I stomped up the stairs, realising that Thermopylae was a long way from my parents' home in Middlesbrough.

3

From the vantage point of my tiny bedroom I saw Mum come home. I heard the door slam and moments later I heard her arguing with Dad.

'But have you heard his side?' she demanded. 'You haven't heard his side. He might have been provoked.'

'Provoked?' Dad exploded. 'He's been suspended! Dunno how I kept my hands off him.'

Shortly after the battle at school and my suspension, war broke out in the distant Falkland Islands. The nation was glued to the news, and it was the Falklands campaign that first got me fired up about a career in the military.

Of course, I didn't have a clue where the Falklands were and I couldn't have cared less why the Argies had invaded. But when I watched the TV news and saw our aircraft carriers sailing from Portsmouth, with the flights of helicopters and Harrier Jump Jets strapped to their decks, I was captivated.

The Union Jacks were flying, families were waving emotional farewells, and I was swept up in the emotion of the moment. One night I was watching the news as the men of the Parachute Regiment – the PARAs – headed off to join the war.

Red berets.

Assault rifles.

Massive Bergens.

Something just clicked.

That's me: that's my dream.

I'm gonna get me some of that.

Mum and Dad might as well know, I thought, so I shared the big revelation with them. I pointed at the TV. 'I'm gonna do that. I'm gonna join the PARAs.'

Dad glanced at me. 'Whoa . . . son, where the hell did that come from? And why not get an education first?'

'Dad, I'm going to join the PARAs,' I repeated.

There was no military tradition in our family – not since my Granddad had been conscripted to fight in the Second World War. Going into the British military just wasn't something that the Heaney household had ever contemplated. I could almost hear Dad's mind whirring: *Of all the units to pick he has to choose the PARAs!*

For her part, Mum was even less impressed. She glared at my Dad, as if to ask why he'd even heard me out. 'You're not going in the Army, and that's that. You'll get yourself shot. Tell him, Joe.'

My dad retreated further behind his paper. It was my turn to be surprised now. 'If he wants to go in the Army, he'll go in the Army,' Dad muttered. 'Let's give the lad a bloody chance . . .'

'Typical,' Mam snorted. 'That's no bloody good, is it?'

It was 5 April 1982 when I made my prophetic announcement. Day after day I was glued to the nightly news. Some 8,000 miles away these massive blokes in camouflage fatigues and bright maroon berets were putting their balls on the block to drive out an invader. They were doing their duty for their country, which gave me a surge of pride I'd rarely experienced before.

I started cutting out articles from newspapers for a school project. The PARAs were in the thick of it, and never more so than in the Battle of Goose Green. We'd taken some hits on our warships, and the worry was that we were losing the momentum of the battle. Then along came Lieutenant-Colonel Herbert 'H' Jones, of 2 PARA, with a selfless act of heroism that set the entire Forces an example.

Jones, who had two boys of his own at home, had attacked the Argentine positions, only for his unit to get pinned down by heavy fire. Undeterred, he'd led a ferocious charge against the nearest enemy gun emplacement. He was shot by a sniper and fell, but he got up again and carried on the charge, until he was hit in the back by a second bullet.

Jones died of his wounds, and was buried in the Falklands. For his actions that day he was awarded a posthumous Victoria Cross. You couldn't ask for a bigger inspiration.

The PARAs were the first troops to enter Port Stanley, the Falklands capital. They'd lost forty dead, with ninety-three wounded, but they looked totally war-bitten and invincible.

They were the Spartans: The 300.

That sealed it in my mind: it was the Parachute Regiment for me, or bust.

I got my mum to subscribe me to a weekly publication: *The Elite Magazine – The World's Crack Fighting Men*. There was one edition devoted to the SAS (Special Air Service) and one to the US Rangers, but my favourite was the one dedicated to the PARAs. I'd sit on the edge of my bed with the mag of the week open at the most dramatic pages, and imagine myself into the pictures.

At that time you could go on a Youth Training Scheme (YTS), taking a week or two out of school to try out the local chemical plants or the steelworks. My mates were all saying: 'I'm gonna do one at ICI Wilton', or 'I'm for British Steel.'

But to me it just didn't compute. The way I saw it, I could either bash hot metal with a hammer or stir vats of chemicals, or else travel the world doing the kind of things depicted on the pages of *The Elite Magazine*. To me it was a no-brainer.

'British Steel?' I'd say. 'No way. I'm gonna join the PARAs.'

My school mates would smirk and shake their heads. 'You in the PARAs! Taken a look at yerself recently? The PARAs are rock-hard. They're big, scary bastards. What'd they want with a streak of piss like you?'

But nothing they could say would deter me. I resolved to get fighting fit and to bulk up. I joined the Middlesbrough Running Club and spent every spare minute running round the track at the Clairville Stadium. There was a gym at the running club where I started trying to pump iron, and Simmo, my stalwart, came with me. He couldn't run for shit, but he was built like a cross between a Neanderthal and Godzilla.

After a few weeks I could see tiny biceps in the mirror, where there'd only been chicken wings before. A few months later I could beat some of my schoolmates at arm-wrestling, and without spraining my wrist. Not only that, but my marginally honed physique was having other, unexpected spin-offs.

There was a girl at school, Wendy Smith, who didn't make a face when I ogled her. She even let me walk her down the street, holding hands.

Simmo decided he'd help me build up some basic skills that would stand me in good stead in the military. The PARAs had a punishing selection course that I'd have to get through, but by building up my skill-sets I'd give myself a fighting chance. We decided to concentrate on reconnaissance and tracking.

Question was, who and what would we spy on and track in and around Middlesbrough? We picked what seemed a suitable target: the humble milk float.

There were several advantages to milk floats, we reasoned. First, they were fairly easy to spot, what with being lit up from tit to toe in the dark; plus you could hear the electric ones coming with a soft 'wheeeeeee' long before they came into view.

Second, a milk float motor packs a mere eleven horsepower and has a maximum speed of twenty miles an hour. We'd never lose one. Third, the drivers had no reason to suspect they were being tracked as they went around collecting empty bottles in the small hours.

One driver always left his float at the top of a particular hill, while he did the rounds. One night I jumped in the cab, inched it slowly forward and parked it out of sight over the brow of the hill. Needless to say, the milkman's face was a picture when he came out and realised that his float had disappeared.

The next night we timed our operation to perfection. We lurked in the shadows on a downhill slope, I powered up the float's engine and it took off surprisingly fast. But then I heard a woman on her doorstep yelling in alarm, as the milkman pounded after us, his face puce with rage.

'Put your foot down!' Simmo yelled.

The slope won the day and the milkman was soon all out of puff. But we were then in possession of a vehicle with a seventy-two-volt battery and a range of sixty miles. Joy-riding a milk float – we were the kings of the road. I was at the wheel, when suddenly a flash of blinding blue filled the inside of the cab. Moments later a police car pulled alongside, an enraged-looking copper at the wheel.

'Pull over!' he yelled. 'Pull over!'

Moments later he was standing at my window, looking about eight feet tall. He started at me in speechless amazement. Then: 'What do you two think you're doing?'

We were nicked. So I figured why not put a brave face on things. 'Driving,' I replied, deadpan.

'Very funny. Joyriding a milk float. A right couple of chancers.' The copper jerked a thumb at the rear of his vehicle. 'Right, in the back of the car.'

Upon arrival at the cop shop, the arresting sergeant was having a right time of it. 'Got Ronnie and Reggie Kray in tonight, lads. Caught red-handed stealing a milk float. Terrorised half the town, they have! Right, better give me the names of your fathers, and their phone numbers.'

I was shoved into one cell and Simmo in another. The seriousness of what I'd done was starting to sink in now. This could be it: a criminal record for theft, and my military career bang out the window. And all for joyriding a milk float. How could I have been so stupid?

Forty minutes later we were let out of the cells. We sat on some plastic chairs in the lobby, trying to look as small as possible so as not to get noticed. Our dads were ushered in. Unsurprisingly, they did not look best pleased. But there was something noticeably different about my father. He looked as if he knew his family's fortunes were hanging in the balance, and it was all down to him to rescue them.

'Joe Heaney, sergeant,' he introduced himself. 'I'm Steve's father.'

The sergeant didn't pull his punches. 'No way to sugarcoat this, Mr Heaney: your son's in a lot of trouble. Theft of a motor vehicle. Driving without a licence. Possession of stolen property . . .' The list seemed to go on and on.

For a moment Dad appeared to buckle under the blows. To me, the arresting sergeant's long string of charges all seemed a bit over the top. Okay, we'd done wrong, but even the cops had seemed to find it funny.

I didn't appreciate the gravity of the situation until Dad spoke. 'What's the worst that can happen to him?'

The sergeant sucked his teeth. 'Well, the courts tend to look more kindly on a first offence. So, taking his age into account, he could get probation if he pleads guilty to all the charges. If not . . .'

My dad seemed to pull himself to his full height. 'Look, sergeant, the lad wants to go in the Army. The PARAs. He's wanted it ever since he hit his teens. He's training for it. It's his only aim in life. You know as well as I do the Army won't take anyone with a criminal record.'

'It's rough,' the sergeant agreed. It was clear he thought my dad a decent bloke looking out for his boy. 'But you have to understand – it's my job to uphold the law.'

My dad leaned forward and lowered his voice. 'I don't know if you've got kids, sergeant, but would it be right for a young man's future to be wrecked by one stupid teenage mistake? He wants to serve his country and that's all he wants to do.'

'I hear what you say.' The sergeant's tone was hardening. 'But your son was caught red-handed.'

'Look, we're a good family,' my dad persisted. 'Is there any way we can make this a warning? I promise he'll never do it again. I'll deal with it. I'll make it go away.'

The sergeant sighed. But something in my dad's words must have touched him. For a long moment he stared at his desk, before casting a look at Dad, which he rapidly switched to Simmo and me.

'Right, make no mistake you two: if you ever end up here again, I'll make sure you go down, so help me God. Be thankful to your dads – and get out.'

I left with the sergeant's caution ringing in my ears. Just as soon as we were out on the streets I went to give Dad a heartfelt hug. I felt as if he'd just saved my life.

There was steam practically coming out of my dad's ears. 'Let's get one thing bloody straight. I will never, ever embarrass myself like that for you again.'

He fixed me with this look: 'It's all up to you now, son.'

4

On the day after my sixteenth birthday Dad took me to Middlesbrough's Army Careers Office. We walked in and the recruiting sergeant rose from his desk, sensing that here was prey. He thrust out a massive, beefy hand.

'Sergeant Davis, Army Recruitment. What can I do for youse?'

'My son's interested in joining the Army,' Dad replied.

'Right,' said the sergeant. 'It'll be the Green Howards for you, lad.'

The Green Howards were the local regiment. They had a distinguished combat history, reaching as far back as the Crimean and Boer wars. With our lack of military service in the family, Dad was thinking: *Who the hell are we to pick and choose?* But he stuck to his guns.

'He doesn't want to join the Green Howards,' said Dad, flatly.

The recruiting sergeant shrugged. 'Right, it's the Engineers. Nothing else for it.'

The Royal Engineers trace their history back to William the Conqueror. Like the Green Howards, they too have strong connections with the Northeast.

'He doesn't want to join the Engineers.'

The recruiting sergeant stared at me for a long second. I could read what he was thinking. Who the f*** does this lanky piece of string think he is?

'Right, it's the Guards, then,' he announced, with a resounding finality. 'They're always looking for . . . tall lads like you.'

The 'tall' remark was clearly the nearest to a positive he could think of.

Dad shook his head. 'Not the Guards, either. He wants to join the PARAs.'

The bull-necked sergeant's eyes practically popped out of his head. 'Right, the PARAs . . . Hard to get into – the PARAs. Tough.' He paused, portentously. 'You sure he wouldn't rather the Guards or the Engineers?'

'No point in trying to talk him out of it,' said Dad. *'He wants to join the PARAs.'*

The sergeant reached into a drawer and pulled out a slim brochure. He slid it across the desk to us – or rather, to me.

'There you go, sonny. The PARAs. Take it home and have a good read. If you still think you want to join them after . . . Well, you're welcome to come back and take the Army's entrance tests.'

I couldn't wait to get home. I stretched out on my bed and devoured that brochure from cover to cover. Mainly I lingered over the pictures. There were photos of PARAs abseiling. Of PARAs scuba diving. Of PARAs travelling the world seemingly having the time of their lives. *Who wouldn't want to join them?* If the sergeant thought this would make me back off, he was very much mistaken.

Brochure devoured, I went downstairs to the kitchen. Dad beckoned me over to the table. It was the first time that I'd sat with him, man to man, to talk about my future. I needed his support, for I couldn't go in as a junior without his signature. He looked at me, silently weighing me up and waiting for me to say something.

I'd always been somewhat afraid of my dad. A year back I'd kicked in the wing of our rusty Cortina, while Dad had been doing some repairs. For sure he had enough to deal with, without his errant son kicking the car in.

I glanced at him now, trying to sound far more confident than I was feeling. 'Dad, it's what I want to do.'

'You absolutely sure?' Each word was growled out in that slow, deliberate way of his.

'It's what I want to do,' I repeated.

'Right,' he said. 'I'll square it with your Mam.'

The next day we were back in the Army Careers Office, facing the same sceptical sergeant wedged behind his desk.

'Look, he's read your brochure and he's convinced,' Dad announced. 'It's the PARAs or bust.'

The sergeant shook his head. 'I appreciate the young lad's *enthusiasm* ... But you need to understand how much more ... demanding the PARAs are than a standard Army regiment.'

'There's no talking him out of it,' my father countered. 'Every lad deserves his chance.'

The sergeant must have figured that he'd lost the first battle but that he'd win the wider war. He'd send me for my initial two-day PARA appraisal, get me posted back to him a reject, and shovel me into the Green Howards. QED.

'Right, you'll receive a letter in the next few days giving you a time and date you need to report to Sutton Coldfield Barracks. You'll get a train ticket in the post, plus a list of things to take.' He paused. 'And your mum and dad will not be included.'

Despite his attitude, I could hardly contain myself. I'd never even been on a train before. And if the seemingly impossible happened and I got through, then I'd be going to Junior PARA, in Surrey – which sounded like a foreign country to me.

In due course forty of us raw recruits pitched up at Sutton Coldfield Barracks. We were divided into two squads and each given an Army cot with a thick and itchy Army wool blanket.

'Right,' barked the company sergeant major (CSM). 'You ugly lot need to be outside in thirty minutes, dressed in trainers, shorts and T-shirt ready for fitness tests.'

We gathered outside. It was a freezing March day and I was shivering so much I couldn't wait to get going. At least movement would mean some degree of warmth.

'Form two groups,' the CSM yelled. 'All going for the PARAs – on the left! All others – on the right! Two groups! NOW!'

Those of us in the PARA group were led to a square. The CSM stared at us. 'Three laps in under twelve minutes thirty seconds and you're good. Any slower, you're fucked.'

The word 'Start' was painted on the concrete. We lined up before it, jockeying for position, and then we were off. I got out in front straight away, feeling invincible. One of the others overtook me and I failed to catch him. But at the finishing line I was second, sailing over at twelve minutes five seconds. I waited while a guy with a stopwatch called out, 'Twelve thirteen, twelve eighteen . . .' all the way down to twelve minutes thirty.

All who arrived after that were peeled away and we never saw them again. The dream they had nurtured had died on its arse in less than a quarter of an hour. This was my first taste of Selection. If you're good enough, you're in. If you're a second late, get on yer bike. This is the only way and it's the right way. It ensures that elite units take only the best.

The same procedure followed in the gym. By the end, twelve of us were in and eight were out. Already, they'd culled almost half. They took our names and details and told us to go back to the billet and get our civvie clothes on. But I wasn't through yet. I still had to be interviewed by the recruiting officer.

He fixed me with a baleful eye. 'Right, Heaney, you've done well on the fitness tests. But tell me – why d'you want to join the PARAs?'

The first question of my first job interview, and thankfully I'd come prepared. It was just what Dad had warned me to expect.

'I watched them on TV in the Falklands: they're the elite; the best. That's why I want to join them.'

The officer was clearly thinking about my age: a not so sweet sixteen.

'Will you stick at it?' he demanded. 'You're young, you'll be away from home. It's gonna be hard, long hours and very physical. Living in a room with fifty blokes and no one to tuck you in. Will you miss Mum and Dad?'

'It's what I want,' I insisted. 'I want to join the PARAs.'

It was my mantra. If I stuck to it for long enough I figured they had to give me a chance. I was dismissed and sent home. No one told me whether I'd passed or not. I may have done well on the fitness tests, but if the recruiting officer decided I wasn't 'PARA material' that would be that.

Regardless, I decided to up my training regime. If I waited to hear whether I'd got in, I'd be leaving it too late. Dad took me to the local Army surplus store and bought me an old pair of Dr Marten-type boots. Then we went looking for a rucksack in Millets. They only had one kind: a bright orange backpack with foam-rubber straps. I tried it for size.

'What's that on your back?' said Dad, laughing. 'A bloody Satsuma?'

And so the nickname stuck: 'The Satsuma'.

Dad gave me some plastic weights that he had, which were filled with sand. I wrapped them in towels and shoved them in the Satsuma. They added 15lb to the load. I put on the heavy Dr Marten-type boots and a pair of black tracksuit bottoms, and took off like a hare out of a trap.

At first I ran along the streets of Middlesbrough, and up and down a beck by some parkland – mile after mile with the Satsuma bobbing up and down. I kept upping the weight and the distance, and soon I was running four or five miles on every outing.

Dad took to driving me out to the Cleveland Hills, which form a doughnut-shaped ring around Middlesbrough. He'd get his *Daily Mirror* out while I strapped on the Satsuma and dashed up and down through the bracken.

I put my all into every uphill climb and when my leg muscles were burning I pictured Junior PARA in my head, and told myself this was the route to entry, and I put on an extra spurt. The downhill stretches were my reward for conquering the heights.

My family and friends; the residents of the streets I pounded; even the dog-walkers I encountered on the hills – all eventually had to accept that the scrawny sixteen-year-old with the orange backpack was serious about trying for the PARAs. But I knew what they were thinking: would the PARAs want me, even if I could run like the wind?

Week after week went by with no word from Sutton Coldfield. I upped the training in the local gym with Simmo, but I couldn't help but notice that he had more grunt in one of his gorilla's arms than I had in both of mine.

'You'll be all right, mate,' he'd say. 'If you want it bad enough, it's gonna happen.'

I'd completed my two-day assessment in the March. April came and went without a word. May was torture – surely they'd have told me by now if they wanted me? I was starting to lose hope when finally, at the beginning of June, a letter arrived postmarked 'Sutton Coldfield Barracks'.

This was it. Make or break time.

5

There was a cold sweat on my palms as I went to open the envelope. The rest of my life would be shaped by the words on that letter. When it came to it, I got my mum to read it out. And joy of joys it announced that they were offering me a place at Junior Parachute Company.

The intake start date would be 7 July – about four weeks away. I was to report to the same Army Careers Office in town to collect my travel voucher.

The pride on my dad's face when he saw that letter was a picture. I felt a swell of exhilaration in my chest, and I couldn't wait to tell Simmo. He looked as pleased as I was. He was right behind me – out of all my mates, he was my chief cheerleader and the one who believed in me most.

As for Neil, he thought it was the best thing to happen since 'Boro' (Middlesbrough FC) had avoided going out of business. Even Mam seemed pleased. At least that's how I read the tears in her eyes.

Everything seemed to happen in a whirl now. Dad came with me to the careers office, where the same recruiting sergeant handed me a train ticket to Pirbright, Surrey, the home of Junior PARA. Did he eat humble pie? A little. But oddly, I almost detected a hint of pride that a Middlesbrough lad was destined for the PARAs.

Not that I was in yet, of course.

The train ticket was one-way – as in not coming back for the foreseeable future – and that's when it started to really sink in. I guess that had something to do with Mam's tears. Wrong 'un or not, she was about to see her eldest fly the nest.

There was plenty to keep her busy, though. The careers office issued me a kit list and sixteen quid towards the cost of the thirty-odd items on it. It included a travel iron, two pairs of smart trousers, formal shoes, a jacket and an electric razor. This was real man-gear, and the kind of stuff I'd never owned before.

'That won't buy the travel iron, let alone the rest,' Mum complained, when I presented her with the Army's cash. 'If we have to spend all this money, you'd better not come back.'

And then her eyes were brimful again.

There was still the small matter of O-levels to sit, but compared to Junior PARA it had become something of a sideshow. I got Cs in English, Maths, History and Geography. Four days later it was time to head south to a foreign country: to Surrey.

I hauled the suitcase onto my bed and placed the precious items of kit inside. Although I hadn't always been the best of sons, I knew that my parents' love had never wavered. They had stood by me through thick and thin, and now they weren't going to be a part of my day-to-day life any more. My mum and dad wouldn't be there to see me achieve my goals, or to pick me up if I failed.

It didn't seem fair somehow – on them or on me.

My dad was waiting at the bottom of the stairs as I dragged down the heavy suitcase. He beamed, sharing my excitement, but knowing that I was nervous about my leap into the unknown. Neil was outside doing keepy-uppy with his football. But Mum was nowhere to be seen.

At the last minute she appeared and climbed into the front passenger seat of the Cortina. Apart from asking if I'd remembered to pack my pants and socks, she didn't say a word. As the train station swung into view her shoulders started to heave, and I realised that she was sobbing. I didn't know what to say.

'So, are you coming, or what?' Dad asked her, when he'd parked.

She shook her head and blew her nose before really breaking down. I felt choked-up to see her like that. All I could do was kiss her goodbye through the open window, then lug my suitcase onto the platform, my father's arm around my shoulders.

'Good luck, son,' he announced, shaking me somewhat formally by the hand. 'You're going to be fine.'

I managed a brave grin for Neil, but I could tell from his hang-dog expression how much he was going to miss having a big bro around to clip him around the ear.

When I arrived in Surrey there were sixty other nervous young lads milling around the platform. The first person from Junior PARA that I saw was a small, angry man with a shaven head beneath a maroon beret, and a massive drooping moustache. His name was Corporal Walt Pearson, and he was going to be my section commander.

The first trial of my new life was to make out what Corporal Pearson was screaming at us in his thick Scottish accent. A white Army bus took us to the Army camp in leafy Pirbright. It was Sunday, 6 July, and far sunnier than any of the personalities that greeted us.

Foremost among them was Corporal George Smith, a legend from his time in the Falklands. When the 2 PARA mortar tubes had sunk into a peat bog, George Smith had propped them up with his own feet so the rounds could still be fired. His feet had been shattered by the force of the recoils.

For such bravery in the battle for Goose Green he was put forward for the Military Medal. Needless to say, amongst the PARAs George Smith was a living legend.

After being issued with uniforms, we had our heads shaved, and were each allocated a bed, a wooden locker and a side table. We were housed in two rooms, each on a different floor, so thirty to a room, which rang to the rafters with our shouting. The men in charge of instilling some discipline looked big, grizzled and scary. Every single one of them was an angry man, but none more so than small, stocky Walt Parson.

Corporal Pearson's speciality was coining nasty nicknames for the new recruits. From the start, I became 'Heinous Heaney', as in: 'Right, Heinous, come 'ere!'

The only bloke who was smaller and stockier than Walt Pearson was Sergeant Anson, aka 'The Troll'. I'm not sure if he was actually christened 'Troll' but I never heard another first name. Troll was the provost sergeant – so the guy you were sent to if you did anything wrong. He gave a lovely speech of welcome.

'Righty, you little fuckers! You've probably heard everyone telling you they're the boss, they're in charge, they're God. Well they're wrong about God – because you just met him.'

Junior PARA started with basic training, in which we learned the nuts and bolts of basic soldiering. It included PT twice a day, with a run, a march, the gym or a swim. Then basic navigation – how to read a map and take grid bearings – and weapons drills. We went out into bracken and heather to learn fieldcraft, plus the tactical skills of operating stealthily, including camouflage and concealment.

Breakfast was at 6 a.m. sharp and we started at 7 a.m., training until dark. That was the routine Monday to Saturday mornings. For homework over the weekend we had to memorise a range of different weapons, map symbols and the Regiment's history. It was all driven by a desire to beast us and run us into the ground, but funnily enough I loved it.

My legs were like sticks still, I was losing weight and with my shaven head my ears were like massive wing nuts. It was not the best of looks. But I was always at the front of the runs: the Satsuma stuffed with weights had stood me in good stead.

We were losing guys week on week. In the bed space opposite mine was the scion of a tyre dynasty. His family lived in a multimillion pound mansion ten miles up the road. The poor sod barely lasted a month.

Next to him was a Geordie called Paul Grahame – a fit, tough, hard little bastard, and seemingly perfect PARA material. I'd have put money on him making it through Juniors. But one day he came out of the instructor's office with a look like death on his face.

'I've quit,' he announced, quietly. 'I don't want to be here any more. It's not for me.'

Admittedly, we were being daily thrashed to within an inch of our lives. There was no mercy from the instructors. And Corporal Walt Pearson – the 'Poison Dwarf' as we'd nicknamed him – was the worst of all, especially where rackets and extortion were concerned.

We were paid £70 a fortnight and allowed to draw £15 of it in cash – you'd get the rest when you went on your first leave. One day the Poison Dwarf came in with a set of shiny gold tins, with a ring-pull at one end. He lined them up on the central table, portentously.

'Right lads, gather round. These are your combat survival tins. You need to carry them everywhere you go. And God help anyone who opens one – not unless you're in a survival situation. And I will tell you when you're in a survival situation. It's five pounds a tin.'

'Yes, right, corporal,' and we all handed over our fivers.

There were twenty-five on our floor and a similar number on the floor above, so he grossed £250 in the one hit. We were looking at our shiny tins, dead chuffed.

'Go and put them in your webbing,' he told us.

Speculation was rife as to what the tins contained. 'Mega. Combat survival tins. Wonder what's in them, though? Something to kill a deer? Knife, snares, flares?'

Whenever we were on parade the Poison Dwarf would bawl: 'Right, everyone take out their combat survival tin.' We'd stand there, holding them up proudly. He'd do an inspection, and woe betide anyone who'd forgotten his.

After five months, twenty-seven of us remained: more than half had been culled. We were nearing the end of our time at Pirbright and we were hauled out on parade.

'On the count of three I want you all to open your survival tins,' the Poison Dwarf announced. 'One, two, three!'

This was the moment. My tin was dented and battered, but utterly cherished. I couldn't wait to see what was inside. Tugging on the ring, I pulled it all the way back. There was no knife and there were no flares. Although I could hardly believe my eyes, the smell confirmed it. I was looking at sardines in tomato sauce.

For a moment I was totally nonplussed, before the realisation dawned, and I was pissed at being made to look so stupid. But the more we complained, the funnier the Poison Dwarf seemed to find it. He walked away laughing his tits off, and leaving us to contemplate our gullibility.

I was due to leave Pirbright that December and start PARA training proper – which was for those aged seventeen or over. But with just a few weeks to go we were told to put together a boxing team. We were to fight the Guards Juniors for a place in the Army championships. Volunteers were called for, and with my distinguished history at scrapping I figured I'd best have a try.

I was put in the welterweight category for boxers weighing 145lb (67kg) or less. The nine of us spent a few short weeks training for our bouts. We had two instructors, George Smith the PARA legend who'd used his feet to support the mortar tubes in the Falklands, plus Andy Gow, the 3 PARA CSM who'd raised the flag over Port Stanley.

CSM Gow was a very large man who hailed from rock-hard Sunderland. It was debatable who was the more scary – him or George Smith. Either way, we were in good hands for the boxing – or big, terrifying hands, at least.

It was the end of November when we faced up to the Guards in the base gymnasium. We'd had twenty-seven Junior PARAs to pick our team from; the Guards, by contrast, had 500 young blokes. Most had turned up to watch and howl for the blood of their mortal enemies – guys like me.

But that was as nothing compared to the pre-match pep talk from Andy Gow. He crouched down so his massive head was at my eye level.

'At the end of the day, lad, you can go in the ring and die, or come out here and die. Because if you don't win, I will kill you.'

The lighter guys went first and amazingly we won the first three fights. But that didn't make it any easier. If anything, it just upped Andy Gow's threat level. As I made my way to the gymnasium my legs felt like splintered jelly. I saw the Guards ranged in every direction, while the Junior PARAs had just two sets of benches on one side.

From the ear-splitting screams of the Guards, I had a fleeting sense of what it must have been like for a Christian entering the gladiator's ring in ancient Rome. Howling for blood, they wanted me battered and bloodied, and at the very least carried unconscious from the ring.

The guy I was facing was the same height as me, but broader and stockier. If he landed a solid punch I was going down. I decided to make like Muhammad Ali – float like a butterfly, sting like a bee. If I pranced around and stayed away from his big haymakers, I reckoned I could pick him off.

Sure enough, by the end of the three two-minute rounds I hadn't been hit, but I'd cracked him a good few times. Each blow was met by a howl of outrage from the Guards. The final verdict was unanimous: victory was mine.

'Right, well done lad,' said Andy Gow. 'You're not gonna die. But next time, fucking knock him out. Got it?'

This fight was just the warm-up: the Army boxing championships loomed large. Having whopped the Guards' arses, next we faced Shorncliffe – a massive Army camp in Kent, with 2,000 Regular Army recruits to choose from. At least we had the home advantage, but that came with one humongous downside.

Some two hundred PARAs had been invited – real, fully-grown, battle-hardened warriors – not least of whom were the regimental colonel, plus the commanding officers of 2 and 3 PARA. If we – *if I* – failed in front of these blokes, including our would-be future commanders, we'd never live it down.

Andy Gow had steam coming out of his ears well before anyone had put so much as a foot in the ring. Slowly, very deliberately, and dripping with menace, he spat out his ultimatum.

'I am from Three PARA. The CO of Three PARA is out there. Don't you fucking even think of humiliating me in front of him.' A long beat. 'You let me down, lad, and I will be wearing your bollocks for a necklace. Now, go out there and prove to me you've got some.'

The first out of our sweaty, fearful changing room was the lightweight. He opened the door and the blast of sound was deafening. I felt a surge of bile hit my throat. One of my teammates jumped up to close the door, shutting off the wall of noise.

Amazingly, the lightweight returned triumphant. One–nil to us. But there was no such luck with the second and third fighters. Both were defeated, and the jeering piled on the agony.

I shook my head, disbelievingly. 'This isn't possible. We're baby PARAs.'

Andy Gow's face was like murder, and I guessed that was two bollock necklaces he'd be wearing from now on. He moved out ringside, in preparation for my fight. It was left to George Smith to fire me up. As motivational speeches went, his was one of the greatest ever.

'Heaney,' he snarled, his gob almost touching my face. 'You'd bloody better fucking bloody win this.'

When the door swung open I was hit by the tsunami of sound. The force of it almost stopped me in my tracks. *Whoaahhh.* Ranks of real-life PARAs were screaming out my name – 'HEANEY! HEANEY! HEANEY!' The deafening chant seemed to shake the very foundations of the gymnasium.

I glanced up to see the COs of both 2 and 3 PARA in their full mess dress, which is reserved for formal occasions. A timeless tradition of military life was unfolding all around me, and for some messed-up reason I was the very centre of it right now.

Parachute Regiment commanders and their men do not expect their elite status to be compromised, not ever. The worst possible environment in which that might happen was when faced with soldiers from a rival British Army regiment. Failure was inconceivable, regardless of whether I was a sixteen-year-old Junior, or not.

It was time to man up.

I forced my legs to move. As I advanced towards the ring, I passed by the rows of guys in their maroon berets. Each was screaming at me, his face a rictus of animal aggression.

'Heaney! Heaney!'

'Go on lad!'

'Go on, son!'

'FUCKING SMASH 'IM!'

I climbed through the ropes and into the ring. All I lacked was a short, stabbing sword and a shield to be a full gladiator.

I perched on my stool.

Andy Gow placed his massive bulk in front of me, so I couldn't see the other guy. He got his face an inch apart from mine, so I could hear his words above the screaming, his massive hands gripping the ropes to either side of my head.

'Just go out there and fucking mallet him.' From the way he screwed up his face, I could see he was feeling the pressure. 'You wanna be in the PARAs, son? Take a fucking look around you. This is your time.'

With that, he stepped aside.

Looking up I saw my opponent for the first time.

I could see why Gow had blocked the view.

He loomed in front of me, a massive guy for his age, muscle-bound and dangerous-looking. And he was shadow boxing, showing off his pecs and the long reach of his powerful arms. From the fact that he was giving it large in the centre of the ring,

I knew he figured he'd got the streak of PARA piss sat opposite him beat.

I stood up, my guts churning like an erupting volcano. *Fuck it,* I told myself. *How bad can it get?* All those scraps at school had to stand me in good stead. Whatever it took, I could not let this fucker beat me.

For an instant we stood face to face, and the referee made us touch gloves.

Then: 'And . . . box!'

We were at each other straight away, toe to toe in the centre of the ring, trading savage blows. Bang! Bang! Bang! Chests pummelled. His head jolted sideways on the end of a right hook from me, then he smashed a fist into my left temple. Stars erupted in front of my eyes.

Bang! Bang! Bang!

Then the shrilling of the bell, and the referee dragged us apart. The first round was over before either of us had gained any advantage.

I went back to my corner, thinking I'd held my own.

But Andy Gow, it seemed, had other ideas.

6

'Have to do fucking better than that, son,' Andy Gow yelled. 'You wanna be a PARA . . .'

I barely heard him. I zoned out his words, and zoned into the threat. I was sorting this out in my own head now. My opponent had the strength, but I had the speed. What I had to do was catch him in the opening seconds of the next round, before he'd had a chance to wake up to the fact that the fight was back on.

I had to hit him with total brute aggression, and finish it.

I opened my ears to the roar of the crowd and let it fill me with bloodlust, and the killer energy that surged back and forth across the ring. As I breathed deeper, drinking in the naked savagery of it all, I could feel my adrenaline rising.

You can do this, I told myself. *Get out there and kill him.*

I stared unblinking at the floor, feeling calm now. My head was crystal clear. Andy Gow's words were just a background soundtrack to what was coming. I knew I had to fight absolutely without mercy. And I was ready.

The instant the bell trilled I rushed towards my target on the balls of my feet, moving with a speed and purpose that surprised him. He wasn't ready for the first punch, which rocketed towards him. It connected with his jaw.

Kaboom!

I saw his head whip back, and for an instant there was fear and surprise etched deep in his eyes. The second blow came a split second later, on the other side of his head, making him reel back still further. This was it – the moment for the kill. I went at him with machine gun punches now – left-right-left-right-left-right-left-right.

To one side of me two hundred blokes in maroon berets were going stir crazy. They were standing on their benches, chanting maniacally, as their fists punched the air.

'HEANEY! HEANEY! HEANEY!' The animal yells washed over me, as my fists pummelled into my enemy's bloodied head.

I could see that he was badly cut. Blood was oozing hot and sticky from his nose and ears. I smashed him still harder – bang-bang-bang-bang-bang! – aiming for the places where already I'd cut him.

The chant from the PARAs changed now, as they sensed bloody victory.

'YOU – HAT – WANKER!'

'YOU – HAT – WANKER!'

'YOU – HAT – WANKER!'

The screams were a deliberate taunt to every single non-PARA in the room. Being an elite airborne unit, the PARAs refer to every other regiment in the British military as 'Craphats', or 'Hats' for short. It's a deliberate insult to anyone who doesn't get to wear the maroon beret – the argument being that all the other hats – berets, bearskins, helmets, whatever – are crap by comparison.

Like it or not, it's part of the PARAs' credo.

The chant went on and on and on, as my fists pummelled the young soldier's head. By the time the referee separated us, the blood was streaming out of the guy's nose and his left ear.

'Back to your corner!' he yelled, forcing me away from my opponent.

I was reluctant to leave him. He was still a big strong lad, and I was desperate to finish him.

The ref motioned for a doctor to come up to the ring. The sight of the medic making an appearance sent the PARAs into an even greater frenzy.

'YOU GOT 'IM, SON!' Gow yelled, as he bent over me on the ropes. 'If he comes back out, go for his ears. Rip his fucking ears off.'

Moments later the referee grabbed me by the arm, and dragged me into the centre of the ring. He held up my bloodied right glove.

'The referee is stopping the fight,' the announcer declared. 'Technical knockout. Winner – Red Corner.'

Red Corner – that was me.

The room erupted like Krakatoa, the PARAs jeering that their gory spectacle had been so cruelly terminated. As I jumped down from the ring and headed for the changing room, wave after wave of deafening noise rolled around the gym.

'Yeah! Fucking CRAP HATS!'

'Fucking wankers.'

'Fucking well done, son, well done!'

To left and right PARAs reached out to slap me on the back. I did my best to stay cool on the outside, jutting out my jaw and hoping I looked the part. But on the inside, I was on fire.

It wasn't just Andy Gow that I'd surprised with my performance: *I'd astonished myself.* The weedy kid from Smoggy Cleveland had just demolished a bloke with double my muscle-definition and three times my swagger. It was all I could do to hold the granite face for as long as I knew everyone was watching.

The applause chased me back to the dressing room.

'Ding-dong!' I announced, as I flung open the door. My team-mates surrounded me, slapping me on the back. All the tension of the fight surged to the surface. I rocked back on my heels, lifted my head and roared.

An hour later the match was all square at 4–4, with one fight to go. We were let out of the changing room for the decider, puffing out our chests beneath smart red boxing gowns. The poor bastard who now carried the expectations of every PARA in the room on his shoulders was Frank Arnold, a blond Cockney lad still in his teens.

Right now, he had way more pressure to deal with than I could even imagine. It all rested upon him.

If he lost, the Parachute Regiment's honour would be forever besmirched. If he went down under his opponent's blows, his future as a PARA was pretty much done for. And by Christ did I feel for the poor little bastard.

The bell rang and the lunatic PARAs worked themselves into an even more bloodthirsty frenzy. Our Great Young Hope leapt into the centre of the ring, an unstoppable force of nature. He instantly went for his opponent, as I had done in round two against mine. Driving the guy back to the ropes, he pulverised him under a rain of savage blows.

All around me monstrous blokes were going insane: 'FUCKING MURDER 'IM!'

After twenty seconds the ref pushed them apart, only for Frank to dart back in and smash the other guy to the ground.

The victorious chants erupted again, only louder than ever now.

'YOU – HAT – WANKER!'

The PARA Regiment officers were trying not to smile. Those from the other – rival – regiment were trying to act nonchalant, like they'd heard it all before. Like the 'you hat wanker' taunts weren't really getting to them.

Both teams were summoned into the ring.

'A great night's boxing in the finest spirit of the Army!' the master of ceremonies declared. 'Let's hear it for the team from Shorncliffe!'

There was muted applause befitting their defeat, but acknowledging that it had been a close-run thing.

'And the team from Junior PARA!' The resulting blast of noise pretty much blew the gymnasium's roof off. We were each given a trophy and a plaque, one that I will treasure till the day I die.

In the base canteen that night officers greeted us with handshakes and murmurs about the great traditions of the Regiment being upheld. On the tables were two cans to go with our scoff – and they were far from being Corporal Walt Parson's 'combat survival tins'.

'Two lagers, lads,' announced Andy Gow. 'You've earned 'em.'

Was that the suggestion of a smile? If so it was the first time I'd ever seen one grace his face.

The day after our triumph we were driven to Aldershot, to start our adult PARA Regiment training. It would culminate in dreaded Selection, better known to all as P Company (Pegasus Company). Upon arrival at Aldershot we stood in the corridor with our bags, looking forward to catching up with the rest of the group.

I thought I recognised the man who presented himself to us – but Corporal Boyd Simpson's welcome was not quite what I'd been expecting.

'Yeah – we were all at the fight,' he growled. 'But if you fucking think for one minute that's done you any favours, you've got another think coming.' He fixed his gaze upon me. 'Takes more than dancing around in a ring to be a paratrooper.'

They showed us to our accommodation. Eight to a room, we were each issued with a metal-framed bed and a thin mattress on which to reminisce about recent glories, and to dream of the future.

We boxers were in the mood to celebrate, but evidently we weren't supposed to mention our win here at Aldershot. It was just as well that we were sent home on ten days' leave – for Christmas and the New Year were approaching. This was our first chance for a home visit since we'd arrived at Junior PARA, six months earlier. I could hardly wait.

I knew we'd be getting a rail card and a train ticket, but there was an early Christmas present that I'd hadn't been expecting. We were each given a fat wad of cash – our accumulated pay. It was £600 – a big sum of money for a seventeen-year-old back then.

Some of the lads were intent on buying a fancy stereo, but all I wanted was to splash out on beer for my mates. As the train pulled into Middlesbrough I could see that Mum had plucked up the courage to join the rest of the family on the platform. I was barely off the train when she enveloped me in the biggest hug ever.

Six months ago I'd have protested and shrugged her off. Now, I let her do whatever she wanted. It was good to be home.

I hadn't thought much about how my family might have been missing me, but I saw it in their faces. My dad had seen me off with a formal handshake, but he greeted me now with a bear-hug. Neil stood there sheepish, but beaming.

They were casting surreptitious glances at me, to see if they could spot how I'd changed. I guess they thought I'd have left a boy and returned a man. But the truth was that I'd gained no weight at all. If anything, I was even more emaciated.

'What have they done to you?' declared Mum. 'Why have you shaved off all your hair?'

I explained how the Army had shaved my head, not me. As new recruits we were regularly shorn bald. It was all part of the rigorous initiation we were being put through. I could tell what Dad was thinking: *Steve was a streak of piss before and he's no better now – but at least he's our streak of piss.*

It wasn't just my news we caught up on. I'd always known Neil was nifty with a football, but his endless hours of keepy-uppy were really starting to pay off. He'd played so brilliantly for school that some serious interest was being expressed by professional clubs, including Hartlepool United.

'I'm getting a right earful in the pub,' said Dad. '*What news of Steve in the PARAs? You think Neil's good enough for the First Division?* Nobody ever asks me about me and your mam any more.'

Beneath the piss-taking, Dad was fair bursting with pride – so much so that I didn't like to remind him that I wasn't through Selection yet. What would he say to his mates in the pub if I didn't make it? After all the trouble I'd caused him, the last thing I wanted was to let him down now.

Before leaving Aldershot I'd splashed out on some new clothes – what PARAs wear when off duty. The outfit consisted of a maroon T-shirt with a PARA badge, faded jeans and desert boots with paracord shoelaces. It made me feel the part, even though I'd never even been on a plane, let alone jumped out of one.

I was wearing the lot when Simmo came round for a big, raucous reunion.

'So tell me, mate, what's it like?' he demanded.

'Truthfully? It's brutal.' I shrugged. 'We're mini-PARAS. We get beasted from sunup to sunset. We don't sleep at night, get fed raw meat, and we get screamed at by these massive Falklands veterans . . .'

Simmo had arranged for us to have some beers with Ken Williams, a mate of ours from our schooldays. The pub they'd chosen was not the most salubrious in town. Its only real merit was having a landlord who was willing to serve pints to seventeen-year-olds. In fact, he'd served me my first beer when I was fourteen.

Typically, when I looked around the pub that night it was crowded with noisy lads in scruffy jeans and even noisier girls in short skirts and high heels, and I'd have been hard-pressed to spot a true adult.

Since leaving school Ken Williams and Simmo had got jobs at Tioxide, one of the biggest chemical plants in the area. I'd admired Ken's fighting prowess while at school, but now he was the one showing all the respect – saying how much he worshipped the Army in general and the PARAs in particular.

Ken kept beckoning lads over. 'Mate! Come take a look! Steve Heaney – he's a real PARA, now!'

I was flattered, of course, but also somewhat embarrassed, so I kept reminding Ken that I had yet to pass Selection for the Parachute Regiment.

The one undeniable advantage I had over my mates was financial. Simmo and Ken were apprentices earning peanuts. Like many in that pub, they'd struggle to make the bus fare home. I was the king of cash, and the big wad in my pocket made me a magnet for allcomers, male and female alike.

'Drinks're on me!' I shouted. 'And what about a bloody kebab, after?!!'

As the night wore on one girl stood out from the pack. It was Wendy Smith, the girl who'd let me hold her hand at school. I'd always fancied her, but now that I'd been away I was looking at her with fresh eyes. She was giving me the eye back, and evidently we both liked what we saw.

By the time I boarded the train to return to Aldershot I was well rested, well-infatuated with Wendy, and pretty much skint. I used that train journey to get myself out of the soft civvie mentality, and back into PARA mode.

P Company loomed large before me now.

P Company puts wannabe PARAs through a week of gruelling tests. There's a ten-mile tab carrying a 35lb Bergen and weapon. That's followed by the Log Race, the Stretcher Race and more. And then there's the dreaded 'Trainasium' – but more of that later.

With P Company on the horizon, Corporal Boyd Simpson took it upon himself to show us the real meaning of the word 'bastard'. The first day back at camp 'Boydy' kicked us out of our cots well before dawn for the first run of the day, across furrows of frozen mud and ice. When we thought it was time for a break and some lunchtime scoff, Boydy told us we had to earn it with a second run, this one through horizontal, freezing rain.

Come nightfall he still wasn't finished. He got us out running again, alternating between the depot's floodlit parade ground and the inky blackness of the surrounding woodland.

'Where are you fuckers?' Boydy screamed, as we stumbled about in the pitch black. 'I've never seen such a group of hopeless scum! *Heinous Heaney* – get your bony arse in gear, you hear me?'

'Yes, corporal! Right, corporal!'

Ten days of beer and partying had taken its toll.

As the days wore on some of the guys formed groups, seeking strength in numbers. I teamed up with a bloke in my platoon by the name of Karl Whitehead. Karl was the same height as me – six feet – but with a far broader physique. He was also five years older, having signed up as an adult. I decided to stick close and see what I could learn from him.

Boydy waited until the coldest morning of that bitter January, before calling for Karl and me. He seemed to have it in for me in particular, and Karl was catching some of the inevitable flak. We were ordered to break the ice that covered the Basingstoke Canal, which runs along the back of Depot PARA.

'You know what we're doing this for, don't you?' Karl muttered.

'Not a clue, mate.'

'How old are you again?' Karl asked, shaking his head.

He had a smile on his face like the ones I used to give Neil, when he'd said something incredibly stupid. But unbeknown to us, Boydy had sneaked up in the semi-darkness. He must have noticed Karl's sardonic smile.

He exhaled in the freezing air – a dragon belching smoke and fire. 'Think this funny? Right, in you go. You've got four minutes to swim to the other side and back. Let's see if that'll wipe the smile off your chops . . .'

I turned to face the water, the surface broken here and there by jagged chunks of broken ice. Corporal Boyd had to be having a laugh. He couldn't seriously want us to swim across that? *Through that?* But then I noticed that Karl was tearing off his uniform and dumping it on the ground.

'Get down to your underpants,' he muttered. 'Quick! Or you'll be weighed down by your sodden clothes.'

He dived in.

He surfaced with a strangled grunt and stretched out into a slow crawl, as if he didn't want to leave me too far behind. Moments later my own head hit the water. I had a fleeting sense of the skin of my face being shredded by shards of ice, before my body was caught in the vice-like grip of the cold.

I felt as if I couldn't move. Even worse, I could barely lift my head above the surface to gulp a gasp of freezing air. I sensed myself getting dragged back under, my limbs too numb to stop me going down. After breathing in a few dollops of the filthy, iced-choked water, I'd be done for.

I glanced at Karl. There was nothing lazy about his crawl now. The cold had got the better of him and he was thrashing ahead. I had to follow his lead. The only trouble was the time lag between my brain ordering my body into action, and my skinny arms actually responding.

Forcing myself to move, I struck out for the opposite bank. But I was so slow I almost smashed my head against Karl's, as I ran into him on his return leg. I saw his blue lips moving feverishly, but I wasn't sure if he was trying to coax me or curse me.

By the time Karl helped me out neither of us could speak. Boydy had been dead right: our dip in the canal sure had wiped the smiles off our faces. A hot shower would have been great, but needless to say the rest of the blokes had gone in ahead of us, and there was only cold water left for Karl and me.

That dunking in the Canal Of Death put the fear of God into me. We'd not even started P Company yet, and this was the kind of thing we were facing. I saw two visions of my possible future. In one, I'd passed P Company. I was grinning for my mate's camera while doing a freefall into some far-flung desert, armed and primed for action. That photo was destined for future editions of the PARA Regiment brochure.

The other vision had me bombing out of P Company with a bad injury, and crashing and burning. Which course would my life take?

Everything seemed to hinge on P Company.

7

I was three months into Aldershot when the fateful day dawned: Day One – P Company. All the trials and tribulations of Junior PARA had led up to this. At the end of the coming week I would know the truth: either I was PARA Regiment material, or I was a reject.

Fitter than ever, I was a streak of wiry, honed muscle and sinew, without an inch of fat. But did I have the sheer grunt and upper body strength – not to mention the mental robustness – to see me through?

The first stages of P Company take place in and around the Aldershot base.

I awoke at 6 a.m. to familiar surroundings, but knowing that the next few days would be anything but familiar. Swinging my feet over the edge of my cot, I felt my stomach churning with nerves. The last thing I felt like right now was food, but I knew that I'd need every calorie for what lay ahead. I hurried to the mess and forced down a massive plate of greasy eggs, fried bread, sausage, bacon and beans.

That done, we mustered outside. I was ordered to daub the number '28' on the left-hand pocket of my green combat trousers – there being twenty-seven guys lined up ahead of me. From now on I didn't have a name. The P Company Staff didn't care who I was. Everything I did – good or bad – would be noted down to that number.

All told there were fifty of us that nerve-jangling morning. As we gathered beside the base football pitch I felt the goose bumps rising. I hoped no one would notice I was shivering – though whether it was from the early morning chill, or nerves I wasn't sure. Karl Whitehead came up beside me, ashen-faced.

'Good luck, mate,' he muttered.

The next minute our first orders were being screamed at us. We dropped to our stomachs in thick mud, waiting for a thunder-flash – like a massive banger – to explode. That was the signal that the first event – the Steeple Chase – was on.

I breathed in the stink of the mud as the seconds ticked by.

BOOM! The blast was painfully loud in the still dawn air.

Before I knew it I'd leapt to my feet and was sprinting across the grass, elbows flying and cracking into the blokes to either side of me, as we jostled for position. Every event in P Company is against the clock, so it was vital to get to the head of the pack and find some space.

At the far end of the pitch was a wall of dark vegetation with a tiny gap that led into the woods. The first man to reach that chokepoint would be fine; the last would be trapped at the back until the crush subsided. In the Steeple Chase we had eighteen minutes to traverse two miles of dense, tangled woodland and deep pools of stagnant water: there wasn't a second to lose.

I wasn't first to the chokepoint, but I sure wasn't last. As I raced through the trees my eyes were searching for roots that might cause me to trip, then flicking up to scan for the way ahead. I leapt over streams and charged through pools of water, pumping my legs hard on the uphill stretches. Accelerating down the slopes, I pushed it to the max – but still I didn't get higher than tenth place.

I'd done it in sixteen minutes, thirty seconds. In my Satsuma days, that would have been an ace performance. Here, it was middling.

Back at our starting point we stripped off our wet gear. We were a pretty subdued bunch over lunch. As we wolfed down burgers and fries with half-a dozen slices of bread, every one of us was thinking about the next event, the Log Race.

If you were slow in the Steeple Chase you were marked down.

But if you messed up on the Log Race, it was an instant fail.

The Log is a like a telegraph pole on steroids, weighing in at 60kg or more. Attached to each side are rope loops – hand-holds. You have to run for one and a half miles in helmet and webbing, the log slung between eight of you. They allow you fifteen minutes to cover the distance across horrendous ground – rough tracks that roller coaster over undulating heath and bog, the lower sections awash with stagnant water.

A fall, a collision or anything else that snatches your hand out of the loop of rope means close to instant death – or at the very least, a big step towards failure. Traipsing into the flat, open sandy bowl where the logs were waiting, we looked like condemned men.

'You eight – log one!' bawled the nearest P Company staffer.

I saw Karl Whitehead fall into line next to a bloke who was several inches shorter than him. Any difference in height would present a severe disadvantage when you were tearing along a track, trying to keep the log level – but the choice of team make-up seemed completely at random.

'You eight – log two!'

Sod's law – I found myself jostled into line opposite the titchiest bloke around. Same problem as Karl, only worse.

There wasn't a minute to gripe or talk tactics. We tensed shoulders, lifted the log and for the second time that day the boom of a thunderflash set us all running. Everyone wanted their team to be first out of the sand bowl and on to a narrow, stony track that rose into the surrounding hills.

'Go! Go! Go!' came the shout from Karl's team, which was nosing ahead of us.

'GET A FUCKING MOVE ON!' I heard myself roar.

My left hand was looped in the rope and I was pushing out my right elbow, to make it hard for anyone to pass us.

Behind I heard someone yelling: 'Push past the bastards!'

A desperate battle ensued, as the two teams directly to our rear fought to avoid hitting the trail last.

My team made the track third out of six. We hit the first climb. This was where the best and worst of my runner's physique was brought home. I knew I had more turbocharge in my legs than most, but my rope-arm looked spindly, compared with the bulging biceps of the others.

The little guy beside me was carrying the log six inches lower than I was. Much more of this and my left arm was going to be ripped out of its socket. As we topped the first ridge and the pain burned up my left side, a voice roared in my head. *Bollocks. Sod the pain. Just get it done.*

The track levelled out, but the grunting and cursing from behind was getting louder. Out of the corner of my eye I saw the next team in line were almost upon us. Their lead runners were barging into the blokes bringing up our rear, in an effort to throw them off balance.

This was the critical moment. The track was only wide enough for one team running at the required pace – roughly ten minutes a mile. If we were rammed and barged off we'd lose vital seconds, and we could easily take injuries.

'MOVE YOUR ARSES!' I yelled at my teammates, and especially the guys in front setting the pace. 'MOVE IT! They're trying to smash us from behind!'

I tried to up my pace, but the harder I strove, the more I felt myself being dragged down by the little guy beside me. *Fucking poison dwarf,* I found myself cursing. *Fucking stumpy!*

But as much as anything, *this* was the test of the Log Race: to see who could work in a team, no matter who he might be paired with. Somehow, I had to make it work with Stumpy, not to mention the six other blokes on my log.

The team behind was neck-and-neck with us now. As sixteen pairs of legs thundered down a steep incline, boots fighting for grip in the wet, we were in danger of snarling up and taking a murderous fall.

Ahead of us, the track narrowed. The ground fell away to either side. I saw an opportunity to seize the moment.

'NOSE RIGHT!' I yelled.

By swinging our log to the right we could slam into our opponents, narrowing their potential overtaking space. Either they'd be forced back where they belonged, or they'd fall. Sure, there was a risk they might take us with them, but I figured it was worth it.

Ponderously, our log swung into our opponents' path. For a moment they faltered. Then a giant of a man with a wrestler's physique barged into my bony shoulder, leading their counter-attack. The impact knocked the breath out of me. I tried hitting back, only to find my arm pinned to my side as he leaned in, trying to eject our team from the track.

I felt the crunch of the bloke's massive boot on my heel. If he could topple the skinny lad, he was thinking, our team would go down and his would have a clear run to the finish.

Well, fuck that.

There was only one thing for it. If I didn't have the muscle, I'd just have to make up for it with speed.

'This is it, lads!' I screamed. 'Get your speed up! NOW!'

They dug deep and responded to a man. Slowly we inched ahead. The gap for our opponents narrowed, and then we were in front, blocking them. Monster bloke couldn't match us on sheer speed.

The cursing and grunting faded. We picked up speed on a downhill stretch, thundered through a knee-deep slough of water, and surged towards the finish. My muscles were burning knots of pain, my lungs were on fire, my throat was parched – but every second brought us nearer to the moment when we could let this cursed log fall.

The Staff running alongside us must have sensed the whiff of elation creeping in. *The sense of the finish.* From out of nowhere I felt a massive crack to the rear of my helmet. It all but sent me pitching forward onto my face.

I had no idea who it was, until I heard the Staff bellow: 'FASTER, YOU LITTLE SHITS! FAAAAST-ERRRR!'

We obeyed the order and fair flew down the hill.

The two teams ahead of us were fighting for first place. Then everything seemed to go into slow motion. One bloke lost his footing and fell heavily. One by one, his teammates crashed to the ground. A couple of guys' hands were ripped from the ropes. Their grim expressions showed how much it hurt.

I scanned the fallers to see if Karl was among them, then spotted him celebrating victory at the finish. We made it in second, and we'd managed to beat the clock.

Never had Army scoff tasted as good as it did that night: roast chicken and spuds swimming in thick gravy. Even the stodgy staple of jam roly-poly and custard went down a treat. Then it was straight to bed. I needed the restorative power of sleep for what was coming next – the Assault Course.

It consists of a dozen obstacles – from a wall higher than your tallest bloke, to a balance beam that you have to run along, six feet above the ground. We had to cling to rope swings, crawl through narrow, stinking tunnels and leap off a high platform into dark, stagnant water – before doing the entire course three more times in our sodden, freezing clothes.

They'd given us seven-and-a-half minutes to complete it. I did it in less, but that was nothing to be smug about. One mega-fit guy finished it in four minutes forty-five.

We were three events down and I was still in the game. More importantly, I was injury-free. Plus my favourite was next up: boxing, better known in the PARAs as 'Milling'.

Milling is something of a legend in PARA Regiment circles. It's designed as a 'test of controlled aggression'. You have to stand toe to toe with your opponent and fight, no ducking or evasive action allowed. You have to take the punishment, give as good as you get, and if you're knocked down get right back up again.

The idea is that if you're prepared to hurt your mates, you'll rip the enemy apart. After the Junior PARA boxing bouts, with Andy Gow threatening to turn my bollocks into a necklace – I figured I could take it.

There's no dancing around your opponent in Milling. We stood there and knocked seven bales of shit out of each other. I took most of the pummelling in the first few seconds, but after that I matched him punch for punch. We landed savage blows but neither of us retreated an inch.

'Good fight, good fight,' announced the P Company staffer, once our time was up.

Compared to what had gone before – the Log Race first and foremost – the next trial was one I figured I was good for. The Speed March is a ten-mile beast under a 35lb Bergen, complete with weapon. We pulled on boots, denims and combat jacket smocks, collected self-loading rifles from the armoury and set off at a cracking pace, the P Company Staff leading.

The Speed March ended with a good pass for me, and still no injuries. But next up was the wild card – the Trainasium, which is an assault course in the air. The Trainasium is an instant pass or fail, and unlike the rest of P Company's tests, there are few if any ways you can train for it.

We gathered below a giant climbing frame – a towering latticework of steel fashioned from scaffolding poles. I gazed up at it, noting that the biggest drops had zero safety nets below them. Anyone who fell was going to end up with some broken limbs or worse.

As luck would have it, I was one of the first to go. The advantage was that I had less time to think about it, and bottle. The disadvantage was that I'd miss the chance to watch other blokes negotiating the twists, turns and death-defying leaps, and learn from their mistakes.

After climbing a ladder I found myself facing a long piece of wooden planking. I was hardly any height off the ground at this point, so what could go wrong?

'Twenty-eight! Get moving! Run!' came the yell from the P Company Staff below.

It wasn't until I was going full pelt that I felt the plank start to move. They'd rigged it up to make it swing, oscillate and shake.

I forced myself to keep going. But the further I went, the more the plank seemed to sway about wildly. After staggering to the left, I corrected my balance, then lurched to the right. I stretched out my arms to either side to steady myself, like a trapeze artist on a high wire.

Then I heard an almighty clatter beneath my feet.

For a horrible moment I thought the whole thing was collapsing. I closed my senses to the fear and surged onwards, holding my balance for just long enough to reach the far end. Ahead of me lay the next big challenge – one that we'd all heard talk of. This was the point where most blokes bottled it.

I climbed higher up the crazy frame and came to a gap in the boardwalk. The only way forward was to leap from one plank to another across six feet of open space – the infamous 'Illusion Jump'. The far plank was positioned to one side and a bit lower. Glancing down, I saw what would happen if I messed up. I'd fall onto a latticework of steel directly below.

I took a series of deep breaths, trying to calm myself. I could hear the Staff yelling expletives at me. Blanking out their voices, I took a run up and launched myself into thin air, trying to keep my body upright and my knees bent to cushion the landing.

My boots hit with a hollow thunk, but the plank was so narrow that my momentum almost carried me over the far side. I let my knees take the impact and gripped with my hands, but even so I almost lost my footing.

Pulse thumping like a machine gun I managed to right myself. I re-orientated, moved ahead, and climbed higher towards the next challenge – the shuffle bars.

As I scurried up the next ladder, I felt the wind tugging at my smock. I climbed to the very highest platform and got a better look. In front of me were two steel poles, like scaffold bars, stretching ten feet or so to the far side. I glanced down. All I could see was a sheer drop to a criss-cross of skull-splitting metalwork.

'Number twenty-eight!' a voice yelled. 'Walk along the bars from one side to the other.'

A gust of wind seemed to carry his words away.

'Repeat!' I shouted back. 'Don't think I heard you right.'

'Walk the bars! Get going! NOW!'

This was insane.

'Go-Go-Go!' came the yell from below.

I forced my best foot forward, and to my horror I felt the rigid sole of my boot slither and slide. The metal was still greasy with morning dew. I threw my arms out to either side, to better balance myself. If my boots slipped I guessed I could try to save myself with my arms, grabbing for the bars as I fell.

'Get moving!'

I inched ahead. A few feet before me lay a knuckle-joint on each bar, which I would have to negotiate to reach the far side. I stood on a trembling right leg while I swung my left over, repeating the process until both feet were clear of the obstacle. Then I adjusted my position, even as the wind rose to a nasty howl.

I calmed my breathing and steeled myself for the final stretch. Then came the call from below.

'Twenty-eight! Stand still, bend down and touch your toes!'

'You've gotta be fucking joking.' It was said under my breath, but I meant every word.

'When you've done that straighten up and shout your name, rank and number! Now! Do it! Other lads're backing up behind you!'

I glanced to my back. No one. But it didn't particularly matter. If I bottled it now that was P Company done for.

I forced myself to do as ordered. Up until this moment I'd avoided looking down. No escaping it now, not unless I closed my eyes, and if you've ever tried to balance on one leg with your eyes closed you'll know how fatal that can be. I shifted my weight onto the balls of my feet, then bent and stretched out my frozen fingers towards the tops of my boots. I felt the rush of blood to my head, as I stared into the beckoning drop.

Two narrow, greasy iron beams – and below that, the abyss.

If I lost my balance now, this would be terminal.

I fought the temptation to jump.

Vertigo. I'd never had much of a fear of heights.

Until now.

8

My fingertips reached for the dull leather of my boot-fronts, my head spinning like a dark whirlpool. I touched my toes, stood slowly and shouted out my name, rank and number – after which I was ordered down.

I had survived the Trainasium.

I had conquered the fear and made it across that final set of bars.

We moved on to the Brecon Beacons, in the midst of the Welsh mountains, for the last tests, culminating in the Stretcher Race – lugging a 15-stone metal 'stretcher' over a ten-mile course.

In due course I stood in line with the remaining recruits to hear the fateful news: who had passed and who had failed. This was the day that everything in my short life had been leading up to. I felt the adrenaline surging through me.

Come on, I told myself, *let's get on with it!*

The P Company Staff seemed in no hurry. It was almost as if they were relishing the last few moments of torture – their final seconds of power over us. After this, we would be relatively free: free either to return to our former lives, or to join the brotherhood.

The lead Staff read out the first name. Recruit Number 1.

'Johnson.'

A figure jumped. 'Sir?'

'Pass.'

Johnson's look of disbelief dissolved into a massive smile. 'Sir!'

Recruit Number 2. 'Greening.'

'Sir?'

'Fail.'

'Sir . . .' I glanced at Greening, hardly able to believe what I had heard. *Fucking hell*, I told myself, *he was flying.*

I was worried now. Shitting myself. As the Staff ploughed through the numbers I started wondering what I'd do if I failed. I honestly didn't know.

There were six fails, then seven, then eight: this was brutal. I was steeling myself for the inevitable: *Heaney! Sir? Fail . . . Heaney! Sir? Fail . . .* Those words would haunt me for the rest of my days.

'Heaney!' the Staff repeated. 'You still with us, Heaney?'

I'd missed the first call.

'Sir! Yes, Sir!'

Then, one word: 'Pass.'

'Sir!' The relief flooded through me, one bruised and aching limb at a time, until my whole body felt like it was glowing. The fates of those who came after me were a blur, apart from one: Karl Whitehead had also passed.

When the final recruit, No. 51, was told his fate – a pass; they couldn't end on a fail – Major Mike Heaton, the Officer in Command of P Company, stepped forward.

'Gentlemen, it falls to me to announce the name of P Company's top recruit, the man amongst you who's amassed the most points.'

He ran his eye down the list, pausing for dramatic effect. I had a few strong boys in mind for the award. Some of them were in their mid-twenties. They were big tough units with a real maturity.

'Private Heaney!' the major announced. 'Congratulations. Step forward to receive your award.'

I was utterly astonished. As I stepped out of line, my legs moved as if by a force I couldn't control. The major presented me with a plaque, and I guess I saluted him and shook his hand – though it was all a bit of a blur.

We marched off the square to the sound of Corporal Boyd 'Boydy' Simpson screeching: 'Left, right, left, right.'

My plaque was gripped in my left hand. I searched out Karl and flashed him a smile, thinking I was far enough forward not to be seen by Boydy. His yell brought me down to earth with a bump.

'Heinous Heaney – you can wipe that fucking grin off your face! You're still a fucking wanker in my book!'

The fails left instantly, their dreams in tatters, while the twenty-eight of us who'd passed were left to congratulate each other. I can't deny I was proud as Punch to be the focus of much of the attention. The lads shook my hand so hard it almost hurt.

'Well done, mate.'

'Cheers, mate. Brilliant.'

'Wow. We're in.'

Then came the moment we'd been waiting for: the order to break out our Parachute Regiment berets.

Nobody – not even Boyd Simpson – could rob me of the pure, unadulterated pleasure of placing that maroon beret on my head for the first time. I didn't mind who saw me walking up to the mirror and beaming at my reflection. A year back I'd been a spotty adolescent in a Middlesbrough police cell, the lowest of the low. A zero. Now I was holding my head high, and perched upon it was that iconic symbol – the beret of the Parachute Regiment.

We now faced three weeks of tactics and live firing training. The Royal Marines of 42 Commando were just finishing a bout of instruction, even as we arrived to start ours. Whenever the Marines and the PARAs come into contact, the long-standing rivalry between the two units inevitably comes to the fore.

The sight of a black Ford Mondeo staff car bearing the badge of the Royal Marines must have been like a red rag to a bull for one of the old and the bold of the PARAs. We were called out on parade by our regimental sergeant major (RSM), his face puce with rage.

'Right, you bunch of fuckers! Which one of you jokers is Sid the fucking Snail?'

We new boys looked at each other in total bemusement. None of us had the faintest clue what the RSM was talking about. *Sid the Snail?*

He ran a gimlet eye down the ranks, his face like murder. 'So, Sid the fucking Snail doesn't want to step forward? No fucking surprises there! For his own fucking good Sid the fucking Snail had better have fucking emigrated. If I ever lay my hands upon 'im . . .'

It turned out that Sidney the Snail was a turd.

He'd been nicknamed Sid the Snail for a variety of reasons: because a 2p coin had been placed on his back, for a shell; because cotton buds had been inserted at the head-end, for eye stalks; because the entire lot had been arranged on the front seat of the – supposedly secure, impregnable and alarmed – Royal Marine Commando staff car; but mainly because behind the whole ensemble was propped a white card bearing the immortal lines:

Sid the Snail.
British Airborne.
In town for a few days.

It wasn't nice. It wasn't pretty.

But as PARA Reg wind-ups went, it was a classic.

I relished every joke and piss-take, but mostly I loved the new skills that I was learning. And above all I wanted to get on to the next course – parachute training – without which none of us could ever wear our prized PARA wings.

Finally, we headed down to RAF Brize Norton, Oxfordshire, the home of military parachuting. In a way, this was the culmination of all that I'd dreamt about, ever since I saw that glossy PARA brochure in the Army Careers Office.

I'd 'won' my coveted maroon beret, but no one could be truly Airborne without earning their Parachute Wings – which proved you were qualified to hurl yourself out of aeroplanes.

Before attempting our first jump we had to go through ground school. We used a full-size mockup of a C130 Hercules transport aircraft to practise exiting from the side doors. We stood and threw ourselves onto the ground, learning to bend our knees and roll with the impact. We leapt from steps and took running jumps from ramps. We clung to a trapeze and swung through the air, letting go on the instructor's command and performing the requisite forwards tumble.

After a few days we could land sideways, backwards, any which way.

The day of my first live jump dawned clear and bright, with just a gentle breeze. A Second World War anti-aircraft balloon was tethered 800 feet above the ground. It wasn't quite leaping from a speeding Hercules – but everyone learning to parachute for the British military starts by jumping out of that balloon.

The excitement I felt was mingled with trepidation. The fear I'd experienced when I'd touched my toes on top of the Trainasium had lasted only a fleeting moment, but the memory of it still haunted me. If I looked down from that balloon, today, I'd see twenty times that drop.

The instructors had given it to us straight. Plenty of guys went all the way up, only to refuse the jump and be hauled down again. None of us really knew what we were made of until the moment of the jump. Would I take the plunge and trust my life to a few dozen square metres of silk, or would I bottle it?

The first four of us boarded the crane that would take us up, up, up. As we rose through the air towards the heights our instructor chatted away, in an effort to take our minds off what was coming.

But I wasn't listening. I was staring at what appeared to be a picnic basket suspended beneath the balloon. It looked more suited to carrying sponge cake and fine china cups than supporting the weight of four wannabe PARAs – plus instructor.

The feeble breeze at ground level gusted stronger as we rose higher. This was something I'd wanted so badly. I'd been convinced that, like Superman, I'd be a natural-born flier. But when the moment came to clamber aboard a wind-blown picnic basket, I found myself wishing I was back at ground level.

One by one our parachutes were hooked up to a cable.

I closed my eyes for a moment, reliving the words of the pre-jump briefing. Our chief instructor had pointed out that what we were about to do was about as bad as it gets. It's far scarier to jump straight down from a static balloon than to be one of a string of blokes exiting an aircraft. You barely catch a glimpse of the ground from inside a dark and noisy Hercules.

In the eerie, windswept silence of the picnic basket I was painfully aware of the drop. I was either fortunate, or grossly unfortunate – for I was the first to be called forward to a gap in the basket's side leading into thin air. Everyone on the course would be craning their necks to watch.

'Steady, lad. Nice and easy, just like in training,' said a voice in my ear – the instructor's. 'Just look at the horizon. Don't look down.'

I felt calmer now that I had some instructions to follow.

'Hands across your reserve . . . and go!'

I'd like to say I leapt heroically into the void. In reality I felt a sharp push on my back – probably the kindest way – and suddenly I was falling. Within moments I accelerated to an incredible speed. My stomach was in my mouth. For what felt like an entire lifetime – but was only a couple of seconds – I was staring at the ground, as it rushed up to pulverise me.

If I hit it at my current speed I'd end up like road-kill.

And then it felt as if I was being wrenched backwards by a giant pair of hands, and my parachute blossomed above me. The panicked near-certainty of imminent death was replaced by this incredible sensation of . . . floating on thin air.

The ground didn't seem to be getting any nearer. Instead, I had a feeling of truly being able to fly, and of having all the time in the world to look around me. So, this was parachuting.

Wow.

The thought didn't last for long. I was getting closer to the ground. There was a drop zone (DZ) safety officer below with a megaphone. He began shouting instructions, which brought me back to reality. Landing time.

'Number one parachutist: pull down on your rear lift webs.'

Corporal Boyd Simpson would have puked at the nice, friendly way in which these RAF chaps addressed us.

'Okay, number one, look around you,' the posh voice drifted up to me. 'There are no parachutists anywhere near. Good. You're clear. Assess wind speed – and . . . you're coming in for a forward right landing. Bring elbows in, feet and knees together, chin on chest and . . . accept the landing.'

I did as instructed. Managing a half roll I bounced straight up on to my feet. Then I unclipped my parachute to make sure it didn't inflate again in the breeze and drag me across the field. It was a near-perfect landing, proof that I didn't need Boydy screaming abuse at me.

If that was parachuting, it was awesome. Utterly fucking brilliant.

The euphoria and the adrenaline rush was the best feeling ever.

All I could think was: *I want to do that again.* As luck would have it a second jump was in the offing – courtesy of those nice RAF chaps – and this time it would be from a real live aeroplane.

I'd never flown anywhere, so this was a whole new experience. But in truth, jumping out of that aircraft was a total blast. The balloon had done its job, just as intended: it had broken our fear.

I'd known it all along, of course: the Parachute Regiment would be the making or breaking of me. But I only realised how much my family had also felt it when they drove down en masse for my passing out parade. My gran was there, as well as Mum, Dad and Neil.

The big news from home was that Neil had been signed by Arsenal, who'd been top of the First Division for most of the season.

My dad was made up about it. Both of his sons were on their way to making their boyhood dreams come true. But Mum seemed quieter, her pride tinged with regret over her prematurely empty nest – Neil having moved to London with the signing.

The morning of the parade I put on my Second World War-style battle dress – a 'No.2' tailored jacket, with brass buttons down the front and matching trousers. It was the smartest outfit that I had ever owned – but it wasn't nearly as smart as the beret that I'd bought from Victors, the local military outfitters.

The berets we'd been issued with were cheap pieces of crap in comparison. My Victors beret had a thick leather band that you could shape to fit your head. In time, it would become my proudest possession of all.

The brass band of the Parachute Regiment struck up what has become the de facto regimental anthem – Wagner's 'Ride of the Valkyries'. We marched onto the parade square in perfect unison, our families gathered on a dais in front of the main hangar. At our head was the regimental mascot, a white Shetland pony called 'Corporal Pegasus' – Pegasus being the winged stallion from Greek mythology.

Like every other passing out recruit, I was staring rigidly straight ahead. I couldn't see Mum, Dad, Neil and Gran yet, but I was conscious of the rows of big, brightly-coloured hats and dark suits and ties beside the hangar.

Major-General John 'Johnny' Frost took the salute for the parade. He'd won the Military Cross (MC) for leading a daredevil mission to steal the technology from a German radar installation, in the Second World War, but he was most famous for his role in the Battle of Arnhem. Frost had spearheaded the 1st Airborne Division's 1944 assault on the bridge at Arnhem, leading his men into one of the fiercest battles of the war.

After four days of being cut off under intense enemy fire, the surviving paratroopers ran out of ammunition. Frost, who'd been injured by shrapnel in both feet, was forced to surrender.

Needless to say, he was a legendary figure in the Regiment.

The bridge at Arnhem had been renamed John Frost Bridge, and Frost was played by Anthony Hopkins in the iconic film, *A Bridge Too Far*. I couldn't have been more thrilled that it was him who was presiding over our parade.

Halfway through, however, the very heavens opened. Major-General John 'Johnny' Frost didn't so much as flinch. His salute – his ramrod figure – remained unmoving. Likewise, we stood stock-still as the rain ran in rivulets down our faces. And the band kept playing, never missing a beat.

The first to break for cover were a couple of the families sat right at the edge of the crowd. But in no time the trickle had become a flood – as men in suits and ladies in nice dresses stampeded for the shelter of the hangar.

But one family remained in their places, utterly unperturbed. I felt one of those rare lumps in my throat, as I risked a glance in their direction. Mam, Dad, Neil and Gran weren't the types to run from a spot of rain.

Maybe that was it, I found myself thinking. Maybe that was the spirit that had seen me through the last twelve months of hell.

As the last of the ladies in their fine hats barged past, my mum's mum, Doris Dring, didn't so much as falter. The giant raindrops were wreaking havoc with her perm, but she didn't care. Beside her was Neil, his shoulders shaking as those middle-aged women struggled to maintain their dignity and their fancy hairstyles, while legging it for cover.

When the band stopped playing Major-General Frost did a wonderful thing. He went over to my family and shook each by the hand.

'Thank you for remaining firm under fire.' He glanced at the nearby hangar. 'You were the only ones.'

It was a gracious compliment from one of the most courageous men I'd ever had the honour to meet. I wasn't sure who was the prouder: my family of me, or me of them. There were hugs, kisses and tears in the NAAFI bar afterwards, and a good few drinks were downed, toasting my future.

I was joining B Company, 3 PARA as a newly-badged PARA – better known to all as a 'crow'.

9

I hadn't been in the Parachute Regiment for long when I first heard whispers of a mysterious 'black platoon' – a secretive elite within an elite. They were based on the other side of the camp, headquartered in an old band room. But you could only ever gain entry into that high-security part of camp if you were of their number – one of the chosen few.

Rumour had it they specialised in missions more often than not set deep behind enemy lines. Reputed to be older than your average PARA, they were more experienced and battle-hardened.

They were supposedly experts at highly-specialised parachute-insertion techniques – HALO and HAHO. In the former – high-altitude low-opening – you jump from extreme high altitude – up to fifty times what I had managed from that Second World War barrage balloon – and plummet to earth, only pulling your chute at the last moment, so as to hide your approach from any watching eyes. As for HAHO – high-altitude high-opening – it was if anything an even more extreme means via which to penetrate deep into hostile territory unseen and undetected.

Formally, this small band of mystery men was called the Pathfinders. They were known by various nicknames but mostly as the X Platoon.

I'd never heard of the likes of the X Platoon. You wouldn't – not unless you made it into the brotherhood of the PARAs. They weren't exactly the kind of soldiers to advertise their existence, and for some reason I felt myself irresistibly drawn to this mysterious unit. But no fresh recruit – no seventeen-year-old kid – was going to be joining their number any time soon.

Instead, I was heading for Northern Ireland.

It was 1989, and the British Army's deployment to Northern Ireland was approaching two decades old. Tensions between loyalists and nationalists, Catholics and Protestants, were running as high as ever. In fact, they'd rarely, if ever, been more murderous or intense.

Recently three members of an IRA active service unit (ASU) had been killed while preparing for a bomb attack in Gibraltar. Subsequently, their funeral had been attacked by loyalist paramilitary types at Belfast's Milltown Cemetery. Two British Army corporals dressed in plain clothes had inadvertently driven their car down the street carrying the funeral cortege. It was flanked by balaclava'd IRA members, who somehow recognised the two men as military. Within seconds Derek Wood and David Howes had been surrounded by an enraged mob.

Before deploying to Northern Ireland we were shown the footage shot from a helicopter. Howes fired warning shots but they had zero effect. The mob still hauled him and his mate from their vehicle. They were dragged through the streets to some waste ground, where they were stripped and beaten. Finally, they were executed in cold blood with bullets to the head, as they lay defenceless on the ground.

I'd never forget the photographs of the priest giving the last rites to Howes, his head and much of his body covered in blood. There was no more sobering a warning than that. It was an incendiary time for us to be heading to Northern Ireland.

Just before we were scheduled to deploy, I noticed a guy wandering through camp dressed in a PARA regimental smock over faded jungle trousers. He wore his scraggy hair long, and I clocked the distinctive DZ patch that was sewn onto his sleeve: red over green with a white arrow driven through it.

I asked around the blokes in my Company. Sure enough, that DZ flash was the mark of the X Platoon – the Pathfinders. The more I asked, the more my eyes were opened. Inside the PARAs – a regiment invariably placed at the tip of the British Army's spear – was a secretive unit whose existence was unknown outside a small, very exclusive circle.

The Pathfinders had been set up four years earlier, and few knew what they got up to. Formed on the black economy, they were a completely off-the-books outfit, one that supposedly didn't exist: they had no official budget or even personnel. On paper, every man in their number remained serving with his parent unit. They also had no official issue of kit – including weaponry or ammo – which meant they had to beg, borrow and steal from other units.

Hence the unofficial name given to them – the X Platoon; 'X' as in does not exist.

The selection process to join the Pathfinders was rumoured to be sheer murder. It supposedly made P Company look like child's play, because it was modelled upon SAS Selection, which pretty much said it all. And needless to say, Pathfinder operations were dangerous and risk-laden in the extreme.

The burning ambition that had got me into the PARAs was suddenly rekindled. I was proud to be in what many argue is the best combat regiment in the British Army – but clearly, I wasn't quite at the tip of the spear yet.

I knew it was utterly taking the piss – I'd yet to be deployed anywhere on active operations, and I hadn't even fired a shot in anger – but I went to see my commanding officer anyway, to ask him if I could be put forward for Selection into the Pathfinders.

My CO's response was three short, blunt sentences. 'Operational tour to Northern Ireland. No men spared. Dismissed.'

And that, for the moment, was that.

It was January 1989 when we were sent 'across the water', as it was euphemistically known back then. B Company was straight into it – kicking down the doors of suspected IRA terrorists, and turning their houses upside down searching for weaponry and explosives. And I have to admit, from day one I loved it.

Shortly afterwards, I was selected for a specialist search-team unit. I was trained by The Royal Engineers to use all sorts of cutting-edge and – back then – secret anti-terrorism equipment, including ultrasound to 'listen' for hidden compartments in walls and under floors, fibre-optics to see around corners and into hidden spaces, and a computer 'sniffer' that could detect the 'scent signature' of explosives.

Most of our time was spent hunting down IEDs (improvised explosive devices) and weapons caches in a never-ending battle to stop the nationalists and the loyalists kicking the shit out of each other – and, not least, out of us lot.

In my first few weeks a Sinn Féin councillor was killed in his car by loyalist gunmen, three Protestant guys were shot dead by the IRA in a garage, and two British soldiers were blown up by a land mine while executing a foot patrol. The IRA also managed to detonate three bombs in Shropshire's Tern Hill Barracks, so taking the fight to the British mainland.

All just to keep us on our toes.

Whenever we smashed our way into a suspect's house and our ultrasound detectors found anomalies in walls and floors, we'd bring in the jackhammers and start tearing up the bricks and concrete, and at times the garden patio too. You can imagine how popular it made us.

We'd been briefed on one of the terrorists' favourite methods of concealment. It was to dig a hole in a floor and lower in a milk churn stuffed full of weaponry and explosives. They'd repair the floor, setting Rawlplugs and screws into the concrete to make a simple cover that could be lifted free and closed again.

Scuffed over with dirt and dust the cover became all but undetectable. Yet all that was required to open it and arm an IRA ASU was to roll a rug aside, unscrew the screws halfway, and then use them as handles to lift out the lid.

On one particular raid I noticed that there seemed to be a break in the surface of a floor. With my heart pounding, I got down on my hands and knees and proceeded to rub the dirt aside. Sure enough, I felt my fingertips uncover two Rawlplugs.

The IRA were known to booby trap their weapons hides, so that anyone attempting to investigate would be blown to smithereens. But there was no way to check this one out, other than by lifting the lid and having a look inside. I was right. The screws proved to be attached to a roughly circular lump of concrete the size of a dinner plate.

Some Royal Engineers were called in to assist with lifting the lid. It came free, to reveal a dark cavity. I switched on my torch and flicked the beam inside. A space had been hollowed out underneath the floor, and hidden inside it was a small war-in-a-box.

First of all I noticed the light glinting on a length of metal pipe inserted into the space at a forty-five degree angle. The interior of the pipe was packed full of explosives and 'shipyard confetti' – DIY shrapnel, like nails, bolts and screws. It was a classic IED, or a 'pipe bomb', as they are more commonly known in Northern Ireland.

I shone my torch further into the gloom, spotting the timers for the device, which were also stuffed into the hole. Then there were the distinctive forms of two AK47 assault rifles, plus a pair of Makarov pistols, a half-dozen clips of ammo, and several AK47 magazines stuffed full of 7.62mm rounds.

Needless to say, it was one hell of a find.

A cache of that order would be used to equip an ASU team of from two to four terrorists, most likely for a multistage attack. The IED would be planted under a car in a busy street, or beside a British Army barracks or police station gate. They would time the explosion for maximum effect – prioritising death and destructive impact.

The ASU – armed with the assault rifles and pistols – would lie in wait overlooking the bomb site. When the security services rocked up to secure the scene, evacuate the wounded and hunt down the perpetrators, the hidden gunmen would open up – hoping to add some British soldiers to the score of dead and injured.

That done, they'd dump their weapons and make their getaway by melting into the crowd. The IRA wore no uniforms, of course, so there were few if any ways to differentiate them from everyday civilians.

And that was why rooting out their arms caches was so important: it was one of the few ways of truly messing up their plans, not to mention their deniability. No family could explain away such an arms cache hidden beneath their kitchen floor!

For making that discovery I was honoured with the General Officer Commanding Commendation (GOC), an award that goes on your Army record.

In due course I spoke to my CO again, repeating my request to get put forward for selection into the Pathfinders. The answer I got was more in the way of a bribe: if I agreed to stay in Northern Ireland and keep serving with the specialist search team, they'd promote me to lance corporal.

It was hugely tempting. In spite of the award that I'd won I was still a private – and a crow – in most people's eyes. But if I earned my first stripe that would all change. I was nineteen years old, and I'd win a smidgin of respect and a small taste of the responsibility that we all crave.

I thought about my parents' reaction. Early promotion to lance-jack would mean something to them: it would signify how well I was doing out here. By contrast, if I told them I was going to try for selection into the Pathfinders – a unit that few outside of the Regiment even knew existed – it would mean jack.

Fortunately, the officer in command of our search unit was Major Pete Fraser, who had been one of the Pathfinders' first ever commanders.

Fraser spoke to me man to man, and in doing so he levered open some of the secrets of the X Platoon. Their primary function was to insert as small units behind enemy lines, to recce targets, or to launch lightning-fast attacks against them. They were trained to do so using all possible means – on foot carrying crushing loads, in light four-wheel-drive vehicles, or – most famously – by high-altitude parachute drops (HALO and HAHO).

Pathfinders were some of the most highly skilled combat soldiers in the British Army. They had to be independently-minded maverick self-starters. Fraser outlined some of the history of the unit. It was the original Pathfinders who'd led the Second World War assault at Arnhem, when 10,000 parachutists had dropped into a heroic, but ultimately doomed, behind-enemy-lines mission.

In that operation – codenamed Market Garden – airborne forces had attempted to seize vital bridges to speed the Allied advance into Germany. But the intel picture had been hopelessly wrong, and the parachute insertion had resulted in thousands fighting to the last bullet and beyond.

After the Second World War a unit had been formed called No 1 (Guards) Independent Company, which continued to perform this crucial, 'pathfinding' role. It had been deployed numerous times: in the 1950s, on anti-terrorist operations in Cyprus; during the height of the Suez crisis, as the tiny vanguard that guided in the massed ranks of Britain's airborne forces; in the 1960s, again in Cyprus; and in Borneo during the anti-Soviet/communist conflict there. The unit had also operated in Northern Ireland, during the earliest years of 'the Troubles'. But for some obscure reason – most likely, one driven by MOD bean-counters – in 1975 the unit had been disbanded, at which point most of the veterans had taken their skills into the SAS.

A decade later it became obvious that a pathfinding unit needed to be reformed. Six to eight of the best blokes were taken from the Parachute Regiment's three Patrols Platoons – those that spearheaded recce and combat operations – and given a 'new' role and identity, being tasked to do what 'pathfinders' had been doing since Arnhem.

The first Pathfinder Selection had taken place in 1986, two years before I first heard about the unit. Major Fraser was brutally frank about what it entailed. It was so gruelling that if six good men volunteered, on average only one would get through. On occasion, only one in ten made it.

To my mind, the odds still sounded worth a punt.

I was nineteen, I'd found the life that I loved, and for some reason I seemed reasonably good at it – as my recent GOC Commendation reflected. And if the PARA Reg was this good, I could only imagine what life would be like if – and it was a big if – I made it into the Pathfinders.

I wanted in, and I told Major Fraser as much. His reaction shocked me a little. I'd thought all that he'd been telling me was the build-up to this moment – the moment of my volunteering.

He cast me this shrewd, appraising look. 'You might not be ready yet. Not quite.'

'But, sir,' I countered, 'I'm keen, fit, and I'm good at volunteering for stuff. If I don't understand something, I'll ask. I'm a good private soldier.'

'Do another year,' Fraser countered. 'You'll be a lance corporal soon. Get some more experience under your belt and apply in eighteen months. You'll be twenty-one – and that's the right kind of age at which to give it a try.'

Of course, I kept pushing. I made a real nuisance of myself, but Major Fraser took it in good grace. Towards the end of 1989 he finally capitulated. I had just turned twenty when he finally gave his blessing to release me from his search unit, and put me forward for Pathfinder Selection.

He made it clear he still felt I was too young. But what was the harm in trying? At the age of sixteen I'd been told repeatedly I'd never make it as a PARA. Yet I'd done it. I'd proved the naysayers wrong. Now I'd been told I was too young for the Pathfinders. But I was going for it, anyway, and I could hardly contain my excitement at being granted the opportunity.

I made a promise to myself, a rash one as it turned out: I would reach the razor-sharp tip of the British Army's spear, or die trying.

10

I didn't have much of a Christmas that year. I spent it pounding the familiar peaks and valleys that surround Middlesbrough ... again.

My poor dad must have thought he'd taken a step back in time: his son asking to be driven into the hills; him sitting there reading his *Mirror* while I disappeared off to punish myself, desperately trying to get into some kind of shape, after spending the best part of a year in Northern Ireland unable to do any real fitness training.

In the back of my mind I knew that Major Fraser was most likely right. I probably was too young. I doubted I had the physical strength, coupled with the sheer robustness of mind, to endure what was coming. But fortunately, I was going to have a perfect partner in crime – for my best buddy in 3 PARA had decided to go for Pathfinder Selection, alongside me.

Dan Miller was a twenty-one-year-old 5' 10" stocky Jock, and a born-and-bred PARA. He was a good-looking fucker, with big dark eyes, curly black hair and a wide, easy smile. Dan could pretty much take his pick of the women, and when he wasn't off being a ladies' man he was invariably getting into trouble with me.

Most weekends in Aldershot we'd get a good few beers in. Our universe consisted of the four pubs where the PARAs drank: The Fives Bar; the Trafalgar Inn – known to all as the Traff; the Ratpit – where they had once made rats fight for money; and, roughest of all, the Globetrotter – or the GT, as we called it. The GT consisted of a dark subterranean cavern, where a cringing DJ used to play records surrounded by chicken-wire mesh, in an effort to protect himself against flying bottles and bar stools.

People got carried out of the GT most nights.

Fortunately, it was rarely Dan and me.

There was always an inch of liquid on the bar – as often as not alcohol mixed with blood and other bodily fluids. The 'reasons' for the fights were as various and imaginative as any PARA could think up, and mostly it was PARAs fighting other PARAs.

One night there was a massive brawl that spilled into the street. That in turn attracted the attention of the Royal Military Police (RMPs). They turned up on horseback, and my reaction was not perhaps the wisest ever.

'Hey, mate,' I shouted at the nearest figure. 'What's got four legs and a wanker halfway up its back?'

Dan didn't appreciate the joke much, either: both of us duly got arrested. Dan got away with it, because while he'd been right into the scrapping he was cuter than me and he didn't make any smart-arse comments. I just wouldn't let it lie. Still pissed when they threw me into the cell, I kept telling anyone who'd listen what I thought of them.

In the end I was put in a cop car and driven back to my unit, where I was handed over to the Provost Staff – reputedly the biggest, hardest guys in the entire Battalion. The Provost Staff are responsible for maintaining discipline amongst several hundred PARAs. They took one look at the charge sheet and decided I was a special case: they referred me to the RSM for 'appropriate action'.

The RSM was a fearsome scouser called Del Amos, with bright red hair and a reputation for showing no mercy to anyone. He decreed that I would go on the CO's orders, and I was told I would serve seven days in the unit's jail. The half a dozen cells were always full, yet the beasting I received from the three Provost Staff was something special.

I was marched from the jail to the main square where everyone could see me. They gave me a Second World War helmet with its insides removed so that it banged around on my head. To that was added a crappy daysack filled with 30lb of sand, complete with tiny shoulder straps.

It was way worse than the Satsuma had ever been.

Next, I was handed an old anti-tank shell, three and a half feet tall and weighing 40lb, and told to run to the other end of the square. At the far end I had to put the shell down, run back to my starting point and do press-ups, until I was ordered to run back and fetch it. Then it was time for squats with the shell above my head, and curls with the bloody thing laid across my arms. Sprints followed with the helmet clanging about and the straps of the day-sack cutting deep into my shoulders.

This went on for thirty minutes; then an hour; then an hour and a half – and still with no water and no break. I was being put through the RSM's very own version of hell, while everyone else went about his daily task having a good laugh at Heinous Heaney's plight.

In truth it was an evil seven days and by the end of it I'd learned my lesson: if you're going to do something, don't get caught.

The moment to register for Pathfinder Selection dawned. It was midday on Sunday, 7 January 1990, and time to report to the home of the mysterious elite unit. I went along with Dan, plus two others from 3 PARA – Joe Greenhill, twenty-two, who was a private, and Steve Rogers, a twenty-six-year-old lance corporal.

There were also four blokes from 1 PARA, and all the rest were from across the Army – five from the Guards and two each from the Royal Engineers and 216 Signals Squadron, plus another couple of infantry cap badges. A pair of officers were competing for the post of second-in-command of the Pathfinders – one from the Blues and Royals, the other from the Guards.

In all, twenty-seven of us reported in that first day.

As I glanced around at the faces – all subdued and anxious, just as I was – I wondered who exactly would be left standing at the finish. If Major Fraser was right, no more than four of us would last through to the bitter end.

It was a hugely sobering thought.

Dan was well up for it. Like me, he craved a new challenge, and he'd spent most of his Christmas running up and down the hills in the little Scottish town that he hailed from. I was glad to have Dan as my wingman. For one thing he was a good laugh. For another, it was going to be good to see a friendly face – that's if we both stayed the course.

'How long d'you reckon this'll take?' he muttered, as we stood waiting in the cold.

In theory, all we had to do was fill in the appropriate forms. The beasting proper would start the following morning. Or at least that was what we'd been told.

The Pathfinder platoon sergeant came out to do the meet and greet. Dave Moore was a skinny bloke who hailed from Burnley in Lancashire. He looked grizzled and evil. His well-lived-in features were adorned by a massive, droopy moustache that curled round his top lip, and all was topped off by a skinhead haircut.

From the get-go he showed not the slightest interest in any of us. There was no shouting or abuse, as there had been from the start of my time in the PARAs, but there was certainly no camaraderie or humour, either.

Facing Dave Moore was like facing a blank immutable wall. This, we would discover, was deliberate. We had to get through this on our own, with zero interaction or feedback from the Staff, and certainly no encouragement.

No one but ourselves was going to help us.

Just as we'd finished filling in the forms and were thinking about our free afternoon and some beer, Moore issued his surprise instructions.

'Get your shirts and jumpers off,' he remarked quietly, almost flatly. 'I want you outside, formed up in boots, combat trousers and T-shirts.'

I exchanged glances with Dan. We hadn't reckoned on this. It was already starting to get dark. Frost was forming on the windscreens of the Pathfinders' vehicles, and as we lined up in our T-shirts we were freezing our bollocks off. We stood there for a full thirty minutes before Moore deigned to speak to us again.

'Right – we're about to leave camp and we have no idea when we're coming back. We're about to start Magic Moments.'

We all knew the song. We'd been bombarded with it all through Christmas, for it was the theme tune for the Quality Street TV ads. But as no one had told us anything about Magic Moments, I didn't have the slightest clue what Moore meant.

If there was one person who seemed to know and care even less, it was the bloke standing next to me. He'd arrived in Aldershot the day before, met some mates and got ming-monged, and was still half-pissed. In a way I admired the bloke for it.

The words 'Magic Moments' must have been the cue for the rest of the Pathfinders to come outside. There were twenty of them – so more or less the full complement – and each was dressed in a red top, complete with the Pathfinder logo.

The oldest bloke in our group was Bob Walters, a twenty-eight-year-old corporal from 1 PARA, and the youngest was me. By contrast, the Pathfinders looked distinctly war-bitten and mature. Underneath the longer hair and the droopy moustaches – which appeared to be de rigueur – they were clearly seasoned guys in great shape.

Like Dave Moore they paid us zero attention, making no eye contact. They just walked around the back of us and stood there silently, waiting.

No doubt about it – this was unnerving.

I'd even have preferred Boydy spitting insults at me, rather than this. At least with Corporal Boyd Simpson you got confirmation that you registered on his anger and disgust scale. With these guys you may as well not even have been there.

Then we heard the dreaded words: 'Prepare to double.'

On Platoon Sergeant Moore's quiet command we ran as a squad through the back gate of this part of the base – Montgomery Lines, named after the famous field marshal – and on to the road leading towards the Aldershot training area. We pressed onwards on a tiny back road, until we reached a hill that was covered in thick vegetation and topped by the Wellington Monument.

The Monument consists of a thirty-foot statue of the 1st Duke of Wellington, the victor at the iconic Battle of Waterloo. He sits astride his charger atop the hill, holding a field marshal's baton. It seemed a fair enough starting point for our own attempts to prove if we were worthy.

We stopped at the foot of the hill while some of the Staff ran to the top and others stationed themselves in between.

'Right,' announced Moore, softly. 'Everyone – up around the statue and back.'

One complete circuit was only a hundred and fifty metres, but it was a steep climb to the top and everyone was fighting to get up there, pushing past each other to avoid falling behind. Back at the bottom, we formed three ranks and stood at ease, catching our breath.

That wasn't too bad, I told myself. *So much for Magic Moments.*

'Right. This time, up and down – two laps.'

Same quiet tone, same lack of eye contact.

As soon as we were back from that, we were off again – three laps.

That done, Moore spoke to us again. 'Right, pick a partner, hold hands, run together up to the top and down again.'

I grabbed Dan and did as instructed.

'Right, this time three of you together – up and down.'

We grabbed another guy and did as we were told.

Then: 'Back to your first partner. Piggy-back. You carry him up and down, and vice versa.'

This was considerably easier for Dan, because I weighed twelve stone on a good day and he was at least thirteen. I cursed my

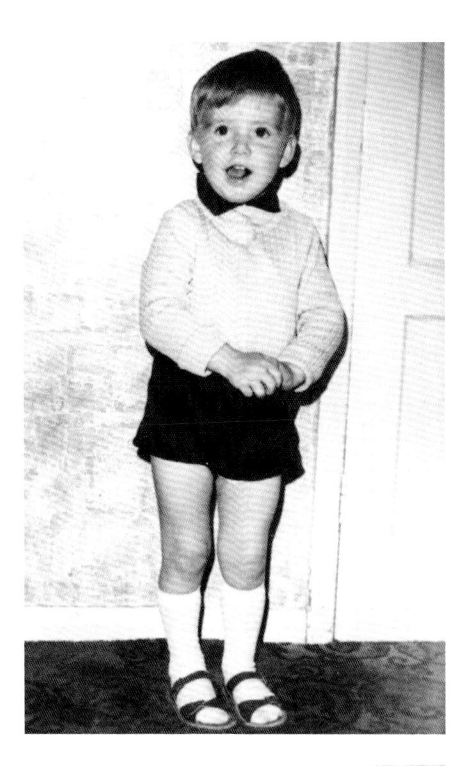

1971, aged eighteen months, and sporting the latest in designer shorts.

The Cub Scouts and my life in uniform has begun. Here I am aged eight and proud as Punch at having won an orienteering competition against other teams.

6 July 1986, standing by the Junior Parachute Company entrance sign at Pirbright in Surrey wondering what I had let myself in for, but eager to get started.

1986 Junior Para boxing team fight in the Army championships against Shorncliffe. This is my fight, and I manage to land a crunching left jab into my opponent's face.

The decision goes my way as I won on a technical knockout (TKO). The crowd was full of Paratroopers from 2 and 3 Para all going crazy as Junior Para won the championship final.

March 1987, RAF Brize Norton, about to complete my first clean fatigue (no equipment) parachute jump on my jumps course. I am on the right of the picture and a fellow recruit, Dave Campbell, is on the left. A C130 nicknamed 'Fat Albert' is in the background.

Pathfinder Selection, January 1990. 'The Fan Dance' on Selection is the first timed event during 'test week', a pass or fail march over the Pen y Fan in the Brecon Beacons. Not so much about your navigational ability, but more a straight race against the clock over the highest mountain in South Wales to the far side and back again – a test of sheer determination and endurance. (Guy Boden)

Pathfinder Selection, January 1990, completing the X Range assault course in Sennybridge. We had been beasted all day on the live firing ranges and then finished with this. I am hanging upside down by my legs on the right of the shot trying to get on top of the wall. Dave Moore watches on from behind me, wearing the brown woollen hat. (Richard Newell)

Pathfinder Selection, January 1990. The X Range assault course is linked with pain and suffering and is an Airborne Forces favourite. Here two guys attempt to crawl through the water tunnels without getting stuck and before they fill with water. My future Belize patrol commander, Andy Parson, is standing upright on the right of the stream. (Richard Newell)

Pathfinder Selection, January 1990. Learning instinctive shooting during the live firing range week phase. I am second from the right as the PF DS Dave Moore looks on with his perfectionist eyes. (Richard Newell)

Pathfinder Selection, January 1990. Patrols week teaches you the necessary skills required to operate as a small four-man team. Here we have gone 'firm' as a patrol. The PF DS is raised up passing on information to the patrol. I am lying on the far left of the picture. (Richard Newell)

The checkpoints for all the marches on 'test week' are usually located on the tops of the highest feature. You must present yourself to the DS to receive your next 'grid reference' on the march. After identifying that point to the DS, you move off quickly, always against the clock.

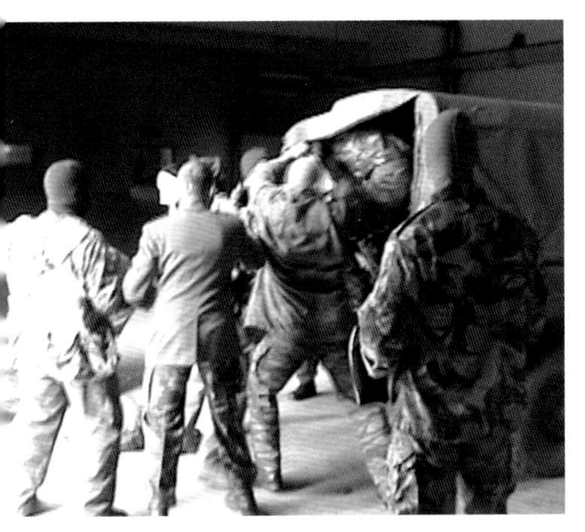

Resistance to Interrogation, or R2I, forms an essential part of selection training for specialist troops who are classed as 'prone to capture'. The guard force dressed in blue jackets drag captured troops off the vehicles and start the R2I process.

Disorientation adds to the shock of capture. This soldier is laid spread-eagle with his head covered. There will be no noise from the guard force as they stand watch, allowing fear and exhaustion to take their toll.

Stress positions, either standing against a wall or sitting crossed-legged, add to the mental, emotional and physical pressure placed upon you, whilst under these conditions you are also subjected to booming white noise to further degrade your senses and ability to resist the questions from your interrogators.

Navigating the monkey bars on an assault course whilst cross-training with the USAF Combat Control Teams – who act as the American military's elite Pathfinders – hoping not to have to drop into the deep putrid water below me.

scrawniness and his pounds of extra muscle, as I staggered past Wellington on his warhorse.

'Giddy up, horsey,' Dan whispered, nastily.

'Shut the fuck up,' I gasped back.

This went on for a good hour. It wasn't like normal PARA training. There was no screaming or shouting nor any word of support, and it was the very silence that was so unsettling. The only time the Staff seemed to bother to speak was when they wanted to persuade one or another of us to throw in the towel.

'If you're gonna be sick, be sick out the back, not beside us,' one remarked to the guy who was ming-monged.

'You chose to be here,' another commented to a bloke who was retching his guts up. 'You volunteered. You can quit at any time.'

Oddly, this kind of thing is generally easier when someone's shouting and screaming obscenities at you. It drives you on. This was a brutal, merciless, never-ending thrashing, and for the first time since we'd joined the Army we had to look to ourselves for all the motivation we needed to get through it.

'Right,' Moore said, when the Wellington Monument torture was finally done. 'Form up in three ranks and prepare to double.'

Fuck. What the hell was coming next?

There was just no way of knowing.

We ran back around the training area, but not to our barracks to recover. Instead we ended up at Engineer's Bridge. This is a military structure that spans the main road into Aldershot, consisting of iron girders with a wooden slatted base.

Wordlessly, the Staff spread out along it.

Fucking Magic Moments, indeed.

Back and forth we were sent. First running, then monkey-running on all fours, then – unbelievably – crab-crawling on our backs. After that it was more piggy-backing Dan's weight to and fro, followed by fireman's carries.

The sun had set long ago. It went on like this into the dark for a good hour. We were two hours into Magic Moments when we doubled back the way we'd come – in the direction of the barracks once more. But all hopes were dashed when Moore veered off into some woods, and like rats following the Pied Piper, we followed.

A member of Staff appeared from out of nowhere carrying a bag full of machetes.

'Half of you on my left, pick a machete,' Moore instructed. 'The other half, stand over there. You lot on the right will do squat thrusts and burpees and press-ups, while this lot chop through their log. The faster they do it, the less work you lot have to do. Those of you chopping, remember the others will be doing it next and you'll be in their shoes.'

It took ten minutes for each guy to chop through his log going like a chainsaw on acid. After that we swopped. By the time we'd finished, we'd been getting thrashed for two and a half hours or more.

We all stood. No one said a word. On everyone's mind was the same thought: *What the hell was coming next?*

'Right,' said Moore, 'understand – the kind of guy we're looking for is someone who doesn't need any encouragement and doesn't need to be told how good he is. He can drive himself. So, is there anyone – *anyone* – at this time who's had enough?'

'No, Staff!' we shouted in unison.

Moore didn't respond in any way whatsoever. It was like speaking to a pillar of concrete. 'Okay, so that's the warm-up done. Is everybody warm? Are you all warm?'

There was zero warmth or concern in his voice.

'Yes, Staff!' we yelled in reply.

'Okay, squad, turn to your right and double march.'

He led the way again. We headed down into one of the wooded areas, upping the pace as we went. At the base of a hill Moore came to a halt. 'To the top. Follow the member of Staff when you get there.'

We sprinted to the summit of the hill, picked up a member of Staff who led us down the other side, then picked up another one and sprinted to the top, and so on and so forth. And so it went on for another forty-five minutes.

When finally we stopped Moore was ready. 'So is there anybody at the moment who'd like to go back to camp? Or shall we keep going?'

'Keep going, Staff!' we cried.

'Okay. Off we go.'

We jogged to another area, this time stopping at the instantly recognisable Spider's Hill. It gets its name from the eight tracks that criss-cross it like a spider's spreading legs. For the Guards or anyone who wasn't Airborne this was their first experience of the hill. But we PARAs knew exactly how nasty this was going to be.

We followed the same pattern. The instructors spread out and sprinted over the top of the hill in relays, while we followed – up and down, up and down, up and down. By now we'd been at it constantly for four hours, maybe more. In the pitch darkness we switched to piggy-backs and fireman's carries, and then, for the sake of variety, wheelbarrows – which required one of us to go up the hill on his hands.

That done, Moore lined us up again.

'Okay, anybody want to drop out? No? Right, turn to your left, double march.'

We ran from there to the Driver Training Circuit, a place where military vehicles are put through their paces. My heart sank to my boots. The Circuit is known for its deep gullies, frozen ridges, clogging mud pits and churned tracks – giving a good imitation of a First World War battlefield after a few weeks of artillery fire.

In fact, it's the kind of place any sane person would least like to have to drive a vehicle across. Or push a trailer for that matter . . .

Five Army trailers, each weighing a quarter of a tonne, were lined up at the end of a concrete track. Each had two wheels at the back and a D-ring shackle at the front. To make things more interesting, the trailers were fully loaded with jerry-cans of water.

This took the total weight of each to around 450kg, or nearly half a tonne.

'Five men on each trailer,' Moore practically whispered. 'Covers off. Haul them up the side, around the top, down through the water gullies and back here.'

There was no way to sugarcoat this: this was going to be 800 metres of sheer unadulterated hell.

11

The two biggest blokes in my group went to the front of the trailer.

They grabbed the shackle and with a Herculean effort lifted more weight than they'd ever managed in any gym. Their job was to keep the trailer level and its load of jerry-cans aboard, while the three of us pushed like hell.

Slowly, agonisingly, we inched that slab of steel with its crushing load of H_2O into painful motion.

All five of us were grunting and howling from the sheer strain. With what my dad called my 'pirate's chest' – 'because it's sunken – boom, boom!' – I feared I wasn't giving as much grunt as the others. But what I lacked in muscle I was determined to make up for in sheer bloody effort.

I poured my heart and soul into the task and worked up as much sweat as the next man. Despite the cold and the damp, it was pouring off me. But if it was this difficult to make progress on the flat concrete, how were we going to get this monster piece of shit around the frost-hard mud ruts that lay ahead of us?

A bit of light would have helped, but it was pitch black. As we stumbled forwards, our clouds of icy breath pooled in the dark air all around us. We soon got bogged down in the mud. The two blokes at the front practically broke their backs trying keep the shackle up, while we pushed like the mad and the damned from behind.

Our boots were constantly slipping in the grime, as we fought our way forward, one foot at a time. Typically, the Pathfinder Staff observed our efforts with a studied indifference. They did nothing either to help or to hinder our progress. I thought back fondly to the Log Race, on P Company. A whack around the head, plus a few choice insults, would have been welcome now. It would have spiked my anger and spurred me on.

But the Staff stood motionless and resolute in the shadows, as silent as ghosts. There was not a word of encouragement or chastisement. And their studied quiet – their seeming ability to ignore us – was the worst of all.

In fact, the only people shouting were us.

At each other.

Desperately.

It took forty hellish minutes of non-stop swearing and torture to get that trailer around the entire course, and without spilling a drop of water. We came in third out of five. In any normal race I'd have been cursing a near-defeat. But not now.

Now, I was just grateful the ordeal was over.

Except that it wasn't.

Not a bit of it.

My boots had sucked up the cold, gunky water and my feet felt like blocks of ice. I was soaked to the skin with sweat and plastered in mud. My T-shirt was so wet it was starting to ice over, freezing to my torso. It was Baltic bloody cold.

Surely this had to be it?

Magic Moments done and dusted?

Was it hell.

'Right,' said Moore, even quieter than ever. 'Remove the jerry-cans from the trailer. They're forty pounds on their own.' A beat. 'Everyone grab yourself a jerry. Off you go. Same circuit, same round.'

From Moore's demeanour, it looked as if Magic Moments was only just beginning. *The bastard.*

The only way to carry the jerry-can was to balance it on your shoulder, but there were two problems. First, H_2O is heavy as hell – doubly so, after all we'd endured. We were exhausted long before being ordered to hoist a jerry and set foot on the track.

As I hefted mine and began to stumble ahead, I could hear guys puking into the darkness. There was only one reason that I didn't join them. I'd had nothing to eat or drink before we'd rocked up at the old band room, because I'd had no idea we were about to be beasted long into the night hours.

My stomach was empty.

I had nothing to vomit.

But I still felt dizzy with exhaustion.

I wove my way down the track, the concrete becoming treacherous, icy mud all too quickly. My jerry seemed to have frozen half-solid on the trailer. It was icy to the touch, and it kept slipping off my shoulder. I had to keep swopping it from one aching side to the other, but even so the searing pain where my arms met my shoulder-blades kept worsening. It felt as if someone was jabbing a red-hot poker into my back.

By the time I staggered over the finish line I had aches in places I didn't even know existed. I was desperate for a breather – for a few precious seconds in which to try to get my shit together for whatever was coming next.

It took a good few moments for me to realise that Moore was speaking – issuing a new set of instructions. At first, I couldn't make out what he was saying. Maybe my brain just didn't want to hear it.

'Jerries back on the trailer,' he announced, repeating himself for those who'd just stumbled in from the darkness. Then, chillingly: 'Find yourself a partner.'

I located Dan, who looked about as bad as I felt. Nothing was said between us. Every precious iota of energy had to be kept in reserve for whatever was coming.

Moore's words came like those of The Apocalypse, whispering out of the empty night. 'Fireman's carry – same course. At the halfway point, swop over. Off you go.'

Dan was bigger than me, but it made sense for me to do the first leg. After four hundred yards of being carried I'd be cold and stiff, making it nigh-on impossible to lift his weight.

He weighed four times as much as the jerry-can, maybe more. The only way to get through this was to draw on my running experience, and what it had taught me. When you're totally and utterly knackered, when you think you're finished and you just can't go on – you've got to blank your mind of any thoughts.

The only way to get through is to concentrate on the next step, one step at a time. Start counting a rhythm in your head, and blank out everything else. Concentrate solely on your heartbeat and your footfalls, almost as if it's a kind of meditation.

That's what I did now.

I told myself it was all in the mind. If my head was straight, anything was possible – even carrying a lump like Dan through four hundred yards of shit.

I made it. But by the time I was done I'd been knee-deep in freezing pools of mud for long stretches. My legs were starting to shake uncontrollably from the exhaustion and the cold. I didn't know how much more of this I could take.

We swopped over.

Dan hoisted me – scarecrow, as opposed to hippo – and I tried to relax into the carry; to find a few precious moments to recuperate. It said it all about Magic fucking Moments when the only moment I'd get to 'recover' was while being carried through the blinding darkness by a guy who was stumbling from frozen rut to frozen rut, and lurching alarmingly from side to side.

Dan was clearly at the limit of his endurance. It felt as if he was going to fall at any moment, launching me head-first into the nearest pool of icy mud.

We reached the finish line for a third time. In spite of the sickness in the pit of my stomach, I was desperately hungry. I needed food. Energy. Fuel.

Moore formed us up into three ranks. 'Right, then, how is everyone feeling?'

'Yep, Staff,' was about all we could manage. 'Still here.'

He eyeballed us for a long moment, running his gaze down our sodden, mud-encrusted ranks.

'Does anyone want to get into the nice, warm Land Rover and go back to barracks?' He flicked his head in the direction of the nearest wagon, the cab light glowing cosy and comforting inside. 'Any takers?'

'No, Staff!'

'Right,' he said, feigning boredom. 'Turn to your right, double march.'

Off we went again, knowing that he was fucking with our heads. What horrors did Magic Moments hold in store for us next?

The reality was that I didn't know the half of it.

We double-timed it through the night, the only sound being the thump of boots on mud and the wheeze and suck of our breathing. We stopped by the side of a country road. A rural lane you'd call it. It was a totally unremarkable place to have called a halt, and at first I couldn't for the life of me see why Moore had brought us here.

He stood before us, King Bastard in all his silent glory. For a long moment he eyed us, the quiet of that night creeping into our souls. But as I listened, soaking it all in, I became aware of another noise running beneath the silence – the bass track to the melody of our suffering.

Water.

Trickling underground.

Somewhere close by.

By the tilt of his head Moore indicated what was coming. Running alongside the road was a shallow drainage ditch. Nothing so unusual about that. But where we had stopped the water was funnelled into a drainage pipe, one just about large enough for a man to crawl through.

We were stood at the start of the pipe.

Where it ended was anyone's guess.

For the first time Moore smiled. It wasn't a nice smile. It wasn't warm. He gestured at that dark, watery mouth that led underground.

'One at a time, in you go. Keep crawling. All the way.'

I couldn't bring myself to look at Dan. I didn't want him to see what I was feeling, because I was in a very dark place. Another beasting I figured I could handle – psychologically. But crawling into a flooded drainage pipe in the pitch darkness, and with blokes piling up to front and rear – that I didn't know if I could manage.

Without a word to anyone I climbed down the side of the bank, Dan right behind me. We dropped into the water. No way would I be first into the pipe. We held back, and I was surprised when one of the older, more experienced guys stepped forwards, ducked low and crawled inside.

Within moments he'd been swallowed by the utter blackness.

By the time the tenth man had disappeared, I understood why the first had volunteered. He would have a free run at it. But the further back you were, the more chance you had of getting stuck in a traffic jam. All it would take was one bloke ahead of you to lose his bottle, and . . .

Well, it didn't bear thinking about. The water would back up behind, its free flow impeded, and the tunnel would flood.

I was number twenty-two to crawl into the waiting abyss. Dan was right behind me, number twenty-three. Down on all fours I felt my hands and feet go numb. I inched towards the gaping mouth of the pipe. It sucked me in, and suddenly the water level rose as it was funnelled underground, submerging me in the one and a half feet of its icy current.

There was about the same gap between the surface and the roof of the pipe. As the water surged around me it was breathtakingly cold – so much so that for a moment the shock of it half-paralysed me.

'Go on, mate,' Dan urged, a touch of panic creeping into his voice. 'We're right fucking behind you.'

I forced myself to elbow and slither ahead, moving with all the grace of a turd in a toilet bowl. The water level grew higher, as more men crammed into the pipe. I crawled forward, trying to push myself up, so that as much of my body as possible was out of the water, but my head came to rest with a thump on the top of the pipe.

Squeezing twenty big blokes in here was like trying to put toothpaste back into a tube. If the water rose any higher, those at the back were going to be in serious trouble.

'Breathe deep,' a voice from out of nowhere echoed through my head. It was my own. 'Stay cool. Just like being on a run, you'll only get through this by putting one foot in front of the other.'

It was easier said than done.

We were several feet in when the faint light coming from the tunnel entrance faded to nothing. Now we were immersed in total darkness, like rats in the proverbial sewer. I shuddered uncontrollably. I'd never felt anything like this before. I was trapped in a pitch black, watery hellhole that threatened to be my grave.

The culvert was there to drain water off the country lane. It was black and shitty by the time it hit the pipe, and by now it was up to my chin. I tried keeping my head tilted to one side, so I could gasp in the air I so desperately needed, but I kept smashing myself against the curved roof of the pipe.

I had to move faster.

To get through this and out of there.

Crawling on my elbows kept me too close to the water. I placed my hands flat on the bottom of the pipe, put all my weight on them, and started to drag myself ahead by my bare palms. A push with my toes at the same time gave a bit of extra propulsion, but the water was so cold my limbs were seized half-solid.

Then came the worst.

I couldn't see anything, so I didn't even realise the problem until my head was up the arse of the guy in front. He'd stopped dead, which only added to the uncertainty and the growing panic. I was trapped, stock-still and in total blackness, with twenty-one blokes ahead of me and five behind.

The water was getting deeper.

Soon it would be up to my mouth.

'Fucking get a move on!' I yelled to the arse in my face. 'GET FUCKING MOVING!'

'Fuck off,' the arse yelled back. 'Got someone stuck in front of me. Fuck right off.'

The water rose higher.

My very blood felt as if it was frozen. I was stuck, I was razor-close to drowning, and there was most definitely no fucking light at the end of the tunnel.

I was on the verge of panicking when I sensed the arse start to move. Hallelujah! I said a short but heartfelt prayer, and forced myself to follow. The rest of the crawl was a total blur. I emerged after a hundred and fifty yards of hell – frozen, shaken and utterly lost for words.

The road lay just a few feet up the bank to my right. I reached for it, so I could haul myself up to its relative safety. To sanity.

But a voice spoke out of the darkness, halting me in my steps. 'Next section. Everyone in. Crawl.'

It was the voice of Moore.

I glanced ahead. A second length of pipe lay before us, just discernible in the gloom. *Oh my God.* I really didn't know if I could do this any more.

One of the DS must have sensed my trepidation; that I was that close to cracking. He bent over me: 'D'you want to get out?' he whispered, voice like Satan. 'Nice warm Land Rover just nearby.'

'No, Staff.'

I didn't know where the words had come from. Every essence of my being wanted out of this shit. The last thing in the world I desired right now was a second crawl through a flooded pipe.

'Off you go, then,' he purred.

In all, there were five stretches of pipe. I honestly do not know how I made it through them all. In a way each was easier than the last psychologically, for you knew what was coming. But each was far tougher physically, as the freezing water sapped whatever reserves of energy you had left.

When I reached the end of the final pipe, I couldn't comply with The Bastard's instructions any more – to climb out. I was too finished. I had nothing left. Below my thighs and biceps I had no feeling in either my arms or my legs. I was shaking uncontrollably, my teeth going like the proverbial machine gun.

'Out you get,' Moore repeated, softly – like Darth Vader on acid.

I turned to Dan and we somehow helped each other to crawl out, then dragged ourselves to our feet.

We formed up.

Surely, that had to be it: Magic fucking Moments dead and buried.

Moore surveyed us. His Freddie Mercury look remained as impassive as ever, betraying not the slightest trace of sympathy for our suffering.

'Right. Here we are, then.'

I was longing to hear those immortal words: *That's it. Well done, lads. Ready for your tea?*

Instead: 'Right, tell me: is there anyone – *anyone* – who wants to go back to camp?'

"N-n-n-n-n-oooooo, S-s-s-s-s-t-t-t-t-aaaaaaf-f-f-f,' we shivered.

Moore shrugged. It was as if he didn't give a flying fuck either way. 'Okay. Turn to your right. Prepare to double.'

As I forced my limbs into motion, I could have sworn I heard Moore start to sing, softly:

Magic moments . . .
When two hearts are caring.
Magic moments . . .

And was that the rest of the Staff humming along to the words?

The bastards.

12

I doubled along the lane, hoping to get some warmth back into my wobbly, frozen pins. Gradually, the icy blood in my veins started to thaw. By the time I'd stumbled through the woods lying to the rear of the Monty Lines – our base – I could hear the reassuring sound of my boots and combats squelching as I ran.

At least it meant that they weren't frozen solid.

More importantly, we were almost home. We were approaching the rear gate of the base. Surely, this had to be it: Magic Moments finally laid to rest?

We doubled back to the Pathfinders' end of camp. It was deep into the night and everywhere seemed asleep. We'd been on the go for pushing six hours when we formed up outside the Pathfinders' office – shit-caked and soaking wet after the longest and most tortuous of beastings imaginable.

'Right,' Moore announced. I'd come to dread that word. It was his signature – his trademark. It meant more shit was coming – but thankfully, it seemed, not tonight.

'I'd like to thank everyone who turned up today to . . . volunteer for Pathfinder Selection. Breakfast is at zero six thirty tomorrow, and then Selection proper will begin. Magic Moments – that was just the appetiser.'

He paused. 'If anybody – *anybody* – wants to pull themselves off the course, make sure you have breakfast first, then bring all your gear here. We will then return you to your unit. Okay, fall out.'

I felt as if my knees were about to buckle. I glanced at Dan. He forced a smile, but it wasn't the usual carefree grin that went with the prospect of a skinful of chilled lager and a bunch of pretty women. It was a grimy, exhausted skeleton of a smile.

We ain't seen nothing yet, it said.

'Everyone on the back of the trucks,' ordered one of the Staff.

We clambered into two four-tonners and drove to a camp at the far end of town. We reached a cluster of ramshackle buildings – ancient-looking wooden sheds arranged around a parade square. The camp dated back to the Second World War, the Staff told us, and it wasn't known for its mod cons. We were herded into a shed with two small wall heaters covered in wire mesh. On the far side of the square were brick showers and toilets.

'Right,' said the Staff, clearly taking his cue from the King Bastard. 'Tonight is the first and last time you will board a military vehicle while here on this course. At zero six thirty tomorrow you will run to breakfast in the main camp. Everything else you need for the day – uniform and webbing – will go on a truck.'

He eyed us. 'Any questions?' He barely paused. 'Right, okay.'

We were left alone, a sodden-wet and crap-covered gaggle of blokes, in our bare and draughty wooden hut. There were mattresses on the bunk beds but no bedding, just maggots – Army sleeping bags.

Dan grabbed a bunk and I followed – him on the bottom, me on top. The number one priority right now was to get out of our wet clothing. Trouble was, apart from a couple of civvie T-shirts, a pair of jeans and some trainers, all I'd brought with me were the clothes I stood up in. Clearly, the most important thing was to have dry gear for tomorrow – day one of the course proper.

I changed out of the worst of the wet stuff, and pretty soon I was down to my boxers. Everyone else was doing the same. We made a beeline for the heaters.

'We can't all sling gear on the heaters,' someone announced. 'Won't all fit. Let's string a line up over. Plus turn those chairs round and hang clothes off the backs. That'll do it.'

We even took the laces out of our boots and slung those up to dry. There's nothing worse than trying to tie heavy, wet bootlaces with frozen fingers, especially when you need to make a quick start on day one of Selection.

By now I was chilled to the marrow. I was so cold that it was slowing my movements. Wrapping a towel around myself, I pulled on a sweatshirt and headed for the showers, to try to warm up. There were zero facilities at this place. No NAAFI. No phones. Nothing. But joy of joys, at the shower block there was at least piping hot water.

It was what I'd been craving – dreaming of – ever since I'd been neck-deep in that drain-water.

I got under the shower, conscious that there was only a limited amount of hot water. We'd each get five minutes, max. By the time I got back to the hut it was 2130. There was no hot food anywhere, and we had no snacks in our bags. Sod all. We'd all thought we were starting Selection on Monday morning. Magic Moments had been totally unexpected.

We were too shattered to go anywhere, let alone head into town for a bucket of Kentucky Fried Chicken. There was nothing for it but to hit the maggots half-starved and zonk out, with the last man in from the showers turning out the lights.

As I closed my eyes all I could see was Spider's Hill and the monster trailer, plus the drowning pipe from hell – and presiding over it all from his spot on the high ground, the Duke of Wellington astride his charger.

Plus, of course, Moore, quietly urging us all to throw in the towel.

The first man out of bed threw the lights on and by 0625 we were standing round like children waiting to be collected from school. When we realised nobody was coming in to get us we went outside to find two of the Pathfinder Staff just standing there.

Day one. Pathfinder lesson one.

Nobody helps you here.

You have to help yourself.

'Okay lads, form up in three ranks,' announced one of the Staff, quietly. 'Turn to your left and . . . double march.'

Never in my life had I found it so hard to break into a run. It wasn't just my legs – my whole body was groaning and screaming. Getting going was like driving down the road in first gear with the handbrake on.

After a few hundred yards the pain started to subside. We reached the Monty Lines at the same time as the Bedford truck loaded with our kit, and made a beeline for the canteen and the mother of all fry-ups. I piled my plate high with carbs. Thanks to King Bastard and his Magic Moments, the tank was beyond empty.

Scoff shovelled down, we traipsed over to the Pathfinders' end of the base. In the former band room they'd arranged one-seater desks and chairs, in four rows of seven. I nabbed myself a place – back of the class, of course – and Dan slid into the seat beside me, just like Simmo used to a few years earlier.

At 0800 precisely the Pathfinders' officer commanding (OC) walked in. This was Major Jon 'H' Hayman, a former SAS squadron commander, a veteran of the Falklands and one of the toughest and most capable soldiers I would ever have the pleasure to meet.

But right now, if Dave Moore was King Bastard, this guy was the Dark Lord himself. He exuded this presence that few men have – a steely-eyed bringer of death, par excellence.

He ran his eye around the room. Utter silence. You could hear the proverbial pin drop. No one was about to flick chewed-up-paper pellets at this bloke, me and Dan included.

'You're all volunteers,' he began. His tone was soft, but somehow so rock hard it sent shivers up your spine. It said: I've eaten scroats like you for fucking breakfast. 'Many volunteer – few are selected. In case you haven't realised by now, there will be no motivation; no help. You are here for as long as you want to be here and you can fail yourself at any time. Do you understand?'

Murmurs of acknowledgement.

Boy, did we understand.

'The course is in three phases,' he continued, in that same, measured tone. 'Phase one here in Aldershot is five days, Monday to Friday. Those of you still here will then go down to Wales, for phase two. That will take three weeks. Then there's phase three, same area. That's all you need to know.'

'One last thing,' he said. 'Voluntary withdrawal – VW. If at any time you want to VW, just approach a member of the Staff, indicate your decision and we will return you to your unit as soon as possible.' A pause. 'Questions?'

There were none. No one risked a single word.

'Right, before we begin: does anyone want to VW?'

You'd be forgiven for thinking Jon 'H' Hayman was trying to crack a joke. You weren't there. For those of us who were, there wasn't even the slightest suggestion of anyone cracking a smile.

'Okay. Let's begin.'

With that, he left the room. Dan turned to me and made a circle with his thumb and middle finger, as if to say: *pure class*. The rest of the morning was devoted to lessons on signals, survival skills and first aid – the kind of stuff we needed to know for what was coming.

As we broke up for lunch, Dave Moore issued an announcement: 'Top tip, guys – don't eat too much.'

I instantly lost my appetite. I turned to Dan. 'I guess have a little bit of everything,' I suggested, nervously.

'Yeah. Plus get hydrated. Get at least half a dozen glasses of water into you, mate.'

We returned from a tense lunch and Dave Moore gave the order. 'Strip your shirt and jumper off, get a T-shirt and denims on, and form up outside.'

He led us off on a five-mile run into the training area and along the hills. We ran as a squad, nice and steady. I was steeling myself for Magic Moments Mark Two, but at the end of the route we simply turned and jogged back again.

We reached the base and Dave Moore gave us our instructions. 'You're done for the day. Have your Bergens packed at first light with forty pounds of kit. That's it.'

After a good feed and a kip, I was up the following morning feeling refreshed and almost eager. We mustered outside the Pathfinder block, our Bergens at our feet, as a Staff came down the line with a spring-loaded set of hand scales. Anyone whose pack was underweight was told to go over to a pile of stones and scoop them into his Bergen, until he'd made up the difference.

My pack was bulging with useful kit and survival gear: warm clothing, sleeping bag, water bottles, torch, knife and food. Thankfully, it weighed in at a good 40lb, so I didn't have to add any rocks to the load.

Dave Moore came and joined us, followed by what seemed like the entire Pathfinder Platoon. Each had a similarly large pack hoisted on his shoulders, weighing the same as ours. The last man to appear was Jon 'H' himself, massive pack strapped to his back.

Day two. Pathfinder lesson two: we're all in this together.

'This is a ten-mile test march,' Dave Moore announced. 'The objective is to stay with us at the front. What we're looking for is your ability to move fast over long distances under a load. You need to demonstrate to us a base level of fitness before we move out to Wales.'

We moved out, rifles gripped in hands, and in no time we were truly shifting it. As soon as we hit the training area the group started to string out. My legs were skinny, but they felt strong. I found that I could stick to the shoulder of the lead Staff, and keep pounding away.

It was the same modus operandi as before.

Zero words of encouragement.

No shouting at stragglers.

We made the top of Spider's Hill and I did a quick scan for Dan. I expected him to be just a short distance behind, like he always was. He was a bit bigger than me, a bit slower, but a powerhouse on any of the heavy-lifting sections, so I was surprised when he was nowhere to be seen.

I figured I must have missed him in the melee, so I pushed on. We climbed up the aptly-named Hungry Hill, where the P Company Log Race takes place. I shifted my weight onto the balls of my feet, leaning into the hill. My calves and thighs were burning, the straps of the pack cutting into my shoulders like razor blades.

The 40lb load felt like eighty uphill, and on the horrendously steep final stretch it was more like a hundred. I hit the summit neck-and-neck with Joe Greenhill, a super-fit Scottish lad, and we led a group of six.

'Everyone close in,' the Staff announced. 'Water break. You've got one minute. Work in pairs.'

There was still no sign of my chief mucker, Dan.

We weren't allowed to take our packs off or put our rifles down, so I turned to Jock Greenhill, pulled a water bottle from one of his Bergen side-pouches and handed it to him – then he did the same for me. I stood gazing down at a long, broken line of blokes struggling up the loose track.

Finally, I spotted Dan. He was way back.

What the fuck was wrong?

This was not good. If you're in the lead group, you get the crucial one-minute rest and water break. If you're not, you're always trying to catch up and there's no break for you. But I had bugger all time to worry about Dan right now.

'Right, let's go,' the Staff announced.

We pounded along a ridge for two miles, then dropped down towards the valley floor. You can't let fly when you're running downhill – especially not with 40lb strapped to your back, but it's a damn sight less punishing than the uphill slogs.

Halfway along the valley bottom we took a sharp left towards a huge hill with a clump of distant trees on top. Ahead of us lay 600 metres of sandy track, straight up. This was The Flagstaff, as they call it. By the time I reached the top I was soaked in sweat and my lungs were on fire. I doubled over, coughing up God only knows what, and spitting onto the track.

'One minute,' said the Staff, coolly. 'Water bottles out. Don't take off your Bergens. Don't put down your rifles.'

This was an unbreakable rule of Pathfinder Selection: never put down your weapon. It was actually good war-fighting training, though I sure didn't appreciate it at the time. If you get into the habit of always having your weapon to hand, you've got more chance of getting the draw on the bad guys.

The lead group was now reduced to three: me, Jock Greenhill and a lad from the Guards called Ted Edwards. Everyone else was strung out over a kilometre or more behind us. I searched for Dan, but this time I couldn't even see him.

'Right,' said the Staff. 'Water bottles away. Let's go.'

Dropping off The Flagstaff with a cold wind in our faces, we crossed a country lane, entered another valley, then followed some deep-rutted tank tracks leading into woodland dotted with pools of frozen water. We came to a ten-foot ditch, frozen solid at the surface. There was only one way through, which was to break the ice and wade in.

Even as we clambered out I could feel my feet starting to freeze in my soaking wet socks. By the time we reached the next high-point – Miles Hill – more distance separated the front of the pack from the rear. The light was fading fast and there was zero chance of spotting Dan.

We thundered downhill, crossed over Engineer's Bridge and headed along the canal – me, Jock and the Guards lad, Ted, leading. A Pathfinder Staff was waiting with a stopwatch. He timed us in.

'Okay, you three, take your Bergens off and go and sit over there.'

The three of us dissolved into a panting, sweat-soaked, heaving mess. It was a good five minutes before I finally spotted Dan emerging from the gathering darkness. He didn't look too hot.

He stumbled through, dropped his Bergen and collapsed next to me.

'You all right, mate?' I asked.

'Yeah. Fine,' he panted, but the way he said it I could tell it was for effect; for the others all around us. Then he turned to me and muttered: 'Knee's buggered.'

Dan had been a brilliant footballer and he'd played for the Army. But recently he'd been kicked in the knee and suffered ligament damage. It had clearly come back to haunt him.

His head dropped. 'I've got real pain in the ligaments, mate.'

I cursed. We were two days in with weeks to go. The primary objective of Selection was to keep yourself free of injury for as long as possible. This wasn't good.

We trudged back to the Pathfinder base side by side, neither of us saying a great deal. It was like a black cloud had fallen over the two of us. By the time we lined up outside the band room it was dark.

'Drop your Bergens; warm kit on,' one of the Staff announced.

While we were changing I spotted two of the guys on Selection heading into the office, only to emerge again a couple of minutes later. They did a silent knife-cut across the throat gesture, before picking up their packs and leaving.

The first two had VW'd.

By the time we jogged back to our Second World War camp that evening, I hurt in places I hadn't even realised a man could feel pain. But my worries were nothing compared to Dan's. We packed out our sodden boots with newspaper, to try to dry them out, hung our sodden kit on the heaters, got some food down us and hit our maggots.

Utterly exhausted.

We were on parade the following morning with webbing kit, boots, smock and helmet, plus weapon. Our orders were to have 35lb of weight in our webbing. Anyone who's in the airborne forces knows what this kind of dress is for: its what you do the Combat Fitness Test (CFT) in.

You have to complete two miles in all this kit, simulating running to battle. The pass mark for the Parachute Regiment is eighteen minutes. For the Pathfinders, we figured it'd be less. Considerably so.

The secret to passing the CFT is not simply to beast it. You can't make it with your webbing scything about on your hips. You have to get your rifle and wedge the pistol grip into your webbing on the right-hand side, so the extra pressure will stop it moving. Then you jam your thumb into a similar position on your left, and start to run.

But as we marched out of camp towards the starting point, I was more concerned about Dan than myself. How he was going to manage a CFT with a buggered knee?

Ted Edwards and Jock were with me as we set off, but Dan soon fell behind. We completed the first mile, did an about turn and headed back the way we'd come. I passed Dan coming the other way, but I didn't even try to catch his eye. The fierce look of concentration on his face meant he was in the zone, blanking out the discomfort and the pain.

I didn't want to risk breaking him out of there.

At the end of the CFT everyone was moaning and cussing. Not a man among us wasn't popping the Ibuprofen – nicknamed 'Brufen' in Army-speak; 800mg, the maximum dose. Then there were the compression bandages wound tight around strained ankles and knees, and two-inch strips of Elastoplast slapped all over backs and shoulders, to try to ease the Bergen sores.

And everyone was slapping Drapolene – the nappy rash cream – over bollocks and inner thighs, in an effort to stop them chafing red-raw. I watched as Dan silently strapped his knee more tightly than ever, and popped the Brufen like Smarties. He was digging in for the long haul.

A third candidate VW'd at the Band Room.

We were down to twenty-four now.

The survivors gathered in the makeshift classroom for Dave Moore's briefing. 'In preparation for Wales, we're not saying you need all this kit, but from experience some of these things may assist you.' He held up a natty-looking head torch. 'All the guys carry one of these: six ninety-nine from your local camping shop. Most of the guys have Thorlo walking socks: two ninety-nine a pair. They're padded and cushion your feet. Less blisters.'

For Dave Moore this was about as kind and caring as it ever got. But it was a bit like a great white shark with a leg in its mouth, enquiring after its victim's health.

'If you make it through the first phase,' he continued, 'a lot of your time will be spent cold and wet, lying still, with little blood circulating. So Goretex socks are a good option. About a tenner a pair. Your boots will be wet through most of the time. You dry your feet, put dry socks on, put the Goretex sock over those, put your wet boots back on – and at least you've still got dry feet.'

He paused to let the alternative sink in: wet boots, wet socks, freezing feet, total misery.

'In the Pathfinders we carry a lot of mission-essential kit and there's no room for luxuries. The Army issue you with a Norwegian Commando top, but once it gets wet you won't get it dry. Most of the guys buy these Helly Hansen thermal tops, 'cause even when they're wet they're still warm . . .'

The list went on and on.

He rounded off with this. 'Look, lads, you're not in the Pathfinders yet, not by a long chalk. A lot of you won't make it. So, I understand the financial implications. It's up to you. Completely. Just a suggestion. Tomorrow you'll get the afternoon off so you can buy whatever you decide.'

He paused, and ran his eyes around the room. 'We leave for Brecon at zero three hundred hours, Friday morning.'

13

The following afternoon – after another morning's beasting – I sat with Dan on the lower bunk of our bed, debating Dave Moore's advice.

'What happens if we don't get in?' Dan complained. 'I'm buying nothing. You?'

'Me neither,' I confirmed. 'If I get in, that's when I'll get some proper gear.'

There was a short pause while we wondered what to do with our free afternoon, now that we weren't heading for Aldershot's outdoor pursuits stores.

Dan grinned at me. I grinned at him. After four days of sheer hell we figured we deserved a visit to the pub.

It was me who put the thought into words. 'Fancy a few beers?'

'Yeah, let's have some Guinness,' Dan enthused. 'Full of iron. It'll be good for us.'

Plan sorted, we started changing into our civvies. To the left and right of us blokes were beavering away, packing gear and writing out their shopping lists. The longest of all belonged to the two Ruperts – officers – undertaking Selection. By the looks of their shopping lists, the guys were going to do Dave Moore proud.

'Fucking come on, Dan, let's go.'

We walked the four miles to the Traff, so we could save the taxi money and spend it on beer. We barged in. It was 2.30 in the afternoon, and after what we'd been through these past few days we each had a thirst to die for.

'Right,' I said, doing my best impersonation of Dave Moore in full flow, 'let's get some iron inside us.' We sat at the bar. 'Let's have some Guinness. Six pints each.'

We downed pints for four hours straight, by which time we were very happy bunnies. All Dan seemed to have needed to sort out his knackered knee was a skinful of ale.

'Dan, I'm going to get a Kentucky,' I announced.

'Good one. Me too.'

I ordered a bargain bucket of Colonel Sanders' Wicked Zingers, three packets of fries, a tub of coleslaw and a jumbo Coke. Dan had the same. We munched our way back to camp. Food never tasted so good – even the bits I had to scrape off my T-shirt.

Fantastic.

We wandered into our wooden hut, bargain buckets wedged under one arm, somewhat pissed and giggling, and bumping about.

In Aldershot, there is an army surplus store called HM Supplies. HM Supplies bags are dark green, and they have their name stamped upon them in big gold lettering. The two Ruperts must have had six bags each from the place. We got the giggles just at the sight of them. They were ever so carefully folding up their new Helly Hansen jackets and Thorlo socks, ready for the off.

I sat there with Dan for a bit enjoying the buzz, before we shoved bits and bobs of kit into our Bergens. A few guys were still coming in from their shopping errands. One was Jock Greenhill, the super-fit Scottish lad who'd been neck-and-neck with me on most of the runs.

'Where've you two been?' said Jock, sniffing the booze on us.

I grinned. 'Been in the Traff.'

Jock shook his head. 'Fucking blokes.'

I eyed his bulging Boots carrier bag. 'What've you got in there, then?'

'Zinc tape, Brufen, analgesic cream. You know the score.'

I figured we'd done rather poorly on the shopping front, but we'd had bucket-loads more fun. For us, at least, it was: day four, lesson four – never regret a few good beers.

The next thing I remember was someone turning on all the lights. It was 0230 and I had a massive head on. I'd never drunk Guinness before: I'm a lager lout. Rolling my head down off the side of the top bunk, I tried to focus on Dan.

'Mate, my fucking head is ringing,' I groaned.

Dan barely grunted a reply.

The Ruperts were already up and they seemed to be doing ballet in their corner. When I looked more closely I realised it was their early morning stretching ritual. Dan unscrewed the top of a Brufen bottle and necked a load.

I reached down a hand. 'Mate, gimme some of them.'

I swigged them down, but boy was I feeling shit.

We mounted up the coach for Wales, and I lay on the back seat and zonked out. Dan was on the seat in front of me, equally comatose. That's all I remember of the journey. I woke up as we crossed the Severn Bridge after three hours' sleep. I felt dog rough, with a throat full of sawdust, and I hadn't touched my 'haverbag' (British Army take-out) breakfast.

'Mate . . . Not good,' I croaked to Dan.

He didn't reply. He was rubbing his eyes and looking totally bewildered.

We crossed the border into Wales in a rainstorm. We climbed steeply for two hours and we seemed to be in one of those mountain scenes from *The Lord of the Rings*.

The third book.

The one where they're deep into Mordor.

The coach picked its way along rain-lashed country lanes and the mist closed in. At 0830 we passed through a tiny village and came to a halt beside two Army Land Rovers, where the road just petered out in the middle of nowhere.

The Pathfinders had driven up separately. Dave Moore poked his head around the coach door. 'Off the coach. Get your Bergens off the wagons, plus your weapons.'

We mustered in the freezing, fog-bound, rain-lashed nothingness. 'Heaney, Walters, Davis, Jones,' Moore announced. 'You're group one. Move over there.'

Dan was in group two.

A small, stocky, war-bitten-looking bloke walked up to my group. 'You will call me Staff,' he announced. 'This is Walkabout One. The aim is for me to assess your navigation skills. There'll be three Walkabouts over the next three days. If I don't think you're up to being safely on the hills alone, you'll go no further.

'I will nominate each of you to take a leg and I will choose the points on the map. You will tell me the best way to get there. You will then lead the group. The pace I expect is four kilometres an hour, whether it's flat, uphill or downhill.'

We all got our maps and compasses out.

'Right, first question. Does anyone know where we are?'

Blank looks all round. 'No, Staff.'

'We're at grid one nine one four zero three, just outside the village of Trefil. Here.' He pointed it out on his map. 'We're now going to move to this point here. Set a bearing, measure the distance and look at the map. Study the ground and see which route you'd take.'

He came around each of us checking our route. I indicated mine, which was pretty much as the crow flies. In truth my head felt so bad I was barely able to read a road sign, let alone make sense of a bloody map.

He frowned. 'All them contour lines are very close together, so that's a bastard steep slope.' He was talking slowly, like he was dealing with a small child. 'It'd be murder trying to get up that. Understand why that would be tough and slow. It's easier this way.'

He indicated a different route, then turned to the last guy in line, Bob Walters, the 1 PARA bloke. He checked Bob's route, and informed him he would lead the first leg. 'I want to be there in forty-five minutes. Let's go.'

Bob took off across the moorland through thick, driving rain and mist. We three followed, with the Staff taking up the rear. That first trek was just a blur to me. Eventually, Bob stopped and declared that we were there. We got out our maps and confirmed we were at the first point.

'Why do you think you're here?' asked the Staff.

Bob described the features he could see – which were precious few in such conditions – and the Staff said he was happy. Sighs of relief all round.

'Next leg. You've got two minutes to give me a bearing, route and time to get there. Remember: if you climb high, you can run along the ridge. Stay high, keep dry. In the valleys it's boggy and marshy.'

The second leg was five kilometres and we had one hour fifteen in which to do it. We climbed higher and higher, our route taking us over marshes and through clumps of bog grass, with just enough space between them to get your feet stuck. 'Babies' heads' – perfect ankle-twisting terrain.

I started wishing I'd eaten my haverbag breakfast on the coach. My last food had been Colonel Sanders' Wicked Zinger bargain bucket, and I could still taste it on my breath.

We made it to our second 'checkpoint', and it was now that I got chosen. Luckily, the terrain, the murderous weather and the exertion seemed to have kicked much of my hangover into touch. I got given a six-kilometre leg, leading up to Point 642, a landmark that has become infamous in elite forces' legend.

We'd all heard of 'Point 642'. The elite forces' rumour mill made sure of that. It's an isolated needle of concrete sat atop a high-point, surrounded on all sides by savage drop-offs. On one side lies the utterly fearsome 'VW Valley', a massive V-shaped chasm that has claimed many a victim on elite forces Selection.

'VW' stands for 'voluntary withdrawal' – the process via which we might cry off Selection at any time, as Dave Moore kept reminding us. Point 642 was synonymous with physical torture, mental collapse and failure.

I didn't doubt that the Staff had done this deliberately. He could probably smell the booze on me. He must have wondered: *Who the hell is this chancer trying to join us lot, the chosen few?*

He'd held the toughest leg back for me.

'That leg – how long's it gonna take?' he demanded.

'Six k? Hour and a half, Staff,' I suggested.

'Right. In one and a half hours we'd better be there.'

Off we went.

You wouldn't have thought it possible for the weather to get any shittier, or the terrain any tougher, but it did. God knows how I managed to get us to the trig point. I guess I was on autopilot: all that running across the Middlesbrough hills sure must have helped.

Either way we reached the godforsaken spot which is Trig Point 642 with just seconds to go before the one and a half hours was up. Another group of four had made it in just a minute or so ahead of us. They crouched there dripping wet and soaked to the skin, looking happy as Larry. But all I could think was – *Yes! Made it, despite the beer!*

The final leg was seven kilometres downhill, at the end of which we caught sight of our coach and the Land Rovers.

Our Staff gathered us for a final summing up. 'Not too bad today. Everyone seems able to read a map. But it doesn't matter how good a navigator you are – it's all about route selection. Read the map, read the ground and choose where to go. Don't rely on fitness to go up and straight over. Navigate round the features. Know when to climb and when to stay in low ground, and which is faster.'

By now, my mind was pretty much clear of the Guinness blowback. A bit of mental arithmetic told me we'd covered twenty-eight kilometres. Not bad going all things considered.

'Tomorrow we'll be in a different part of the Beacons,' the Staff continued. 'Same thing, but further. If anyone wants to jack, do me a favour – don't jack on the tab, 'cause once we're on the hills there's nowhere to go, so you have to finish anyway. Jack at the start of the day over breakfast, or at the end of the day – not in the middle.'

I figured that was about as near as we'd ever get to a dollop of compassion from this bloke. I sat at the rear of the coach. Dan got on and walked towards me, laughing and shaking his head.

'Mate, I think it was lunchtime before I sobered up.'

I grinned. 'I'm still only half there, mate.'

We headed for Sennybridge Camp, of Sidney the Snail fame. They'd allocated us a single-storey wooden hut, twenty metres long by ten wide, with a hard-backed wooden chair and a radiator at either end. Crammed into it were twenty metal bunks. We got in and fought for a bed.

I elbowed my way to one end and grabbed the bottom bunk positioned immediately next to the rad, bagsying the top one for Dan. It was the prime spot for the simple reason that it was furthest away from the door, which would let in a blast of cold air every time someone got up in the night for a piss.

Colin Hines, a chirpy Cockney from the Royal Signals, bagged the space two down from us, bottom bunk. Time for a little wind-up, I decided.

'The Signals,' I remarked, picturing their cap badge – a guy in silver holding a silver globe. 'Nice cap badge, mate – the little ballerina.'

'You gotta love the PARAs,' he retorted. 'Strong in the arm, thick in the 'ead.'

'Yeah, not like us Engineers,' a hulking great monster of a bloke added. He'd taken the bed next to Colin's. 'We're the thinking man's Army. We got us a trade.'

What a fucking numbskull. Dan managed to nail him proper.

'Engineer, you say? Best get on with it, then – go build us some shitters.'

Dan joined me in declaring our end of the hut a 'Blood Clot Zone' – a term we use for PARAs grouping together in a gaggle. We got Jock and Steve, the two 3 PARA lads, installed on the bunk opposite, plus Bob and Ian from 1 PARA on the bunk next door.

Strangely enough, the two Ruperts with their rakes of Gucci kit had taken the bunk right next to the door. It was going to be slamming shut all night, and blowing Baltic around their heads. I sensed we might have some fun with the both of them, as Selection really got under way.

Kit and bunks sorted, Dan pulled me aside for a quiet word. 'Mate, either I keep drinking six pints of Guinness, or my knee's gonna torture me. It's hurting like hell right now.'

'Like how bad?'

Dan's brow furrowed. 'Like bastard bad sore.' The twenty-eight klicks up and down the mountains had clearly done it no good at all. 'Guess I'll just tape it up tomorrow and pop some more Brufen.'

'Nothing for it: you're just gonna have to Reg it out.'

'Reging' it out was Army-speak for what you do when the going gets tough – like it had done for Dan: you Reg it out.

We headed down to the canteen for some hot scoff. That meant shovelling in meat stew, pasta, potatoes and bread followed by sticky pudding and custard – as much as we could stomach. At the far end of the canteen were the Pathfinders, studiously ignoring us. There was no talking, no fraternising.

I noted my Staff was there among them, shaven head bent over a massive heap of food. There was something of a hobbit about him. Something that suggested he'd spent much of his life underground. No, correction: it wasn't a hobbit. He was more Gimli the dwarf.

From that moment onwards he became Gimli in my mind.

We'd just about done eating when Dave Moore wandered over. 'Right, brief for tomorrow. There's a pile of maps on the table in the corner. The Black Mountains. The routine is parade zero four thirty, breakfast zero four forty-five to zero five hundred. Then go get your weapon. Zero five fifteen on bottom square with Bergen to weigh forty pounds. All kit to be useful; no dead weight. Collect haverbag at breakfast.

'Right. Does anyone need to speak to me before tomorrow morning? Does anyone want to VW?'

Murmurs of 'No, Staff.'

'Okay. The rest of the night is your own.'

We grabbed maps and headed back to the hut. Dan and I started to pack. A sleeping bag went in first, plus waterproof survival bag. If you got lost on the hills in bad weather you could crawl into your maggot, get inside your survival bag, and last out the storm. Warm clothes went in on top of that, followed by webbing, water bottle and food.

That way, the heaviest gear was where you wanted it – high on your shoulders.

We waxed our boots to try to increase waterproofing and ensure they didn't crack. Then we slapped Drapolene all over our manly bits, Vaseline up the bum crack – it's the only way to stopping chafing in there – and plenty of talc on our feet.

We did it now, because there sure as hell wouldn't be time in the morning.

14

The Ruperts were the first up, God bless 'em. They threw on the lights a good hour before we needed to be on parade, and started stretching and pirouetting and pointing their toes. I burrowed deeper into my smelly maggot, determined to snatch thirty minutes more shuteye.

Over breakfast, we had our first no-show. Dave Moore had just sat down to a mountainous fry-up, when one of the blokes rocked up in front of him: 'Staff – can I have a word?'

'Yep,' said Moore, barely lifting his head from his plate. 'What?'

The guy had clearly wanted a private word, but Moore was having none of it. If you wanted to VW, you did it out in the open where all could see. By the time we'd finished breakfast and were back in the hut, that guy had already packed his gear.

He glanced our way – towards the Blood Clot Zone – and shook his head. 'Nah, not for me, guys. I VW'd.'

That left twenty-three out of an original twenty-seven.

It was sheeting down by the time we threw our Bergens into the two waiting trucks. If anything, the weather was even worse by the time we arrived in the Black Mountains. True to their name, a dark crown of clouds swirled around the peaks, threatening to swallow up anyone who ventured forth.

Our Staff – Gimli – called us over.

'Before we go anywhere,' he began, raindrops dripping off his nose, 'does anyone wanna jack? 'Cause I'll be pretty fucking pissed if anyone does it halfway through.'

'No, Staff, we're good.'

Today was pretty much a repeat of Day One, only we had the 40lb packs lashed to our backs. We tore up and down hillsides like demented mountain goats. I was as wet on the inside of my clothes as I was out. The sweat poured out of me, bleeding through to the rain seeping in, and the two fused into a sodden, freezing blanket.

We stopped at midday in a derelict stone barn. It had no windows, but at least the tin roof kept out the worst of the rain. We sat on our Bergens, shivering, while we crammed down our haverbag lunches: two cheese sarnies, a bag of barbecue flavour crisps, three Jammie Dodgers, an apple, a bar of chocolate, plus a can of Panda cola.

By the time we were done eating, my teeth were chattering and my legs were shaking uncontrollably. Either we got moving again or I would freeze solid.

I was well chuffed when the second day's Walkabout came to an end, and I'd kept up with Gimli and the others. The conditions could hardly get any more inhospitable, so maybe this was as bad as it could get? If so, I figured maybe I could do this: I could get Pathfinder Selection whooped.

But one look at Dan when we got back to camp dashed my good spirits. The usual spring in his step was no more. We stripped off our wet gear and threw it on the radiators, after which Dan plonked himself down on the lower bunk – my bunk.

He was staring at his knee. It had swollen up to twice its normal size. I didn't know what the fuck to say, and Dan didn't seem to want to say anything in front of the others. He popped a horrendous number of Brufen, then glanced up at me. I was shocked by what I saw in his eyes. For a fleeting moment there had been the flash of . . . *defeat*.

'Mate, what're you gonna do?' I asked.

'I'll just keep trying to strap it up, and crack on.'

There wasn't much else to say. No matter how much I might will him on, Dan was going to have to do this for himself.

Day one. Pathfinder lesson one. Nobody helps you here. You have to help yourself.

We were all of us suffering, not to mention beyond tired. The canteen was like a morgue, as everyone was concentrating on piling on the calories, before racing to get their heads down.

The next morning Dan was up well before me, which was odd. I couldn't find him anywhere. I walked up to breakfast on my own. He came in just as I was tucking into a humongous plate of fried egg and beans.

The first thing I noticed was how badly he was limping.

Then I saw the look of utter desolation on his face.

He knew it. I knew it. Dan was finished.

'You all right, mate?' I mouthed at him.

It was a good candidate for the world's most stupid question. He stared for an instant, then did the slash-across-the-throat gesture. *I'm done.*

I just couldn't believe it. I dropped my knife and fork and walked over to him.

'Mate – *what?* You can't be.'

He shook his head. 'I can't walk, mate. I really can't walk.'

'But you're Dan fucking Miller. You can't *VW*.'

He shrugged. 'I can mate. I have to. I can't bastard walk.'

Early that morning Dan had been to see the camp doctor. He'd been told that it was hopeless. His knee was kaput, and only a long period of rest would sort it. I couldn't think of anything I could do or say to help. Maybe the only thing left was to accept that Dan was done, to make it easier on him.

'Okay, mate. Okay, buddy. But who the fuck am I gonna drink Guinness with now?'

Dan tried to crack a smile. He didn't quite make it. I could tell that he was hurting real bad. But what was torturing him most was the pain of having to face up to what he would see as his own failure.

He hobbled across to the Pathfinders' end of the canteen. I couldn't bear to watch. He stood before Dave Moore and I could imagine what the poor bastard was having to say. I felt devastated. For Dan and, if I'm honest, for myself too.

I was losing my wingman.

My brother-in-arms.

It was a massive blow.

The worst was – I couldn't even hang around to see Dan off. We had fifteen minutes for breakfast. If I waited I'd miss the trucks, and they'd most likely fail me.

I went up to him. 'Dan, I've gotta go, mate.'

We shook hands. He looked me fair and square in the eye. 'Good luck. I think you'll do it. *Do it for me.*'

All through that third twenty-eight-kilometre walk my mind was on Dan. I thought about how we'd boozed and scrapped and soldiered hard, living the PARA dream; about how we'd decided to go for Pathfinder Selection together; about how we'd fuelled ourselves on ale and a belly full of Colonel Sanders' Wicked Zingers, that first day out in the Welsh Hills.

That's what had united us: the shared spirit to do the unthinkable and the unexpected, and sometimes the downright stupid, and to come through it all laughing. I imagined him being driven out of camp, head down, with his dreams in tatters, and with nobody there to say a few encouraging words.

I lifted my head into the driving, wind-whipped rain.

I had to bastard beat this; I had to – *for Dan.*

15

'Right,' said Dave Moore. 'Right.'

It was starting to get a tad annoying.

It was the evening, Dan was well gone, and we who remained had just traversed the hell of the Elan Valley. I didn't mind if I never set eyes on the place again. And why they called the place the 'Elan Valley' I didn't know. It was the Valley of the Shadow of Death, if ever I've walked it.

It's a place of swirling clouds, hanging cliffs and thick, disorienting mists. A nightmare; a torture garden; a shitehole. And no matter where you are, it all looks the bastard same. But right now, I had other things to worry about.

'Right,' said Dave Moore, for the third time. 'That's the Walkabout phase over. Tomorrow we start Test Week.' He stroked his droopy moustache and stared. 'First test is the Fan Dance.'

Everyone who knows anything about elite forces Selection knows about the Fan Dance.

'The Fan Dance,' Moore repeated. 'On the Fan, if you fail to make any of the timings, you'll be withdrawn.' As if we didn't know. 'Right: the Do's. Do stick to the route and stay as an individual. It's an individual test. Don'ts: don't use out-of-bounds areas like roads, don't move as a group or a pair, and whatever you do – don't get caught cheating.'

Back in our wooden hut I laid out my kit on the top bunk – where Dan's should have been. It felt wrong doing it, but the extra space was proving damn useful. Plus I knew that Dan would have wanted it. *Do it for me.* I packed my Bergen, got my head down and fell into an exhausted sleep.

I was up the following morning at 0430. Those of us who still remained climbed in the waiting Bedford truck and drove to the base of the Fan. All around us the landscape was shrouded in thick banks of low cloud, mixed with freezing fog. Here and there I caught glimpses of the rock-faces towering above us, between thick, black curtains of rain.

The conditions couldn't have been more unpleasant. We lined up next to the trucks with weapons and Bergens. Two of the blokes were underweight, and Dave Moore proceeded to give them a right royal bollocking. He barely raised his voice, but his tone would have made hell freeze over.

'Right: you two. Listen. If you can't follow simple instructions about the weight required in your Bergen, how can you be expected to lead a patrol behind enemy lines? Think long and hard about it, as you carry your extra rocks up 'n' over the Fan.'

One of the Staff came along and plonked a small boulder into each of the offending packs. No effort was made to check whether it took them hugely over-weight or not. Dave Moore bent over the rocks and signed his signature on each with a big black marker pen.

He straightened up. 'Just so you don't get any clever ideas, and try to swop 'em with a lighter one when you're out of sight.'

We all knew what lay before us. The route of the Fan Dance leads straight up a near-vertical climb to the peak of Pen-y-Fan. You then drop down to Windy Gap, beast it along a stony track called the Old Roman Road, reach the turnaround point, and do it all in reverse.

It's twelve kilometres out, twelve back again. Time allowed: six hours. Average speed required: four klicks an hour. And all in the most appalling January weather imaginable.

'Right: Bergens on,' Moore commanded. 'Everyone ready. Let's go.'

We hit the bottleneck – the stile at the top of the car park – and the lead guy was sucked into the mists ahead of us, disappearing completely. I crossed the stile, set my head down and began to climb – some four kilometres more or less straight up to the Fan.

I was swallowed by the low cloud. I could only see twenty feet to left and right, and ten ahead. I immediately regretted bringing my trusty woolly hat, which quickly became waterlogged, sagging down in front of my eyes. I'd had it since my earliest PARA days, and it was now worn and out of shape. Although I kept trying to push it up, it just slipped down in a soggy, shapeless mush again.

Eventually, I ripped it off and shoved it into the side pocket of my Bergen. What I wouldn't do now for one of the Ruperts' smart new Thinsulate hill-walking hats. Maybe I could ambush one of them in the thick murk, and steal it. The thought made me smile, the smile lifted my spirits, and it spurred me on.

The Fan Dance has a reputation for setting calves, shins and thighs on fire. I could feel the pain start as soon as I hit the slope and there was no respite. I had decided to allow myself one hour to hit the top; and five hours forty-five minutes to get all the way there and back again. That would leave a quarter of an hour leeway in case of any unforeseen emergencies.

As I climbed, a bitter wind drove the rain into my face. Once again, I found that I was sweating and shivering all at once, with my trousers and inner fleece plastered to my body. My shoulders were burning with the effort of the never-ending climb. I bent forward, shuffling the Bergen higher onto my back, and trying to get some blood flow back into my deltoid muscles.

After what seemed like an age I reached the last hundred-metre stretch, the way ahead of me becoming practically sheer. I felt this burning temptation to use my weapon as a walking stick, but that was at the top of the banned list. If I did that and was spotted it would be an instant fail.

Instead, I kept one hand gripping my rifle, while the other pushed against my thighs, to help drive me uphill.

A tiny green tent was pitched on the flat expanse that marks the summit of the Fan. I stumbled towards it through a howling gale, expecting at any minute to see it ripped away in the wind. As I bent at the entrance, my heart was pounding and my lungs were heaving fit to burst.

Two of the Staff were in there, snug in their maggots. They were playing Radio 1 on a little tranny, while they used their big Army radio to keep a track of who was between which checkpoints – just in case anyone got into serious trouble.

I reported in. 'Heaney, Staff.'

'Okay, Heaney, d'you know where you're going next?'

'Yes, Staff.'

'Off you go then.'

When I set off again I was practically blown across the remainder of the summit. I juddered to a halt on the brink, at the top of what is known as Jacob's Ladder – a near-vertical drop of fifty metres, one you have to inch your way down. At the bottom you hit a bowl-shaped depression, leading to the start of the Old Roman Road.

I was two-thirds of the way down the Ladder when a savage gust of wind blew me off balance. While trying to right myself, I missed my footing and tumbled the last fifteen metres or so. Luckily, I came to rest on a patch of boggy ground, the soft, squelchy surface serving to break my fall.

I climbed to my feet, brushed off the worst of the mud and shit, put my back to the wind and set off again. They hadn't named this area Windy Gap for nothing. It was a battle just to stay on my feet, let alone keep moving. But after five hundred metres of fighting my way along a faint sheep track I hit the start of the Old Roman Road.

It may have been covered in jumbled boulders and rocks, but to me the Old Roman Road was a godsend. Running broad and straight for a good five kilometres, it was mostly downhill. This was where I figured I could really make up time. I hunched my shoulders, accelerated into a semi-jog and pressed on.

It was murder on the knees, but I knew the return leg – uphill – would be far harder, and it was now that I had to make like a racing snake. I caught sight of a figure up ahead of me. Visibility was so bad I had no idea who it was, and strive as I might I just couldn't seem to close the gap between us.

Next thing I knew two figures shrouded in the finest Goretex tore past, going like the proverbial steam-trains. For a moment I feared it was the two Ruperts. That would seriously twist me. But then I recognised them as Pathfinder Staff, even as they pressed ahead into the murk and left me for dust.

They'd said not a word as they'd burned past.

Not one teeny-weeny hint of encouragement.

The bastards.

I started hearing that infernal song again – *Ma-gic mo-ments* – echoing through my head, and I used the anger as fuel. My thighs pumped like pistons, my knees thrashed away, and my boots ate up the miles. *I'd magic-bastard-moments them . . .*

As it happened, I'd been a bit hasty in my judgement of those two Pathfinders. I reached the turnaround point, and – as impossible as it might seem – there they were, crouched over a pair of steaming tea urns.

I stomped up to them. Dark suspicions swirled through my mind. Maybe the urns were there for the psychological torture value; the ultimate sickener. *Fancy a brew, Heaney, lad? Ooops, it's empty. We must've had the last cup.*

I reported in. 'Heaney, Staff.'

'Right, Heaney: there you go.' They gestured at the urns. 'There are cups by the urn. Go grab yerself a brew.'

I still didn't believe them.

I dropped my Bergen, grabbed a disposable Styrofoam cup and turned the tap on the nearest urn, sceptically. Unbelievably, a thick, brown stream of liquid came gurgling out.

Tea; sweet, milky and steaming hot.

It was a total bastard miracle.

There was a God, after all.

Buoyed by two cups of the best brew that I had ever tasted, the return stomp to the summit of the Fan didn't seem quite as brutal as I had feared. Once I'd scrambled up Jacob's Ladder I got a massive psychological boost: I knew it was all downhill from there on in.

I bent at the green tent for a second time. 'Heaney, Staff!'

'Okay, Heaney, you know where you're going: back to the Storey Arms.'

I had an hour to get off the Fan and I was in a good place. Once I'd stumbled down the hundred-metre face I hit a sheep track, leaned back into the hill and let my legs go. I began to trot my way down, zigzagging from left to right to try to ease the pressure on my thighs and knees.

Oddly, I almost found myself enjoying this.

There is something distinctly primeval about being on your own, isolated in the wilderness, and relying on the most basic of navigation skills to get from point to point. That sense was massively heightened when doing so in the midst of a hellish, storm-lashed January.

No sane person would ever be out on these hills on a day like today.

That made me and the handful of others the chosen few.

It might have been totally insane.

It might have been crazy.

But it was most definitely my kind of insanity. And it would have been Dan's, too, if only he hadn't been carrying that injury.

As I hammered down the Fan, the mist cleared and an incredible vista opened before me. The rolling green hills and the winding valleys were lit up by piercing shafts of sunlight. Somehow, they had penetrated the heavy, iron-grey blanket of the sky, like searchlights shining from the heavens to light up my path ahead.

No doubt about it, I was hooked. The four days we'd had in Aldershot had been a right beasting. They'd done the job: they'd served to weed out the slackers. But we'd moved up to a whole different level now. PARAs are used to working in a pack under orders. This – this was out-there, lone wolf, warrior territory.

What I was experiencing here for the first time was total self-reliance. I was sore – bastard sore – and I was utterly exhausted, but at the same time I was totally elated.

I reached the waiting truck.

'Okay, Heaney, there's a tea urn down there,' one of the Staff announced.

I was the second in and I'd done it in five hours forty, so with twenty minutes to spare. Gulping the tea – pure nectar – I counted down the seconds to six hours dead. We hit the mark, and twenty of us had made it in.

'Anyone who comes in now – is that a fail?' I asked.

I could scarcely believe that the next guy in from such a gruelling trek would be ejected as unworthy.

'Six hours plus – that's a fail,' Dave Moore confirmed.

After scoff that evening, he asked the three guys who were late in to stay behind. They returned to the hut a few minutes later looking utterly crestfallen.

'That's us,' one of them said.

'We're done.'

'Didn't make the time on the Fan.'

They packed their kit ready to leave the next morning.

Three more guys with their dream snuffed out.

16

The bloke who'd beaten me on the Fan Dance was the 1 PARA bloke, Bob Walters. He was something of a phenomenon. It wasn't just the razor-edge bright ginger hair that made him . . . striking. It was his age. He was twenty-eight years old, which made him seem ancient to lads of twenty like me.

It was that – plus the fact that he always had a ciggie in his mouth – which made him the enigma. I just couldn't fathom how quick the guy was over the hills, when he kept sparking up a smoke at every opportunity. He seemed to be the fittest of us all.

He was stocky, with thighs like tree trunks, but he was no gym queen, and his voice had a thick Cornish burr – hence the nickname we'd given him of 'Cornish Bob'. By his own admission he could drink as much Cornish cider as any self-respecting Cornish yokel – which, indeed, he was.

For the start of the next day's forced march – back to the Black Mountains – the order in which we had completed the Fan Dance was reversed. The slowest guy went first, with ten minutes separating us – which put me second to last, and Cornish Bob hard on my tail.

We were facing a twenty-four-kilometre route march with a 45lb Bergen – 5lb more than the day before – and we were up against the clock. I sat on my pack and took a minute to study my route. As visibility was low, I tried to create a 3D image of the landscape in my mind. I was hoping for a break in the mist, but none came.

I set off, counting my footfalls as I went. If I counted one hundred and twenty left footfalls, I'd know that I'd covered roughly a hundred metres, which was a basic method to keep a record of distance covered. After navigating to six checkpoints I hadn't seen a soul between any of them. Although I was totally alone, I was loving the self-sufficiency and the solitude.

I was the second guy in again, with Cornish Bob right on my shoulder – and in terms of cumulative times he was still ahead of me. Two guys failed to make it in time, and they were duly binned.

We were down to eighteen.

In the military, these kind of forced marches get called 'tabs'. Tab stands for 'tactical advance to battle': in other words beasting it in on foot under a crushing load, to where battle can be joined with the enemy. We were two tabs down on Test Week and I was still very much in the game.

Our third tab took us back to that most hated of places – the Elan Valley. The peat bogs that litter the hills are notorious throughout the Army. It's said that if you fall into some of them you'll never get out again. The main difference since my last visit to this cursed place was that I'd be alone, and carrying a 50lb Bergen – so up 5lb on the previous day.

At least there had been a 'dramatic' improvement in the weather – for this part of the world anyway. There was a steady drizzle falling from a slate-grey sky, and I told myself it was about as good as it gets for around here in the depths of winter.

Once more, I was second to last to be set free, with Bob placed ten minutes behind me. I set off from a picnic area – *who would ever want to picnic here?* – and was soon into a patch of drizzle-soaked woodland. Emerging from the cover of the trees I began the first of several long, exposed climbs.

It was weird, but again I found a part of me was almost enjoying the slog through the Valley of the Shadow of Death. As my legs pumped and my lungs heaved in the moisture-sodden air, I hauled myself through the worst of the swampy ground, comforting myself with the thought of how I was making good time.

Yet when I approached the last and final grid point, who should be waiting for me but Smokin' Cornish Bob, with a big grin on his face.

'Fucking hell,' I panted. 'How the fuck did you get ahead of me? I never even saw you.'

'Not bad for an old 'un, eh?'

That was what I liked about Bob. Clearly the fittest and the most capable of the lot of us, he never boasted. He was a man of few words – and when he spoke, you listened. And he never had a bad thing to say about anyone, either – not even me, the young upstart snapping at his heels.

The eighteen of us who remained had made it through the Elan Valley relatively unscathed. We gathered for that evening's scoff. That was when Moore delivered the bombshell. Pathfinder Selection was but a few years old, and so few had attempted it that word was yet to get around about what exactly it entailed. None of us knew what was coming.

'Right. The next tab will be a Point-to-Point on the Beacons, with fifty-pound Bergens,' Moore began. 'But for all of you who get through tomorrow, be warned. You'll be coming back to camp for your evening meal as normal, but reveille after that is midnight.'

He let that word hang in the air. *Midnight*: that meant three or four hours sleep, at best.

'You'll be here in the cookhouse for a very early breakfast,' Moore continued. 'Your Bergen must weigh in at fifty-five pounds – minus food and water. You'll be leaving for Endurance at zero two hundred.'

He ran his eye around the lot of us. 'So, is there anyone who wants to VW? Anyone? Better now, than halfway through what is coming.'

There were subdued murmurs from all: 'No, Staff.'

With that, he spun on his heel and was gone.

I turned to Cornish Bob. 'What the fuck? What does that mean?'

The way Bob saw it, the aim of the Point-to-Point was to bounce us around the Beacons with the purpose of wearing us out, prior to starting Endurance.

'Endurance is the big one,' said Bob, in his soft Cornish burr. 'We'll go over the top of the Fan and do sixty-four kilometres. We'll get twenty hours to make it. Any longer and you're done for.'

'What, with three hours' kip before starting?'

Bob smiled. 'That's the idea. Break you down and mess you up for the Big One.'

My priority on Point-to-Point was to complete it just in time and to avoid any injury. I finished the four legs – twenty-odd kilometres – just before the cut-off point. Bob was right, of course. Point-to-Point wasn't supposed to be hard to navigate: it was simply a long, nasty slog designed to exhaust us.

Endurance was all anyone could talk about on the truck drive back to camp. If we made it through this, we were over the worst. Test Week completed – and Pathfinder Selection pretty much done 'n' dusted.

Or so we thought . . .

I got back to the hut and stuffed an extra water bottle, half-a dozen Mars bars and a couple of Cornish pasties – a Cornish Bob inspiration – into my Bergen, on top of all the usual gear. When I was done I had a 65lb pack to lug 64 kilometres over some of the harshest terrain Britain has to offer – and all to the clock.

I crawled into my maggot at 1830, knowing that every minute's sleep was precious. But for a while I lay there thinking: *This is it. Endurance. Go grab it. Go do it for Dan.*

Reveille was midnight. We ran to the cookhouse, stuffed our faces with a massive fry-up, then grabbed ourselves two haver-bags each. They too went into the Bergens.

Then it was time to leg it to the armoury to grab our weapons and on to the trucks. The night was cold and crisp for a change and – miracle of miracles – it wasn't raining. For the first time since we'd arrived in Wales the stars were twinkling bright above us.

Maybe it was a good omen.

It took twenty-five minutes to reach our starting point, a picnic area by a reservoir. We were called off the truck one at a time. I was second to last and Cornish Bob was after me.

I took a series of deep breaths, psyching myself up. Fitter than I'd ever been, I was injury-free. *I could do this.*

'This is it, mate,' I muttered. 'This is fucking IT. Twenty hours. Just twenty hours and you're in.'

We were setting off from the opposite side of the Fan to the Storey Arms, facing a nine-kilometre climb to the summit. I headed off into the crisp, clear darkness, following a path winding through thick bracken and heather. There was just enough ambient light to see by – from the moon and stars – but my Bergen sure felt bastard-heavy.

It wasn't as if we'd had time to recuperate after the Point-to-Point. My shoulders hadn't had a chance to loosen up and neither had my legs. With sixty-four kilometres still to go, they were aching like hell.

Focus, man, focus, said a voice inside my head. *Blank out the pain. Focus on the climb.*

I followed a sharp ridge – the obvious route to make the summit. Halfway up, I caught the guy ahead of me, pushing past him without a word. This was no time for niceties.

At the top of the ridge I turned left onto a track, heading for the summit of the Fan. I could just make out its dark silhouette against the starry sky. Far below in the valley a few lights twinkled on the farm buildings, but up here all was dark and deathly quiet.

I was alone in the world.

This was me against the elements.

Nothing else and nobody else mattered.

To my left rose a steep hillside; to my right a sheer drop fell away. By the pale light of the quarter-moon I could see maybe a hundred yards ahead, so I figured I could navigate well enough to avoid stumbling into the abyss. I crested a ridge, and hit terrain that I instantly recognised: Windy Gap, the final approach to the Fan itself.

Breaking into a semi-jog, I pounded across the Gap, which for once was all silence and stillness. I passed a second guy as I began the climb up Jacob's Ladder. I hit the top with my breath smoking like a dragon, and strode towards a torch-lit tent.

Kneeling beside it was a bloke who'd had a twenty-minute head start on me. I told myself that if I'd made up that kind of time already, I was doing all right. I'd started off at 0245. It was 0500 by the time I reached the tent.

I stood, hands resting on my thighs to try to give my shoulders some relief: 'Heaney, Staff!'

'Okay, Heaney, let's see your map. The next grid is three four eight four five five.'

I plotted the grid, identified it as the trig point at Fan Fawr, the second highest peak in the Beacons, and showed the Staff where I was heading. As I moved away the bloke who'd had a twenty-minute start on me was still fiddling with his map and compass. On Endurance, racing against yourself and the clock, you couldn't afford to linger.

I charged past him and was gone.

As I picked up the pace on the downhill, I warned myself to be extra bloody careful. Last thing I needed now was an injury. If I buggered-up a knee, as Dan had, I'd be done for.

Half way down the drop off the Fan I caught sight of the next bloke in line. He just beat me to the next checkpoint, on the summit of Fan Fawr, but I'd been snapping at his heels all the way. Telling myself I'd pass him early on the next leg, I crouched down to report in and get my next grid from the Staff.

I plotted it. It was a cairn known as Spot Height 619, and from the summit of Fan Fawr I could actually see it far in the distance. I took my Bergen off for the first time since starting Endurance, treated myself to a Mars bar and some water, then hefted my pack and slipped down the far side of Fan Fawr.

I hit a sheep's track, and followed that all the way to Spot Height 619. By the time I reached it I'd passed the guy I had been chasing without even realising it. He must have taken a different route.

The next grid was the Cray Reservoir, some nine kilometres distant. I studied the terrain, which was a series of rolling hills. There were no massive climbs, so this was a golden opportunity to gain time. It was getting light, and I figured it would take me eight hours in total to reach the reservoir. That left me twelve to get back again, which should be doable – taking fatigue into account.

Jogging along a winding sheep track into the valley, I crested a few rises and dropped down to the Reservoir. I made it there in seven hours forty-five minutes in total, which put me a quarter of an hour ahead of schedule.

The next grid was a parking area ten kilometres away, where the route passed over a tiny lane. God, this was going to be a long leg. I could feel the tiredness creeping up on me now, gathering in force as the sun rose.

I decided I could afford a ten-minute break, to get a hot drink and some food into me. Breaking out my Hexi stove – a foldable metal cooker, that burns hexamine solid fuel blocks similar to fire lighters – I set a metal mug of water to boil. Then I got the contents of the first haverbag down my neck, and followed that with two mugs of tea.

I felt energy flooding back into my veins.

That tea-break was a total life-saver.

I stood up in a twisting motion to try to avoid muscle cramp, and went to reach for my Bergen. It was then that the pain hit me. The moment I put any weight on my feet, the soles felt burning sore. Hot-spots were forming on the undersides of my feet – the start of blisters.

I cursed myself for taking that break. If I'd kept going, the pain wouldn't have hit me so bad, but the exhaustion would likely have done for me. It's only when you stop and have to start again that the pain really strikes. I forced myself to get going again – to stomp through the pain.

The sun rose above me and started to burn into the shadowed corners, zapping away the thick crust of crunchy frost. It lit up the hills, leaving no doubt about the distance still to cover. But at least the visibility was good. It didn't bear thinking about undertaking Endurance in the kind of weather we'd experienced over the past few days.

By the time I'd topped the first hill I'd caught up with a figure ahead of me. It was one of the two Ruperts. As I went to overtake him I thought about how snug he had to be in his brand-new Helly Hansen jacket, and how blister-free his feet must be in those lovely, padded Thorlo socks.

What was that they said about the British Army being a great leveller? Well I was about to level Rupert Number One, and figured I may as well take the opportunity to twist him.

'All right?' I said, as I passed him, deadpan.

'Yep,' he gasped. 'You?'

I nodded. 'Livin' the dream.'

I'd hit the halfway stage of this leg, a high-point – five kilometres to go to the car park. Down below to my left was a massive, sweeping valley. I caught sight of a figure halfway across it, struggling through what was obviously a very nasty bog.

Although I couldn't quite tell, I fancied it was the other Rupert. *Stay high, keep dry.* I repeated Gimli's mantra, the one that he'd taught us on our first Walkabout.

Hand-railing around the high ground of Fan Fraith, I overtook my seventh guy as I motored towards the next checkpoint. I figured Cornish Bob was still behind me, and there were several blokes to my front. No one was kidding themselves: with Endurance, most likely no more than the first half a dozen would make it through.

I was 33 kilometres in, with 31 still to go and approaching the turnaround point where you head back east. Exhaustion washed over me like a leaden death, but I forced myself to up my pace as I approached the next checkpoint. I needed to move up the field still more to guarantee that I'd make it.

The next checkpoint was marked by a Land Rover. As I approached, the side window of the cab slid open, and immediately I could smell this delicious, mouthwatering aroma wafting out.

'Heaney, Staff,' I reported in.

'Okay, Heaney, good to see you. Is everything okay?' The Staff's tone was strangely soothing. It was the first bit of warmth that I'd ever heard from their direction. It wasn't until he spoke again that I realised the trap.

'If you're not okay, you can always come in.' He waved his flask at me. 'Hot soup and bread rolls. Nice warm Land Rover to sit in. Come on in. VW. You know you want to.'

I shook my head. Violently. 'No, Staff!'

I'd forced out the words, for the voice of temptation was not easily resisted right now.

'We've got sandwiches in the back,' the Staff went on. 'You can get in, crawl into a maggot and sleep. Why not get in and have a rest? No need to crack on if you don't want to.'

They were trying to Magic Moments me all over again. *The bastards.*

'No, Staff. Don't need a rest. I'll crack on.'

He shrugged. His tone went back to normal: flat; devoid of any emotion. 'Okay, the next grid is three two three four five zero – the Beacons Reservoir. Right, off you go.'

The route to get there was a complete bastard. If I kept to the high ground I'd have to go twice the distance, as compared to heading across this massive valley that lay before me.

But my inner voice just kept repeating: *Stay high, keep dry.*

I started to semi-jog around the rim of the ridgeline, which would take me in a looping detour, but keep me at altitude.

Glancing down into the depths of the valley, I could see that one at least had chosen the 'shorter' option. Thank God I hadn't done likewise.

He looked to be in a terrible state. I twice saw him slip from the solid ground and fall into the water, after which he had to fight his way out of the waist-deep shite. He was making little or no progress, and for him I figured Selection was over.

Ahead I caught sight of two figures. Like me they were skirting around the valley rim. If I could keep my eyes fixed on them it would give me something to aim for. A goal. Something to blank my mind from the pain that was now throbbing through the soles of my feet. I didn't doubt that the blisters had burst, soaking my socks first with their fluid, and then with blood.

The exhaustion hit me in waves. I'd never felt anything like it. From my calves to my shoulders, I was burning up as if the Devil himself was jabbing me with a red-hot poker.

I didn't know how many miles I had left in the tank.

When I crested a ridge I could see two tiny black dots running down the slope ahead of me. *Catch them*, I told myself. *Catch those fuckers.* If I did, I'd be four or five from the front – which had to put me in reach of the impossible; of completing Endurance in time.

I just caught the slower of the two as we made it to a waiting Land Rover – our next checkpoint. When I got given my next grid – the infamous Trig Point 642 – I reminded myself of Cornish Bob's words of wisdom, which he'd imparted during the truck-drive in.

'Keep scoffing,' he'd said. 'Take that little bit of time to get some extra fuel in the tank.'

I moved away from the wagon, dropped my Bergen and plonked myself down on it, my body feeling like a mass of red-raw nerves. On a whim I pulled off my left boot and emptied out the water. I levered out the insole and beat it against a rock, before replacing it, doing the same with the other boot.

They'd be wet again just as soon as I set off and hit the first patch of boggy ground, but at least I'd have dryish feet while I got myself a meal. I brewed up, and wolfed down my second haverbag, relishing the feeling of a fuller belly.

Cornish Bob appeared, checked in, then stumbled across to where I was. Dropping his Bergen he lowered himself painfully into a sitting position.

I glanced at him. 'All right? How you doing?'

He grunted. 'I'm fucked, mate.'

'Me too. Feet are fucking on fire. So, is this the same route the SAS use?'

'Yeah.'

'We through the worst of it?'

He looked at me as if I was mad. 'Through the worst? You fucking kidding me?'

I shrugged. *What did I know?*

He shook his head, wearily. 'VW Valley, mate. It's still to come. You and it – you're about to get acquainted.'

17

After cresting the ridge at the near end of VW Valley, I suddenly knew what Bob had meant.

Falling away from me like a massive yawning chasm, VW Valley dropped six hundred metres more or less straight down. It was like a giant had taken a slice out of the earth, cleaving it with a massive axe and leaving a similar climb up the far side. Running along the valley bottom I could make out a small river, and I could see a couple of figures had forded it, and were just starting the long climb.

They were the guys I had to chase.

I would have given anything to be where they were now, but there was only one way to reach the river: straight down. For a moment I glanced to left and right, searching for some alternative route. But it only served to confirm what I knew already: there is no detour that gets you around VW Valley. It would be eight or more kilometres in either direction, and that would mean a fail.

Endurance – done for.

I lowered myself into the descent. According to Bob, this was the last real obstacle before the finish. It was early afternoon, and VW Valley is so steep the sun had barely got to burn off any of the frost. Mostly, it was still thick and silvery underfoot – not to mention treacherous.

The pressure on my knees felt like murder. I'd tightened my laces at the last stop, but even so I could feel my feet getting forced to the front of my boots. My toenails were getting ripped and more blisters were bursting from the pressure. I tried to crab down sideways, but that put unbearable pressure on my knees.

Any which way I approached this, I knew it was going to be sheer agony.

I started yelling at the top of my voice. 'Fucking hell! Fucking hell! Fucking hell!'

The shouting and screaming seemed to help ease the pain.

Suddenly, I lost my footing and had to scrabble desperately at the frost-bitten grass with my fingers. My nails ripped through frozen mud, as I fought to slow myself. I went down twice more, and twice managed to stem the fall before I finally reached the valley bottom.

It was now I faced the next challenge. From the high ground the river had looked Legoland tiny. Up close I could see it was six feet across, plus deep and fast flowing. I couldn't jump it in one and I didn't fancy wading it. I found a place where I could use two stepping-stones, before jumping the final stretch. I'd just made it across without falling in, when Bob appeared on the far bank.

I indicated where I'd forded the river. 'Cross there, mate. It's easier.'

Bob did as I'd suggested and joined me. We surveyed the climb before us. Sheer murder. I started off with Bob on my shoulder, but in no time he was powering past.

'Keep going, mate,' he urged me. 'Keep pushing it.'

I told myself I just needed to stick to Bob's coat-tails, and he would drag me up and out of VW Valley. But every now and again I had to stop to readjust my shoulder straps and ease the pain. Bob did none of that. Slow and steady he just powered up the hillside, taking the most direct route possible. I zig-zagged up, trying to keep in Bob's wake, but every minute he was pulling away from me.

By the time Bob crested the valley rim I was a good hundred metres behind him. I got to the high-point, gasping for breath and feeling like I was dying, and already Bob was nowhere to be seen. Glancing behind, I could see two blokes descending into the Valley. One was definitely the Rupert that I'd passed earlier.

It had taken me one and a half hours to traverse VW Valley. That was how far behind me those blokes were. *God, but we were strung out here.*

I pushed on.

I followed an undulating track that threaded through a series of peat bogs. To either side was this thick, oozing mud like treacle. It was late afternoon by now and already the light was beginning to fade. I made Trig Point 642 just as Bob pushed on into the gathering darkness. If I could just make it to the next major feature – an old Donkey Track – it would take me down to the woods above the Pontsticill Reservoir, and I would be almost there.

I needed to find that Donkey Track in the light, which meant forcing myself on.

The sun sank bright and crisp, dipping over the horizon. I pushed ahead, but with each footfall I felt as if someone was beating the soles of my feet with a hosepipe. It was sheer fucking agony.

I hit the Donkey Track just as the last light faded into dense black. The way ahead switchbacked ever higher, until it hit the thick, dark woodland. I entered the pine forest, my eyes straining in the gloom. I spotted a guy ahead of me, limping along at one side of the track. As I stumbled past him at a semi-jog, he looked to be in a real bad way.

'You all right?' I shot over my shoulder.

'Yeah. Yeah. Just a really sore knee.'

'Okay, mate, just keep going. Crack on.'

I hammered through the dark and silent woods, the pines to either side deadening any sound. I broke through the lower wooded slopes, coming out into a moonlit swathe of a valley, with a lake glinting gun-metal blue below me: the finish line – the Talybont Reservoir. Ahead lay the wall of the dam, and across it ran a road.

Halfway along the road I spotted a figure. It was Bob and he was maybe five hundred yards ahead of me. I looked beyond him, and there were the vehicles: a gaggle of Land Rovers and Army trucks. Either that was the finish, or I was done for.

I shuffled onto the concrete of the dam wall. My feet felt as if they were on fire. At least the terrain before had been comparatively spongy underfoot. The concrete was rock-hard and totally unforgiving. I hobbled onwards. Six hundred yards; five hundred; three hundred ... Every step was murder, but at least the finish line kept creeping closer.

I was crying out every time I placed a foot down. 'Fuck! Jesus! Fuck!'

Hobbling onwards I could finally see the wagons. I could hear voices; the sound of vehicles' doors opening and closing.

So close now.

I stumbled up to the nearest truck, thinking to myself – *my God, I've made it.* Then a voice reached out to me from the shadows.

'Right, Heaney, is it?'

It was Dave Moore.

'Heaney, Staff,' I confirmed.

'Heaney, you ready for your next grid?'

I stared at him, confusedly. Through the open truck back I could see Cornish Bob, plus the 1 PARA lad, Ian, getting their warm kit on. *My God, had the two of them jacked? If this wasn't the end, they must have ...*

I groped about for my compass and my map. 'Yes, Staff.'

'Next grid – three zero one four eight two. Show me where it is.'

I plotted the co-ordinates. If I'd got it right, it was the very summit of the Fan ... again. There was no way that I could make it. It would be nine kilometres straight up – again. I half collapsed at the thought of it.

'Show me where it is on the map,' Moore repeated.

'It's here, Staff.'

'You okay to continue? Or you want to VW?'

'Yep. I'll go on.'

'Before you set off, I have to ask again: do you want to VW?'

I shook my head, obstinately. 'No, Staff.'

'Right. Off you go.'

I hobbled off. I could not believe that Bob and Ian had jacked. It was impossible. But it was equally impossible that I would make the summit of the Fan . . . again.

Yet I would not VW. I would not fail myself. King Bastard would have to order me to stop, before I gave up on this thing.

'Heaney!' The call came from behind.

I halted. 'Staff.'

'Come here.'

'Staff.'

I hobbled back to where Moore was standing.

He nodded towards the open truck. 'Heaney, get over there and get your warm kit on.'

I shook my head, confusedly. 'What – is this the end?'

'Yeah, it's the end. For now. Go get your warm kit on. You're done with Endurance.'

'Staff.'

I hobbled over to the truck.

Bob grinned. 'Don't worry, mate, they did exactly the same to us. The bastards.'

'Mate, it was gonna take me a month to get to the top of the Fan.'

Bob glanced at Ian. 'Yeah, us too.'

With Bob and Ian's help I clambered into the rear of the truck. I unlaced my boots and slowly peeled them off. The undersides of my socks were blood red. I eased on a pair of dry trainers, and lay back in the truck.

I was so exhausted I doubted if I could move.

18

Twelve of us made it through Endurance – including Cornish Bob, Ian Johnson the 1 PARA lad, plus the two Ruperts. Two weeks had passed since we'd started Selection, and I could barely remember Magic Moments. It felt like a lifetime ago.

Thankfully, we now had a week in the Sennybridge classroom. Anything more physically demanding would have been pretty near impossible. After Endurance we were taped up and bandaged up and limping like the walking wounded.

In the classroom we studied 'patrols and tactics', in which you basically start to learn the Pathfinder's craft. Never a natural-born fan of the schoolroom, I actually found myself loving this. I was learning the skills of elite forces soldiering, and I figured that unless I dropped a complete bollock I was through the worst.

I was in.

In truth, I didn't know the half of it.

Patrols and Tactics ends with Range Week – several days of live firing exercises. This was where we started to learn how to move and fight fluidly, and instinctively, as a four-man patrol – the basic operating unit of the Pathfinders. When the Staff demonstrated it to us, it was incredible; they moved and fought like the guys do in the awesome bank raid scene from the movie *Heat*.

Aping them, we worked in singles, pairs, then groups of four, learning close-quarter battle manoeuvres – starting off in the open, before moving into closed areas, like woodland. We learned how to shoot instinctively, in the spirit of the moment, when the weapon becomes almost an extension of your body – like a fifth limb.

After Range Week came the grand finale of Pathfinder Selection: Final Exercise Week. Rarely does anyone fail patrols and tactics or even Range Week. They're more designed to teach you the Pathfinder's craft than they are to fail you. But Final Exercise Week is different. It's where all the previous trials and all that you've learned are rolled into one, and pushed to the limits.

Make no mistake, with Final Exercise Week we were back in 'pass' or 'fail' territory, big time.

We were broken down into three groups of four. I was teamed up with Ted Edwards, from the Guards – a six-foot rake of a bloke who hailed from the Windsor area. Needless to say, I liked winding him up about being a 'southern woos'. Next was Rob Lee, a short, stocky bald-headed bloke from 216 Signals Squadron. Rob had a face like a sack of claw-hammers, and suffice it to say he was not exactly easy on the eye.

The third member of our team was Pete Stanley, another Guardsman. He was 5' 9", good looking and married. Known as a 'pad' – meaning he lived with his family on base – he could be fiery and snappy if pushed. All of them were in their mid-twenties, which made me – at twenty – the baby.

The four-man team is the basic Pathfinder unit. Being the youngest I was appointed lead scout – the guy who fronts up the patrol. That was the place to put the freshest face, for he was likely to be first onto the enemy's guns. Your lead scout should by rights be the patrol member you could most afford to lose. After me came Ted Edwards, the patrol commander, Rob Lee as patrol signaller and Pete as medic.

Dave Moore briefed us on the 'mission' that would form the core of Final Exercise Week. 'Insert; locate enemy building from which they are launching attacks; report on location to HQ with a 'be-prepared' to bring in main force for direct action, or attacking as a platoon. Find, fix and strike.'

We packed our Bergens, grabbed our weapons and were driven out into the wilds. The insertion march was ten kilometres across night-dark terrain. As lead scout I had to find the way, and we had a Pathfinder Staff – Gimli the Dwarf – taking up the rear, to keep a close watch. Luckily, my feet had recovered well enough, and the night was clear and crisp.

I led us direct to a large barn that formed our target. It lay in a clearing in the midst of some dense woodland. Sticking to the edge of the trees we completed an initial recce, then decided where to site our observation post (OP). We chose a shallow ditch, broke out some chicken wire, and began to construct our camouflage.

Each of us had carried in a square of wire, folded over and over and strapped into the very top of our Bergens. Unfolding all four pieces, we twisted them together at the edges, and made one large sheet of wire six feet square. We laid that sheet over the ditch, pinned it down with sharpened branches and gathered bracken, fallen twigs, leaves and moss to thatch it over.

By the time we were done, the OP position had been rendered completely invisible.

All this time Gimli had been watching us wordlessly, and taking note of everything we did. Knowing that the rest of the Pathfinders were out and about in groups of four, hunting us, we crawled into the three-foot-high space beneath the chicken wire. We hid in there during the hours of daylight.

Pushing the Bergens to the back we settled down to a watch routine. One guy would be on sentry covering the rear of the OP, two guys would be on watch on the target, with one guy resting. Like that we logged any enemy movement, and tried to remain undetected. As we couldn't afford to move we were on 'hard routine' – so pissing in plastic Coke bottles and shitting in cling film.

That, plus the cold, made it pretty unbearable. I was wearing every item of clothing I possessed, but still I was freezing cold. The longer you lie still in a chilly and damp OP, the colder and colder you get. I'd got wet and dirty building it, and I could feel my feet going numb with the chill. But that was nothing compared to what was coming.

As the sun dropped below the horizon so the temperature plummeted. Soon, frost covered everything. One guy crawled into an Army maggot to try to sleep, while the rest remained on watch. There was every chance the enemy would remain active during the night hours. By dawn we were frozen stiff, and no one had managed more than a couple of hours' sleep.

I'd spent most of the night cuddled close to the others, trying to share body warmth. After radioing in a report on all that we had seen, we were ordered to withdraw to a grid where we would link up with the other patrols. We were to do so after sunset, so we could move under cover of darkness.

At dusk we collapsed the OP, devegetating the chicken wire and packing it into our Bergens once more. Nothing would be left at the OP site – not even any human waste. We gathered at the RV, linked up with the other patrols and prepared to launch a simulated night attack on the enemy position – the barn.

H Hour for the attack was 0200. On the dot the night erupted with fire, as all three patrols went in to hit the place. Our objective was to gain entry into the left-hand wing of the barn and sweep through and clear the bottom floor, while the other patrols took out the remaining areas.

We'd just completed the simulated attack and were pumped to the max, when we were issued new orders. They gave us a grid to head to, for a 'rapid extraction' – which had to mean a pick-up by helicopter or vehicles. As we hammered through the woods, the yells from the Staff rang about our ears.

'QUICK! Bug out! Bug out! HEAD FOR THE GRID!'

Gimli was screaming at the four of us to follow him, as he charged off into the darkened woodland.

'MY PATROL! Bergens on! FOLLOW ME!'

We flitted through the darkness, feeling a growing tension and confusion pulsing through the air. It was just starting to get light by now, so I presumed we were heading for the trucks, and that Exercise Week was over. We arrived at a small patch of woodland, with a barbed wire fence strung around it.

Gimli knelt before us in the half-light. 'Okay, wait here. I'll go forward and see if pick-up point's clear.'

I felt a flood of relief. Great. We were that close to done.

We'd been there for five minutes or so, kneeling in a silent circle, when from behind us this horde of figures broke out of the darkened wood and charged forwards. They were screaming and shouting, and within an instant they were upon us.

Four guys pounced on me. They forced my head into the dirt, face-first. 'GET DOWN! GET FUCKING DOWN!'

I felt powerful arms pinning me down, as one guy wrestled my weapon off me. They forced me so deep into the dirt that I was choking on it. *Fucking hell, they were going to suffocate me.* I tried to lift my head so I could breathe, but all I succeeded in doing was attracting a series of savage kicks and punches.

'Keep fucking down!' the same voice screamed. 'Get your fucking face in the dirt! Who the fuck are you?'

Then: Bang! Bang! Bang!

Wild shots fired off into the darkness.

What the fuck was going on?

I felt panic rising within me. I didn't have the slightest clue what was happening, and I couldn't breathe. Trying to break free, I elbowed my attackers, and screamed: 'Get fucking off of me! GET OFF!'

'SHUT THE FUCK UP!' the voice yelled back.

Smash! Smash! Smash!

A rifle butt cracked into my shoulders, as whoever these fuckers were forced me into the dirt once more. Another assailant grabbed my arms and pulled them so far back they felt like they were coming out of their sockets. I was still getting smashed and punched around the head, even as the guy holding my arms lashed my wrists together bastard-tight.

The next thing I knew someone had grabbed my hair and yanked my head backwards, pulling me up and out of the dirt by its roots. Before I could see anything much, I felt a bag go over my head. A string was pulled tight around my neck, and everything was suddenly dark.

In a flash I was dragged to my feet and propelled helter-skelter through the woodland. *What the fuck was going on?*

I didn't recognise a single one of the voices that I'd heard yelling and abusing me, and the main guy hadn't even sounded like a Brit.

I stumbled down a bank and fell.

'GET FUCKING UP! FUCKING UP!'

I was dragged to my feet and hustled down a long shallow slope, at the end of which I could hear vehicle engines. Through the sandbag I could just make out two sets of headlamps, piercing the darkness. That was all I could see.

For a moment I was thrust into the lights, and then wham! They'd slammed me into the side of a vehicle.

I collapsed onto the ground.

'GET UP! GET ON YOUR FUCKING KNEES!'

I was forced into a kneeling position, with the headlamps no more than two feet in front of me, shining directly into my eyes. The bag was whipped off without warning. I was blinded, but someone held me gripped by the hair, forcing me to face the light.

Questions were yelled in my ear. A foreign accent. I couldn't see who was doing the asking.

'Who are you? What are you doing in this country? What's your name?'

It just did not compute. *What the fuck was going on?*

'What's your name?' the voice screamed. 'What's your name?'

'Heaney,' I croaked out a reply.

'Heaney? Okay, Heaney, what is your rank? What rank are you?'

'Two four seven five four four two two Private Heaney.'

'What fucking unit are you, Heaney?'

I told myself I could not give him this shit. We'd had it hammered into us during the patrols and tactics phase that if ever we were captured all we could reveal were the big four: name, rank, serial number and date of birth.

I shook my head.

Not answering.

'Are you fucking British?' the voice screamed. 'Are you the British fucking Army?'

From somewhere I found my voice. 'I can't answer that question, sir.'

The screaming resumed, and for several minutes the voice continued to abuse me. Getting no further answers, he ordered the bag back on again.

'Get him fucking away from me,' the voice snarled. 'He's no fucking use to me. You know what to do.'

With that I was dragged around to the rear of the truck, lifted up and thrown aboard. I landed in a heap, aching from every blow they'd rained down on me.

There was a scream and a yell, and a second figure was thrown in beside me. They'd captured and bagged another of my patrol. No one had ever said anything like this would happen. No one. Not even Cornish Bob – and he seemed to know all there was to know about Selection.

So what in God's name was going on?

Two more guys got hurled in, each landing with an agonised thump. I presumed that was all four of us taken captive now. Hands forced me up into a sitting position. Cross-legged, not leaning against anything. I could hear the other blokes' laboured breathing, and I could sense – almost taste – their fear.

I tried to alter my position, to ease the pain. Smack! Someone had whacked me around the head from behind. Nothing had been said, but I knew now that I wasn't allowed to move. I'd been put in a stress position, one designed to slowly torture me.

I'd been sitting there for ten minutes or so, my whole body burning, when the truck gave a sudden lurch and began to move. The unexpected movement threw me over onto my side. I was instantly cracked around the head several times.

Blam! Blam! Blam!

I pulled myself back into the sitting position, but we hit a rut and I was thrown onto my other side.

Smack! Bang! Bang!

Elbows and boots rained onto my head, forcing me upright once more. How long this went on for I do not know, but whenever I tried to drop forward or lean back someone put his hand on my forehead and his knee into my back, and ripped me into the stress position again.

It was sheer agony. Pain like I'd never known. Unbelievable.

What the fuck was happening?

19

For what seemed like hours there was zero noise, other than the throb of the truck engine and the sound of kicks and punches, plus our laboured breathing. And the rush of the passing air.

Suddenly we stopped. The tailgate crashed down. There were yells of pain from those nearest, as they were dragged out. I tensed. I felt hands grab me and drag me backwards, and then they let me fall to the ground.

Fuck that hurt.

I felt myself get dragged away from the truck. They pulled me along by my arms for maybe fifty feet or so. I was trying to see if there were any voices I recognised, but there were none.

I could see by the brightness filtering in through the bag that it was daylight now. But all of a sudden it went totally dark again. *Horribly, horribly dark.*

I was dragged through a series of hard right and left turns, along what seemed to be a gravel floor. Then a door opened and I was hit by a deafening wall of 'white noise' – as if a TV had been left on after all the programmes had ended, blasting out the electronic zumm at top volume.

I felt the ties holding my hands get cut. Two blokes dragged me over to a wall. They got my arms positioned shoulder width apart and fully extended, my fingertips just touching the wall. My legs were kicked out and apart until I was leaning heavily, then my head was jerked up and backwards so I was almost staring straight at the ceiling.

They walked away: I could tell by the scrunching their boots made on the gravel. I was left in that position, white noise blasting through my head, and as far as I knew I was all alone now.

I'd been in that agonising pose for a good ten minutes when I first tried to move. My first instinct was to get off my fingertips and get my palms against the wall, to relieve the pain and the cramps. But as soon as I attempted it I felt a swift rabbit punch to the kidneys.

I screamed out in pain.

Someone forced me back into the same position. After an hour or so my limbs were shaking uncontrollably from the exhaustion and I was cramping up big time. All of a sudden I was kicked out of that position, and I collapsed onto the floor. Hands forced me to sit up, legs crossed, with my arms held behind my head.

Not a word had been said.

The white noise was still blasting.

The moment my arms and head started to sag, I felt a knee in my back and an arm on my head, forcing me back into the upright position. Again and again and again it happened. After an hour of that I was forced back against the wall, into the first position. And so the rotations went, until I'd lost all track of time.

Without any warning I was picked up off the floor and dragged to my feet. My head got forced onto my chest, and my thumbs were jammed tight together, and like that I was led out of the room. I was propelled through a series of confusing right and left turns, moving at the double, and then pushed into a room.

I felt myself get shoved into a chair.

Silence.

Was I alone?

Was I there a minute?

Or an hour, or maybe more?

What was happening? Would someone kick the chair out from under me? Smack me around the head?

I had no idea where I was, and I had no idea who exactly had got me, or why. The next moment the sandbag was ripped off my head and the lights flashed on.

Blinded, I tried to look around to see where I was, but it took an age for my sight to adjust to the dazzling brightness. I started to make out details. In front of me was a wooden desk. On the desk was a white plastic mug with what looked like tea inside it. Sat on the opposite side of the desk was a small fat bloke, dressed in civvies.

He was the last thing I had ever expected to see. His hair was grey and so was his beard, and he looked to be in his late fifties. He was so nondescript I doubted if I'd even recognise him again, if I saw him in a crowd. I'd expected to face a group of thugs armed with pickaxe handles, or worse. This – it was utterly bizarre.

The room seemed completely empty apart from him, me, the desk and the cup of tea. It looked to be perfectly square, like a cell, with grey-painted walls. There were no windows, and the metal door was set behind me.

In the patrols and tactics phase we'd been given some conduct-after-capture training, being told to accept food or drink if offered it by your captors. Yes, it might be poisoned, but why bother? It's far easier just to shoot you. The room was cold and I was still dressed in my damp grungy kit. I stared at the cup of tea, watching the wisps of steam rise from it, alluringly.

I felt the bloke staring at me. 'Have a drink, if you want a drink. Have one.'

The voice was utterly calm. Totally unperturbed. The accent was one I couldn't place.

I shot my hand out, grabbed the disposable cup and necked it. It wasn't scalding, or poisoned, as far as I could tell, just hot, sweet milky tea. I finished drinking and put the cup back on the desk. He stared at me.

Utter silence.

'So, tell me – how did you find yourself here with me? How have you got here?'

What kind of a fucking question was that? This was the kind of thing I should be asking him. I was about to blurt that out, but stopped myself just in time.

'I'm sorry, I cannot answer that question, sir.'

His facial expression didn't change. 'Well, if you want me to help you, you are going to have to talk to me. Let's start by making you comfortable. You look wet and cold. Are you wet and cold?'

'I cannot answer that question, sir.'

'Tell you what – look behind you.'

I did as asked. On the floor was a pair of green coveralls and laceless black training shoes.

'Take your clothes off and put those on.'

This I figured was a 'reasonable request', and changing into dry gear didn't contravene any of the post-capture rules that we'd been taught. I stood up and he continued to stare at me, as I began to strip off my wet gear.

'Throw it all there and put that warm clothing on.'

I took off my sodden top, plus T-shirt, and stepped out of my camo trousers. Dropping it all in a soggy pile I stepped into the overalls, put my arms in and closed the press studs at the front. That done, I slid my feet into the plimsolls. They were massive; three sizes or more too big. But at least they were dry.

He was still staring at me. 'Sit back down.' A pause. 'So, what are you doing in my country? Why are you in my country?'

I forced myself to give the same answer. 'I cannot answer that question, sir.'

He sighed, as if bored. 'Well, I tell you what you are doing here. You are here to harm my people. So why are the British in my country? You are British, yes?'

'I cannot answer . . .'

'It does not matter,' he cut in. 'My men have your equipment. We will search your equipment and we will find something. What is your name?'

'Heaney, sir.'

El Centro, California, September 1990. A group shot of the course with five Pathfinders and five guys from 22 SAS: the only two units in the British military that are trained to conduct high-altitude parachute operations. I am standing far right on the back row, the tall guy standing in the centre of the back row (five from the right) is Big Mal. Five months after this shot was taken, he was paraded as part of the ill-fated Bravo Two Zero guys captured in Iraq. (Richard Newell)

El Centro, California, September 1990. The five musketeers on our HALO course after passing PF selection. We are sitting on the ramp of a C130 about to complete a night HALO jump from 18,000 feet. I am on the far right of the picture, next to me on my right are Bob Walters, Ted Edwards and Rob Lee, and on the far left is Ian Johnston. (Richard Newell)

Aldershot, 1993. Conducting General Purpose Machine Gun (GPMG) Sustained Fire (SF) training. This is a technique that mounts the machine gun on to a tripod for more effective and accurate fire role. It's a specialist skill and all Pathfinders are taught how to do this as part of their training. I am looking down the weapon sight, Wag is on my left shoulder wearing his beret.

Belize, 1990, conducting live firing Close Quarter Battle (CQB) training with my pistol.

Our patrol waits as we prepare to deploy on our anti-narcotics operation to the Belize/Guatemalan border. As Lead Scout I am at the front armed with my M16A2 with M203 Grenade Launcher fitted; behind me is the patrol commander, Andy Parson, Karl 'Beano' Dennis is number three in the patrol, and sitting at the rear is Johno.

Belize, 1990, during PF continuation training. The patrol consisted of (l-r) Patrol Signaller Graham 'Wag' Wardle, Lead Scout Yours Truly, Patrol Commander Lt Robert Mackenzie-Hill, Medic Bob Leon (deceased).

Belize, 1990, during PF jungle training taking a jungle-line resupply of food and equipment by parachute. Often the only way of receiving such stores is by airdrop.

Belize, 1990. The three amigos: I'm on the far right kneeling, Wag is in the centre and Bob Leon on the far left. We have just received our resupply by parachute. Then we bury the parachute canopy and packaging, load up the resupply and move off the drop zone.

Belize, 1992, during the Gurkhas training trip that would take a very unexpected turn and see our patrol deploy to the Belize/Guatemalan border on an anti-narcotics operation. I am sitting (in the middle) in the back of a transport vehicle heading into the jungle with the rest of the PF patrol. A Gurkha soldier sits on my left side and the patrol commander, Andy Parsons, is on my right. Karl 'Beano' Dennis is visible over my left shoulder and Johno is sitting behind Andy.

Belize, 1992. A Puma helicopter waits patiently on the helipad in Rideau Camp as our four-man patrol prepares to insert into the jungle and make our way to the Belize/Guatemalan border on our anti-narcotics operation.

April 1990, conducting helicopter abseil-training. The Scout climbs to a height of 120 feet with four operators (two on each side) and they descend rapidly down the abseil rope. This technique is used to get men into restricted areas very quickly.

Malaya, 1995, on joint training with the Group Gerak Khas, Malaysian Special Forces. My team (l-r): Rich James, Nick Bentley, Yours Truly, Sean 'Biscuits' Brown.

Belize, 1990, conducting PF jungle training. Myself and Wag on the left making traps out of natural material during the survival phase of the training.

Florida Disney World, 1990, on R&R after continuation training in Belize. I'm second from the right in the white T-shirt. Dave Moore is second from the left and Andy Parsons is on the far left.

Empuriabrava , Spain, 1991, conducting freefall training with three PF operators. I am in the blue freefall suit. Continuous freefall training is essential for maintaining your skill level. Four weeks parachuting on the Spanish coast is not all bad.

'So how old are you? How old are you, Mr Heaney?'

'Ten, nine, nineteen sixty-nine, sir.'

'What unit are you with? Who are you here with in my country?'

'I cannot answer . . .'

He cut me off. 'Well obviously, it's evident you're not going to help me. If you won't help me to help you, you will have to go back to the other room.'

I hadn't heard the door open behind me. In fact I hadn't heard a bloody thing. All I knew was that the bag was suddenly whipped over my head again.

The shock of it all but gave me a heart attack.

Whooaa . . . FUCK! Where did that come from?

I was yanked to my feet, and without a word from the fat guy I was dragged out of the room.

20

My head was forced down onto my chest, as I was propelled left-right-left-right around the series of sharp turns – and back into the white noise room. Someone kicked my legs from under me, I fell towards the floor, and was forced back into the same stress position as before – sitting crossed-legged with my hands behind my head.

I could hear nothing but white noise. I could taste and smell nothing but my own bile. I was just cold and scared and hurting like I'd never hurt before. On an impulse, I started trying to sing songs in my head – old numbers, ones that I remembered from my teenagehood.

I thought if I could keep a record of how many times I sang them I could keep some track of time. But I was tired. So tired. My head started nodding, double tapping, as my chin slumped onto my chest.

The next moment I was jerked savagely awake, as someone ripped me onto my feet. *God I was in agony.*

I had zero time to worry about that. Instead, I was shoved out of the door, and whipped left and right down the corridors again. I ended up being thrown into a room and slammed down onto a chair. Moments later the bag was ripped off.

I was expecting to see the fat man again for a second session of Mind Games. Instead, standing next to a chair and desk, and facing me, was a drop-dead-gorgeous blonde. She was well over six feet tall, looked about thirty years old and was dressed in a white blouse that was one size too small. From where I was sitting I could smell her perfume.

'Hello.' The voice sounded eastern European. Russian, almost. 'You are very handsome. Very beautiful boy.'

She frowned. 'You have spoken to my friend, Dimitri. But you did not help him. Maybe you will help me?' She thrust out her ample bosom. 'Will you? Help me?'

I stared at the wall, willing the words to come. 'I'm sorry, I cannot answer . . .'

'Will you not just tell me your name?' she wheedled. 'A very handsome boy like you.'

'Heaney, sir.'

'Ah, yes, Heaney. Ten, nine, sixty-nine. So, that means you are twenty? Are you twenty?'

I tried working out if I was permitted to answer that question, but I didn't have a fucking clue, so I just repeated my DOB: 'Ten, nine, sixty-nine.'

As I said it, she raised herself to her full height, in silence. Out of the blue a voice screamed in my ear-hole: 'ANSWER THE FUCKING QUESTION!'

Hands punched me out of the chair. I fell to the floor, landing awkwardly, and I was absolutely shitting myself.

'GET UP OFF THE FUCKING FLOOR!'

I had a quick glimpse of a stocky, balding guy in a dark pullover, as he reached to drag me up. He was of medium build but he looked immensely powerful. Slamming me back into the chair, he melted back into the silence.

Meanwhile, Helga the Ice Maiden hadn't so much as flinched. She glanced in the direction of her enforcer, and they exchanged a few words in a language that sounded like Russian. Not that I was fluent in any language but English, of course – and there were those who'd argue I wasn't fluent in that, either.

Finally, Helga turned back to me. 'Look, there is no need for this. All we want from you is what you are doing here and how many of you there are.'

'I cannot answer . . .' I began, but Helga cut me off.

'All we need to know is what you were doing here.'

'I cannot . . .'

'Look, if you will not co-operate things will become very difficult for you.'

The instant she said that the sandbag was whipped on again. I felt my head slammed down onto my chest, my thumbs were jammed together, and I was on my feet being propelled left-right-left-right towards what I figured was the white noise room once more.

I was shoved back into the stress position. I was shivering uncontrollably, I was tired beyond belief and the pain was unbelievable. I felt as if I had daggers jabbing into my arms, my shoulder, my arse, my coccyx – hell, everywhere. I'd had no food for God only knows how long, and my last liquid was the fat guy's meagre cup of tea.

I was horribly disorientated.

I felt like I was cracking up.

At some stage someone sat me down on the floor. The bag was lifted up just enough to get a cup to my lips. I smelled tea. My head was forced back as they poured it down my throat. It was followed by a slice of bread. Then another. They rammed some more in, pulled down the sandbag, and shoved my arms onto my head, putting me back in position.

I had a few last chews.

Swallowed.

At some stage later I was lifted up and marched out again. I was propelled into a room and plonked on a seat. The sandbag came off and I was facing the fat guy once more.

On the desk in front of him was my notebook, lying in its protective camouflage pouch. As part of our training we'd been shown how to encode vital information. All the intel in there should have been coded, but was I entirely sure? I stared at it, willing myself to remember what exactly I'd written in there.

Fat boy reached forward, picked up the notepad and flicked through it, almost absent-mindedly. He came to a halt halfway, then looked at me.

'Six seven five four three seven. Is that a grid reference? What is this? Is this a position on a map?'

I shook my head. 'I cannot answer . . .'

'One five six seven four three. What is this? Is this another grid reference? I will get the grids checked and once we have them checked on a map I will know where you have been.'

He put it down again. 'But anyway, we have your friends. We have Corporal Edwards.' *Fuck – they'd got Ted.* 'We have Corporal Lee.' *Fuck, they'd got Rob.* 'And those two – they are telling us everything.'

I sat there thinking: *Fucking hell, I am utterly fucked now.*

The one ray of hope was that they didn't seem to have captured Cornish Bob. There had been no mention of the iron Cornishman from fat boy.

'So really, we don't need you any more,' he continued. 'So, you can go back to your room while I decide what to do with you.'

Slam! The bag went on again. They had just ripped me out of my chair, when I yelled out that I needed a piss. I was busting.

'Take Mr Heaney to the toilet area. You see how reasonable we can be? But you must co-operate, like your friends. Or we will decide what we will do with you.'

My head was thrust down, my thumbs were jammed together and I was whisked left-right-left and pushed through a door. The smell inside confirmed this was a toilet block. I felt hands undo me at the front, so I could urinate. I still had the bag on so I had no idea where to aim; I just let go and started to pee.

Suddenly I heard a voice. It sounded so familiar that it completely threw me.

'Hello, mate. You all right, mate? It's John. The name's John. Bastards in 'ere, aren't they? So what's your name?'

I was still peeing, and it was the familiar accent plus the lingo that had so thrown me.

'Mate, I'm 2 PARA. Lots of us in 'ere are PARAs. What lot are you with? Quick, mate, let me know before the fucking guard returns and I'll see what I can do for you.'

I didn't answer.

'John's' whispering stopped.

My head was shoved down, my thumbs were jammed together again and I was dragged along the series of bends back to the white noise room. When I was forced into the sitting position I went to put my arms behind my head, as before. But instead, someone manhandled me onto my left side. My left arm was placed underneath my head, like a pillow, and I was curled into the foetal position.

The white noise suddenly stopped and the room was filled with a ringing, echoing silence. I couldn't hear a thing any more. It was utterly quiet. Not a soul seemed to be walking, talking or breathing even. Behind the bag I shut my eyes. All sorts of thoughts were shooting through my head, but they were jumbled up and scrambled so none made any sense.

All perspective was gone. I was beyond agony now. Beyond thought. Beyond reason.

Like that I must have drifted into a troubled sleep.

I was wrenched out of my dark dreams without warning. When I came back to wakefulness, I was still in the land of the living nightmare. I was dragged to my feet – head down, thumbs together, and shoved left-right-left-right down that hateful corridor.

I was pushed into a room. Utter silence.

The sandbag was ripped off.

Before me was Dave Moore. He was wearing a white armband and bizarrely he started trying to do some sort of a Mr Nice Guy act on me.

'Right, Heaney, you know who I am, don't you? It's Dave Moore. Don't worry. Take it easy. You see the white armband? I am the umpire. It's over. It's finished.'

I shook my head. *Why the hell should I believe this fucker?*

'Look, it's Dave Moore – Pathfinder platoon sergeant. I am not trying to trick you. It's over. It's finished.'

I shook my head again: *Fuck you.*

'Heaney, it's over. Do you understand, Heaney? It's over.'

A bare whisper. 'Yeah.'

'Are you okay?'

I shuddered. 'Yeah.'

'Okay, go out that door and join the others.'

21

Getting to my feet, I stumbled towards the doorway. I felt dizzy, confused and nauseous, my body was a mass of agony, and I was physically and mentally drained as never before.

I stepped outside the room and there, lined up against the wall, were Cornish Bob and Ted Edwards, dressed in overalls and plimsolls just like me.

Gimli nodded towards a tea urn set on a table. 'Heaney, get yourself a brew and a sandwich and sit down.'

Silently, I did as instructed. I glanced up from my tea as Helga the blonde waltzed past. Not a word.

Next, Dave Moore stepped out of the room. 'Right, lads, follow me.'

We walked outside and I found myself standing in the blinding daylight, next to some kind of a massive hangar.

Dave turned to face us. 'Right, okay – well done. Right, how long do you think you've been in there?'

'Twelve hours?' Bob murmured.

'Ten,' whispered Ted Edwards.

'Sixteen,' I muttered.

Dave Moore looked at his watch. 'It's now four o'clock on the seventh of February. You've been in there for thirty-six hours.'

Thirty-six hours.

Fucking unbelievable.

The bastards.

Twenty-four hours later we were back in Aldershot. We'd just completed what is known as 'R2I' – resistance to interrogation training. If any one of us had turned around at any stage and said the following, we'd have got binned: 'I was at this grid with eight guys and our mission was to do X.'

Neither Cornish Bob, Ted Edwards nor I had done so. But even now, none of us were through this yet.

At Aldershot we grabbed a quick shower and a change of clothes. It was eight o'clock in the evening when we gathered at the Pathfinders' band room office. We sat there, the twelve of us who remained, waiting to be called into the OC's office.

Cornish Bob, Ted Edwards, Rob and Ian went in before me. The way the room was set up, it must have had another exit, for I didn't see any of them leave. Then the time came for me.

'Right, Private Heaney, you're next,' Dave Moore announced.

Sat behind his desk was the Pathfinders' OC, Jon Hayman. He glanced at me. 'Okay, take a seat, Private Heaney. Right, so how d'you think you did?'

'I think I've done okay, sir. I think I did well on ranges, I understood all the tactics, conducted myself well during Final Exercise, plus I think I did okay on R2I.'

'Okay.' A pause. 'You do understand you're still very young and fairly inexperienced?'

I thought: *Shit, this is it – they're failing me.* 'Yes, sir, but . . . but . . . but . . .'

He held up a hand to silence me. 'No buts . . . *That's* what we're looking for. We can do the rest; we can shape you into what we want. You performed well in Aldershot. Clearly you're fit. Good times on Test Week. Considering your age and fairly limited amount of experience, you acquitted yourself well on tactics. You are a team player – which is crucial. You had a good Final Exercise. And you got through R2I relatively unscathed. So, congratulations – and welcome to the Pathfinders. Go join the other guys that are outside. Once the interviews are finished we've laid on a bit of a celebratory party.'

He stood up and shook my hand. 'Well done.'

I turned and left, feeling as if I was walking on clouds. As I exited, Dave Moore was there. I went to pass him, but he thrust out a hand.

'Welcome to the Pathfinders, Steve.'

That was the last time he ever called me Heaney.

'Oh . . .' I stammered. 'Thanks, Staff.'

He went: 'It's Dave. From now on it's Dave.'

I walked out feeling ten feet tall. There was Cornish Bob, puffing away on a ciggie. There were Ted, Rob and Ian, grinning like Cheshire cats. They gave me a thumbs-up.

'Yeah. Pass,' I confirmed.

'Mega!'

'Mega, mate!'

'Well done.'

Next out was Pete, the Guardsman. He raised one hand and did the victory salute. 'Yeah!'

Pete was the only one so far who hadn't earned his wings, so we figured we'd twist him.

'Fuck me, they let you in?'

'Standards must be slipping . . .'

'All you got to do now is get through P Company.'

Next out was one of the Ruperts. His face said it all. He shook his head, morosely.

'Didn't make it.'

'Did they give you a reason?'

He shrugged. 'They felt I didn't contribute enough during the Final Exercise. As an officer, I should have been more forward with my advice.'

'Oh, right. So what happens now?'

'OC said I'm welcome to hang around and have a drink. I probably won't. To be honest I've got my car and I'm just gonna pack and shoot off.' He shook everyone's hand. 'Congratulations – well done. You all deserved to pass.'

He turned and walked away. As Ruperts went he was one of the better ones, that was for sure.

Next out was the other officer. Surely they couldn't have failed them both? But he too shook his head.

'I only just scraped through the test tabs. Only just making times. There were doubts as to my aptitude during live firing – not aggressive enough. They felt I wasn't strong enough in my patrol. But – congratulations to you guys.'

One by one the guys filtered out who remained. They were all fails. 'Not assimilated enough knowledge . . . Not good enough in a small team . . . Not able to fit into small team operations . . . Not showed enough aggression . . .'

My entire patrol from Exercise Week – Ted, Rob, Pete – had passed. So had Ian and Cornish Bob. That was it. Six out of twenty-eight were through.

When the last man had been processed, Dave Moore walked out and joined us. For the first time since we'd met him he gave a genuine smile.

'Right then, guys – let's go and get drunk.'

We walked to the nearby bar, which was part of the base. On the way someone asked him what would happen next.

'We'll get drunk. Then over the next few days you'll go back to your parent unit, and get cleared by them. The day after tomorrow you'll go in front of the Brigadier, who will present you with Pathfinder DZ flashes. But for now, let's hit the bar.'

I held back. I wanted to call home.

It was late, and I could tell that I'd woken my dad up.

'It's me,' I said. 'I've passed.'

'Mega. Brilliant. Well done, son.'

Mum grabbed the phone. 'Yeah, Mam, I'm in.'

'Brilliant. What you doing now?'

'I am going to get blooted.'

Mum said to me what she's always said since the day I started drinking. 'Just you be careful when you're drunk, lad.'

Laughing. 'Okay, Mam.'

I walked up the stairs into the bar.

By the time I staggered out of that place the sun was well up. And I had just started my first day as a Pathfinder.

When I did finally manage to catch up with Dan, he was genuinely pleased for me. I asked him if he would try for Selection again. He told me the knee would always trouble him, and in any case he was getting married and planning to have kids.

We shot the shit. Reminisced.

And we've been mates to this day.

22

Having passed Selection I moved onto Continuation Training. As a Pathfinder you have to be able to do everything required of any member of a patrol – in case someone gets captured or killed. First I went on the Signals Cadre, to learn the art and craft of signals. I stripped radio kit to nothing and built it back up again, finding out how radio signals work, about frequencies, and how to erect antennae.

I learned to encode signals and how to use Morse Code, which is a vital piece of tradecraft. If all other signals fail Morse will nearly always get through, as we would repeatedly go on to prove. I did a Medical Cadre – when I was taught about intensive first aid – and a Mobility Cadre – to gain knowledge about vehicle-mounted operations – and then I moved onto the next big challenge – six weeks of jungle training.

I flew to Belize, in Central America, and had my first close encounters with the rainforest. I learned jungle demolitions work – using explosive charges to fell trees, and carve out a helicopter landing site (HLS) from the virgin forest; live firing and close quarter battle in amongst the dense vegetation; river crossing; caching stores and ammo; jungle close target recces (CTRs); and tracking.

I was shown how to cut winch-holes in the canopy to bring in stores from a hovering helicopter, I learned how to use a tethered air marker balloon to ID the winch-hole for the approaching helo. Finally, I learned classic jungle survival – so what to eat in terms of monkeys and snakes and that kind of stuff. And I loved it all.

I did my first HALO – high-altitude low-opening – course in the September of that year, so seven months after having passed Selection. We headed for El Centro, deep in the Californian desert, to a base where we could dive out of a C-130 Hercules from the roof of the world. And just like the jungle, I loved it.

I did three stints on exchange with the Americans, whereby we embedded one of their blokes in the Pathfinders, and they did the same with yours truly. I trained with the US Air Force Combat Control Teams (CCTs) – their nearest equivalent unit to the Pathfinders, and the blokes who are first-in to guide in Delta Force and the SEALs.

I trained with and competed against US Navy SEALs, Delta Force, US Air Force CCTs, the US Rangers, the French Foreign Legion, the Canadian Pathfinders, the Italian Special Forces, and elite units from as far away as Indonesia and Thailand. And in all of that we – the Pathfinders – more than held our own.

A high spot was two weeks' instruction at 'Billie Joe's Killing House'. Billie Joe was ex-Delta Force and he served as the CIA's chief pistol instructor. He owned a ranch in North Carolina and was reputedly the world's best pistol instructor. His party trick was to have his pistol holstered with four rounds in the magazine. He'd draw, fire four rounds, load a second mag, fire those off, and all within three seconds.

All eight shots would be bang on target.

Unbelievable.

The accurate range of a pistol is about fifteen to twenty metres. Billy Joe would lie on the ground 100 metres from his target. He'd angle his pistol to compensate for the range, and he'd adjust it minutely to account for wind speed and air temperature, both of which can affect the accuracy of a 9mm round. Like that, he'd hit his 'fall-down' target every time (it falls over every time you hit it).

I was eighteen months into being with the X Platoon by now, and I believed I was at the very top of my game – or at least well on my way to being there. Under the guidance of the Pathfinders' veterans, Dave Moore first and foremost, I was doing my Sponge Bob act: I was soaking up all there was to learn.

I was serving in a small, tight-knit, beautifully formed unit, under the guidance of such men: it just didn't get any better. But somewhere in the back of my mind there was a little voice telling me: *Dave Moore – he's got the best job in the world. He's the Pathfinder platoon sergeant. He gets to mould and shape this unit to his design. One day, I want his job.*

But any which way I diced it, that was a long way off right now.

The modern-day Pathfinders were formed to fulfil a role seen as lacking in the wider British military: covert insertion deep behind enemy lines to recce DZs and guide in the main force, and for capture, sabotage or direct-action missions. The unit's formal role is to 'cue the deep battle'; to go forward into enemy territory and guide in the main force and battle assets: fixed wing warplanes, helicopters, mortars, artillery and rocket-fire systems.

We also act to divert enemy forces, by hitting their command and control nodes deep inside their own territory, using sniper rifles and other precision weaponry. Accordingly, Pathfinders have to be mentally and physically tough enough to operate as small teams in isolation over protracted periods of time. We would also be doing six HALO jumps to most other elite operators' one, and that simple fact made us unbeatable at what we did.

We were a twenty-seven-strong unit by now, and Jon 'H' Hayman decided that we needed to expand our number so we could form a Mountain Cadre, to augment our existing Air (parachuting) and Mobility (vehicle operations) Cadres. With my love of jumping out of aeroplanes I'd wangled a place in the Pathfinders' Air Cadre, but we all wanted a role in shaping this new arm.

It was winter and the regular Pathfinder Selection was about to take place. All Pathfinders in-country attend Selection. They do so to act as Staff, to get some extra fitness and to set an example to the raw candidates. We figured this year we'd combine Selection with forming up the new Mountain Cadre.

Someone had the bright idea of bringing in an American who was an expert in high-altitude mountaineering. The idea was that he'd help train up the Mountain Cadre. The guy's name was Hank Goodman, and he was supposedly a Spiderman when on a rock face. Hank was a US Ranger, so we figured he'd more than know his stuff.

Inevitably, he earned the nickname 'Hank the Yank'.

He flew over to the UK and headed down to Aldershot, where Jon H briefed him in. Jon proposed to put him through our forthcoming Selection, just so he could learn our SOPs (standard operating procedures). That way, he could deploy with us on operations if the need arose. Hank seemed happy with that, so off we went to the Beacons.

It was a horrendously shitty January, but with my fitness being as good as it was I was allotted as the Staff to take some of the more punishing runs across the snow-covered hills. We started with a brisk ten-miler, and pretty quickly those undertaking Selection were spread out behind me like mad man's shit.

I decided to 'pull a sickener' at the end of the run, just to really twist them. When we reached the supposed finish line where the vehicles were parked up, I allowed the main body of runners to stream in. Giving them just enough time to figure they'd made it, I set off again . . . heading back the way we'd come.

I only intended to run an extra mile, but no one knew that. The sickener was psychological. It was all in the head. As far as they knew I might be leading them all the way back again.

Just as I was approaching the end of the extra mile, I saw Hank the Yank coming the other way. As we neared each other, I could see that the front of his top was streaked with vomit and mucus.

'Keep going, mate,' I urged him. 'Not far now.'

Strictly speaking, it wasn't Pathfinder ethos to offer any support – but Hank was a guest on Selection, so I figured I could bend the rules a little.

He threw me a look. 'Eye of the tiger, Steve,' he gasped. 'Eye of the tiger.'

The following morning we were up long before the crack of dawn, parading in the bollock-shrivelling freezing cold and darkness. As I surveyed the ranks of those still with us I could see no sign of Hank. We headed over to the canteen for a very early breakfast and there was a bang on the door.

Hank popped his head around. 'Say, guys, I need to see the OC. Need a private word.'

We motioned him towards a small anteroom, where Jon H was busy prepping the day's schedule. Fortunately Hank left the door ajar, so we could hear every word.

'Sir, now hear this,' Hank began, grumpily. 'I am not doing your crazy fuckin' Selection course. I am fuckin' going back to bed.'

With that Hank turned and exited, leaving Jon H utterly speechless. It was day two of Selection and we'd yet to have more than a handful of lads bale – yet Spiderman himself was crying off.

Jon sent Cornish Bob to try to talk Hank out of it. Bob was back a couple of minutes later.

'Yeah, boss, it's no good,' he declared. 'He won't get out of bed.'

Hank eventually emerged from his maggot at 1100, so a good seven hours after the rest of us. Jon H didn't have one iota of mercy or remorse. He sent Hank directly back to Aldershot and that was the last we ever saw of him.

For the remainder of Selection we kept throwing that line at each other: *Eye of the tiger, Steve, eye of the tiger*. Like the best of lines, it never ceased to be funny.

Jon H was perfect for what an outfit like the X Platoon needed. He fought tooth and nail to get us the best equipment and weaponry, for which we had no official budget or allocation. Somehow, he managed to blag enough M16 assault rifles to equip the entire Platoon, which was a total godsend.

The British Army at the time was using the SA80-A1, which had only recently come into service. Prior to that we had the self-loading rifle (SLR), a heavier, longer weapon, which fires 7.62mm ammo, as opposed to the SA80's 5.56mm round. We'd heard the arguments for replacing one with the other: the SA80 was lighter and shorter – making it good for operating in close terrain – and it packed a thirty-round magazine, as opposed to the twenty-round mag of the SLR.

But the SLR had one crucial advantage: it was 'soldier proof'. It had simple iron sights, was bullet-proof reliable, required little maintenance, was sturdy and solid, and with the larger-calibre round it would drop an enemy every hit. By contrast, the SA80-A1 felt plastic and tinny: it had a distinct 'Made in Taiwan' feel about it.

As time and experience would show, the SA80-A1 was an utter pile of crap. It could pose as much danger to the user as the enemy, suffering from any number of faults – the worst being the habit the magazine had of falling off. Because of the weapon's dog design, all you had to do was go into a tight fire position, hit the magazine release button by accident, and off it would fall, spewing out the rounds.

The weapon was also horribly prone to rust, which was especially problematic for a unit like ours, which worked in the jungle, amongst other humid terrains. The moving parts that force the rounds into the breech tended to rust up in moisture-laden air, and jam solid. By contrast, if moisture, dirt or rust got into the M16, it would rarely stop the gun from churning out the bullets like a good 'un.

Unbelievably, the SA80 also couldn't be operated left-handed. Due to the positioning of the cocking handle it could only be used by a right-handed person. Those Pathfinders who were lefties – and we had a good number of 'em – tried using the SA80, and quickly showed how impossible it was for them to fight effectively with it.

The SA80-A1 was manufactured by Royal Ordnance at a cost of £850 per rifle. At that time the M16 was being produced in the UK under licence, at £150 a throw – but for some incomprehensible reason the MOD felt it better to saddle the regular British Army with a costly crock of shit like the SA80.

They had tried to do the same with us. Jon's answer had been simple: *Fuck that!* Instead, he'd blagged us a bunch of M16-A2s.

Our first impressions of the American assault rifle were entirely positive. It could be fired from either shoulder, just like the SLR. The safety was set on the left of the weapon, where it was easy to operate, but hard to trigger accidentally, and the magazine release catch was well-positioned and user-friendly. Also, the working parts broke down into four simple units. With the SA80 there were numerous small pins you had to prise out in order to dismantle it, which were all too easy to lose.

As a massive extra bonus, our M16-A2s had an underslung M203 40mm grenade launcher – something the SA80 just didn't have. In short, the M16-A2 weighed about the same as the SA80, was ergonomic and far easier to use, felt strong and robust, required little tender loving care, and packed a far greater punch.

One was an Aston Martin, the other a Fiat Punto.

As matters transpired, we were incredibly fortunate to have got our hands on those American assault rifles – for we were about to deploy on the first ever combat operation of the modern-day Pathfinders. For what was coming, proper, usable, soldier-proof weaponry would be crucial; a life-saver. But none of us had any idea what lay ahead, for it all started out as a bog-standard training mission.

And it was one that I only made by the skin of my teeth.

23

Something real nasty must have been munching on me during my week's of training in the Belize jungle – only I didn't know it at the time.

I had been back in the UK for two months or so when I developed a small spot with a pus-filled head on the topside of my left hand. At first, I didn't pay much attention to it. Still only twenty-one years old, I was only just out of my gangly, spotty youth, so I presumed it was a last gasp throwback to those times.

But then it started to grow.

Over the space of a week it got bigger and bigger, until it was an open, weeping sore the size of a pound coin. It had also started to pong. PARAs never are the sweetest-smelling bunch, but this reeked of rotten flesh and God only knows what else.

I went to see the camp doctor. He prodded and poked around a bit, but in truth he had no idea what it might be. Then he asked me if I'd been anywhere exotic recently. I told him about the Belize jungle training, and he sent me direct to the Hospital For Tropical Diseases, in London.

They identified it pretty much right away. Apparently, it was cutaneous leishmaniasis – in other words, the site where a sand fly had bitten me and laid its larvae, so they could feed off my living flesh.

Nice.

We'd been warned about the sand flies, but there are few preventative measures you can take. Mozzie repellent doesn't work. And anywhere the tiny critters can get a chomp at exposed flesh – so hands, face, ankles – they will lay their brood. Worse still, if not treated properly the larvae spread throughout your body and resurface in your oral and nasal passages – so your mouth and nose – by which time it's incurable.

The only treatment is a long series of injections of Pentostam – sodium stibogluconate, a highly toxic drug. The first injection felt as if the nurse was pumping acid directly into my veins. It was sheer bloody agony.

I had to endure two such fire-injections every day for two weeks. Worse still, the drug is so toxic it can damage your heart and respiratory system – so I was banned from any physical activity for three months thereafter.

All due to a tropical mite the size of a bloody pinhead.

The treatment literally starves the sand fly larvae to death. What the injections do is kill the flesh all around the wound, so the bugs have nothing to feed on. Once the nurses had declared the critters well and truly dead, they bound my wound with sterile bandages, to enable the flesh to regrow – after which I faced three months of doing nothing.

For a young lad fresh into this dream outfit – the Pathfinders – those long weeks of enforced inactivity were torture. Catching cutaneous leishmaniasis hadn't exactly made me enamoured of the Belize jungle, either. So it was top news when I learned where I was being sent next – that's if I recovered well enough to deploy.

I was heading back to the jungle.

Belize, again.

A company of Gurkhas under the command of a former SAS officer was in need of a stint of jungle training. I was to team up with three other Pathfinders, so we could run them through a six-week course – covering patrolling and navigation, contact drills and ambush, camp attack and direct action, survival and living off the land, tracking, and river crossings.

In truth, the jungle is entirely neutral. As I'd been taught during my continuation training, it is neither inherently hostile nor friendly. But if you learn its ways, tune into its resonance and become at one with it, the jungle can prove a fantastic refuge and friend.

During my six weeks in Belize I'd thrilled to the idea of surviving in – *and fighting in* – such a wilderness, one devoid of all trappings of human civilisation. From the first time I'd stood beneath the awe-inspiring canopy, it had felt ancient and primordial and somehow totally compelling.

But I could sure do without the sand flies.

By now, my left hand was almost healed, a red and angry scar replacing the festering wound. Typically – and rightly – Jon H considered me fit enough to go. With Jon there was never any praise. He was a remorseless taskmaster. You were there to do your job and be the best, no excuses – not even a spot of cutaneous leishmaniasis.

In short, he was exactly what the Pathfinders needed, and I liked him.

Our four-man team was commanded by Lance Corporal Andy Parson, a 6'-4", 17-stone mixed-race lad, of Fijian and British descent. Andy was built like your average Fijian, so the proverbial barn door. He liked to tell the girls he hailed from the 'Fijian Islands' – for it sounded far more exotic than the truth, that he'd grown up in Birmingham.

'I'm from Fiji, like,' he'd tell them, in his thick Brummie accent.

Most seemed to fall for it.

Go figure.

He sported the cropped-haired, bemuscled Fijian rugby player look, and I have to confess it was far more successful with the women than my own. Andy was young, free and mostly single, and his pride and joy was a flame-red Ducati 916 Sport, only twenty of which were ever imported into the UK. Top of the list to get one had been a British Formula One motor-racing champion. Second had been Andy.

Andy treated it better than most blokes do their wives. It was kept in the Pathfinder office with a blanket thrown over it. He polished it every day, caressed it, started it up, blipped the throttle a few times and then turned to us, grinning: 'Wow! Will you listen to that . . .'

It got worse. He tape-recorded himself revving the engine, and then he used to sit alone in his room and play it back. Sometimes he'd grab a bloke and make him come listen.

In short, Andy was a motorbike perv.

One day he headed down to a national bike show, somewhere near Andover. The parking area was a field, so he chained up his beloved and wandered around enjoying the sights. When he got back all that remained of his bike was a broken chain and padlock.

It turned out a professional gang had driven over from France, targeting the show. They'd stolen fifteen prestigious bikes – Andy's being one of them. After bolt-cropping the chains, they'd wheeled the machines into a horsebox and headed back to gay Paris.

Because of the horrendous waiting list Andy could never get another Ducati 916 Sport. We tried to comfort him by telling him that at least he had a recording of the engine noise – something to remember his beloved by. He cried for a month and was just about coming out of mourning when we were warned off for Belize.

Andy was a real character in the unit. When not lamenting the loss of his Ducati he was funny and charismatic, with an uproarious, coarse sense of humour. Like any number of Pathfinders he was something of a loner, and he was very much his own man. His dress sense was horrendous, but he didn't give a shit. He wore shorts and florid Hawaiian shirts all year round, and it was quite cool in a way.

Seven years older than me, at twenty-eight, he'd been in the Pathfinders a good few years. He was a very capable, experienced soldier and a real workhorse. In short, as patrol commanders went Andy was about as good as it got. He appointed me lead scout for the Belize mission.

The four-man patrol is the smallest Pathfinder operational unit – four being the least that would ever deploy. As lead scout you front up any patrol, because the other patrol members – the commander, the signaller (radio operator) and the medic – are far less dispensable. That's why they make the freshman the bullet-taker.

My role as lead scout was to select the route and to navigate. With only four men on the patrol I doubled as the demolitions guy. That was fine with me: after leaping out of aircraft, blowing things up was my next favourite pastime.

The patrol signaller was Karl 'Beano' Dennis. No one seemed to know for sure how he'd got the Beano nickname, and he certainly wasn't telling. Presumably it was something to do with Dennis the Menace being the beat 'em up character in the *Beano* comics. Either way, it suited Mr Dennis to a T.

I'd never met anyone quite like Beano. He was the wealthiest squaddie I'd ever known, and the most careful with his money. He never drank, and the only thing he ever used to spend his hard-earned cash on was chocolate. Allocating himself a £1 daily allowance, he'd spend it at the NAAFI on that day's supply of Kit Kats and Mars bars.

He'd arrive at the Pathfinders' base with his carrier bag containing the standard six bars of chocolate. Once they were gone he'd never buy any more. He never went out, and had no girlfriend and no car. On top of that, he walked everywhere – if you ever tried to accompany him you had to warn him to slow down. He was 5' 10", weighed 14 stone, didn't smoke and had not an ounce of fat on him, which was a miracle considering his chocolate intake.

Beano's monthly expenditure we figured was around £30. His only other love in life was heavy metal. He used to lie on his bunk listening to AC/DC and Motorhead, and playing air guitar.

If you paused to listen outside his door you'd hear Beano going: 'Woowewwnahng . . . I'm on a highway to hell. Wnoowewwnahng . . . I'm on a highway to hell.'

And then you'd hurry on by.

Funnily enough, I liked Beano. He was around Andy's age, but far more experienced in the military. He was an acquired taste, but what I recognised in him was an extremely capable operator, plus a top-class signaller. Oddly, he kept people at a distance, calling everyone by their surname – 'Ah, Heaney' – but I warmed to him because he was such a character.

Andy and Beano had come to the Pathfinders direct from 1 PARA. Our fourth patrol member was from 2 PARA – Jonathan 'Johno' Jones. Johno was a fit-as-fuck 'racing snake' – a long-distance runner. He hailed from London, and was also a bit of a boy. His philosophy was work hard, play hard. He liked his beer, had a very short fuse and was known as a bit of scrapper.

What I liked about Johno was his sense of mischief. He was the ultimate prankster. He was a 'pad' – that is, he lived in the married quarters on base ('on the pad'). His two wild kids, boys of four and six, were the spitting image of their father.

One time he put his cat through its parachuting course. The British Army has something nicknamed a 'Schermuly'. It's a hard plastic tube with a firing lever at the bottom, and it's used for putting a flare up over the battlefield, to illuminate it at night, under a parachute. Or at least it should be. Johno worked out a way to attach his cat to the parachute, and Puss in Boots duly went airborne . . . safely returning to earth after his epic descent.

But perhaps his best ever wind-up was when a crew from ITV came to shoot an episode of the 1990s TV drama series *Soldier, Soldier* on his estate. They got all the roads blocked off, positioned their lighting rigs just so, and set up multiple cameras. But just as the director called 'Action!', Johno sent his boys running through the set, yelling out 'CRAPHATS!'

'Cut! Cut!' yelled the director. 'Where did those bloody kids come from?!!'

Johno's boys tore around to the rear of his house and in through the back door, ready for a second run. Just as soon as the director called out 'Action!' again, Johno set them running, as unstoppable as meerkats. Eventually, the director had to stop all filming while they called in some security.

Talk about a bunch of misfits and vagabonds in the X Platoon.

As was so often the case, the Belize mission fell to us as a result of personal connections. The Gurkha commander was a Lieutenant-Colonel Nick Stanley-Price, and he was a good mate of Jon Hayman's. They'd served together in the SAS, and it was the lieutenant-colonel who had asked Jon to send out a Pathfinder team to Belize, to help train his men.

The jungle is by far the toughest environment in which to soldier. It's the hardest in which to remain combat effective and survive. In the Arctic you're fighting against the extreme cold, but specialist kit enables you to remain warm and operational.

In the desert it's fairly similar – you're pitted against the extreme heat. The key challenges are staying out of the blistering sun and drinking enough water to keep alive. You move at night and lie up during the day in whatever shade you can find. If necessary, you make your own shade. Whether you're in the snows of the Arctic or the desert sands navigation is usually fairly simple, for you can nearly always acquire a GPS signal.

By contrast, the jungle offers myriad dangers – ones that nowhere else seems able to equal: dehydration, fatigue, disorientation, infections, trench foot, cuts, sores, bruises, bites, disease-ridden insects, murderous mosquitoes, rakes of hungry predators, millions of leeches, plus a whole universe of snakes.

In the jungle you are forever fighting the close, suffocating terrain, which makes navigating by GPS all but impossible (beneath the canopy it's mostly not possible to get a GPS signal). That's why after the Beacons, Pathfinder Selection continues in the jungle. It's the most difficult terrain imaginable, making it the perfect environment in which to test the ultimate soldier, and to refine his or her skills.

The Gurkhas are a class outfit, so to be tasked to train them in any combat environment was an honour. But to be asked to do so in the jungle was doubly so. The Gurkhas hail from Nepal, which does have its own jungle terrain. Unless we could live up to Jon H's credo – to do our job and be the best – sending us out to train the Gurkhas could have a similar effect to sending Hank the Yank on Pathfinder Selection.

Very quickly our usefulness – or lack of it – would become obvious, and we'd be out on our ear.

24

It was early October 1992 when the four of us – me, Andy, Beano and Johno the Joker – jetted out to Belize.

Having spent a few days acclimatising in Airport Camp – the main British Army base, located just outside Belize City – we flew south again, and were dropped in Rideau Camp, in the southern Toledo District of the country. There we boarded a helicopter and were flown out to the Gurkha's jungle base, situated at Guacamayo Bridge, about forty minutes' flying time northwest of Rideau.

The Gurkha Company consisted of some hundred-and-sixty soldiers. Our mission was to train them all, in four batches of forty, and we had six weeks to get them through the course. The modus operandi would be to head out from base camp each day, train hard in the jungle and return for the night, to eat, do admin and sleep.

Little training would be conducted at night, for one simple reason: no one operates in the jungle during the hours of darkness. It's next to impossible to move through the jungle at night, and you leave every sign for an enemy to follow. It's pitch black beneath the canopy, so you can't use night-vision equipment. You need light to move, and anyone using light can be seen, tracked and ambushed.

Everything in the jungle stops for the night hours – or at least, everything human.

We began by teaching the Gurkha lads the absolute key to jungle survival: navigation. Modern GPS units need to be able to 'see' the sky to be able to acquire satellites and work properly. They can't through thick jungle canopy. The only way to navigate is using a compass and a map, and via a process known as 'pacing and bearing'.

We started by finding an open area a hundred metres long. Each Gurkha was tasked to walk the distance, counting how many left footfalls it took him. We then got him to do it again, but carrying a heavy Bergen. If, like me, it took a hundred left footfalls to do it unencumbered, it might take a hundred and twenty to do it under a full pack. This is because your legs don't open as widely when carrying a heavy load.

We repeated the exercise, but going steeply uphill, which might take a hundred and thirty paces. By contrast, a downhill slope might only take eighty-five. To navigate in the jungle all of this has to become second nature – because the only way to find your way is to pick a bearing, count your footfalls, measure off each hundred metres covered, and note your progress on a map.

In practice, you develop a system for recording each hundred-metre section covered – ten of which equal a kilometre – and you mark your position accordingly.

If ever you hit an open patch of sky – say that provided by a river bed – you break out your GPS, to double check that pacing and bearing is working. But in the intense heat and humidity of the jungle, GPSs have a habit of malfunctioning. Batteries get corroded. Moisture seeps into electrical circuits. So the GPS is only ever used as a backup.

Confirmatory recces are also vital. You go firm at a location and send out guys in various directions. The first pair will look for a particular feature identified from the map – say a ridge line, lying 300 metres due east. The second will be heading for a waterfall, 250 metres due west. Hopefully, both will return having located those features, proving you were where you thought you were.

Next we taught the Gurkha lads how to move tactically through the terrain – so leaving little sign for an enemy to follow. Of course, all Gurkhas are used to wielding blades: each carries a curved, razor-sharp knife about a foot long – the Kukri. They proved well adept at wielding a machete, but the trick of jungle patrolling is to keep such use to an absolute minimum.

Cutting through the vegetation is a dead giveaway. As well as leaving a path to follow, it also makes a lot of noise and is exhausting. Instead, you learn to select the easiest route, taking the time to note obstructions that you'd otherwise have to cut through, like vine thickets or thorn groves. Generally, the higher you move the thinner the vegetation gets, as the ground tends to be drier. By contrast, low gullies and ravines tend to be sodden and clogged with undergrowth.

Much of what we were teaching was the ability to use the head, and not just brawn. The key was to get tuned into the jungle terrain. If you needed to head north and a ridge ran due north, then take it. It would invariably offer better going. Likewise, a riverbed running in the right direction might offer an easy path to follow.

That done, we taught the basics of tracking and the different kinds of signs left by an enemy. 'Ground Sign' is any kind of a trace below ankle level: a footprint, a boot scuff, or something on the side of a rock. 'Top Sign' is anything above ankle height: so where a Bergen has caught on a vine, or scuffed the side of a tree, or where a patrol has stopped for a smoke and left a weapon leant against a bush, crushing the vegetation.

Most soldiers who haven't received specialist training will stop for a rest and lean against a tree. They'll generally prop their weapon beside them, butt to the ground. If the indentation on the ground and the barrel scuff-mark are both visible, you can measure the length of the weapon, so giving you a clue as to its identity. If it's of a certain type, it may indicate whether it's friend or foe.

'Transfer' is where someone dislodges something and carries it to another part of the jungle – so most likely a piece of vegetation or a leaf. 'Discardables' are foreign objects brought into the jungle environment by whoever you are tracking: so a cigarette butt, or a fragment of cleaning cloth smeared in gun oil, or even a deposit of human faeces.

We impressed upon the guys how vital it is to note everything, no matter how seemingly insignificant. By doing so you build up a picture of the enemy: what brand of cigarettes they smoke, what kind of weaponry they carry, their numbers, and you could even get a sense of their discipline and morale.

Once the basics were grasped we formed up an 'incident stand' – a ten-metre by ten-metre patch of terrain. We marked off the box with 'mine tape' – a warning tape more normally used to mark off an enemy minefield – and we allowed the Gurkha lads to mooch about the perimeter, observing, with pen and notebook in hand.

'What do you see?' we'd ask.

'Footprint,' one would reply.

'Okay. Good. Footprint. From that what can you tell?'

They'd look closer. 'Footprint there and footprint there.'

'Good. And that gives a direction of travel,' we'd confirm. 'Now, ask yourself how many people is it? One or more? Is it military? Is it a boot or a sandal? Do a little sketch in your notebook of the tread pattern. That way if you come across more footprints you can tell if it's the same bunch of guys again.'

Once the basics of tracking were mastered we moved on to river crossing. We broke the men down into teams of four. Each carried a Bergen, inside which was an Ortlieb canoe liner – a tough, rubberised bag, which served to keep the backpack's contents dry. But the canoe liner could also double as a flotation device.

We showed them how to clip four Bergens together end-to-end, using carabiners – a D-shaped metal ring with a spring-hinged clip – so they formed a square. This makeshift raft would be put together on the 'home bank', at which point you'd slip it into the water with one guy on each of the four corners.

Before the launch, you'd tie your main weapon – your assault rifle – to the nearest carabiner, using paracord, a tough nylon cord about the width of your average washing line, just to ensure you didn't lose your weapon in the drink.

With your left hand holding onto the straps on top of your Bergen, and your right grasping the pistol grip of your weapon, you could in theory kick your way across, while still being able to put down covering fire. Having swum and drifted from one side to the other, you'd make landfall on the 'away bank', dismantle the 'raft' and continue with your patrol.

Having taught the basics, we moved on to fighting in the jungle, which by its very nature means close-quarter battle (CQB). We established CQB lanes, with wooden targets to either side. We used Figure 11 and Figure 12 targets – used to represent a standing and a kneeling man.

The trainee had to walk the lane, and react by opening fire from the 'patrol alert' position. This means firing from wherever is comfortable – so most likely the hip – aiming to be first to get down some rounds.

Bringing your weapon into the aim at the shoulder is all good in theory, but in practice it would most likely cost you your life in the jungle. Most contacts take place at a few yards' distance, due to the dense vegetation, and being first on the draw is key. The aim is to hit your enemy, or to force him to dive out of the way, which gives you a second or two to get into a proper fire position.

We taught the Gurkha lads to take two steps to left or right before doing so. If the enemy survived your first shots, he'd look to nail you where he last saw you – hence the move. In short the drill was to ID target; instinctive shooting; side step; then unleash aimed shots – at which stage marksmanship and weapon handling skills would come to the fore.

Once the Gurkhas had mastered doing it singly, we switched to pairs, and then patrolling and live firing in patrols of four. My impression of the Gurkhas was that they were rugged and strong, with fine instinctive skills. But they tended to wait for orders from an officer, without which they'd rarely take the initiative.

Under orders, they'd follow what they'd been told with utmost bravery.

They made a fine infantry unit.

There were few better.

We'd been through three rotations of the Gurkhas – so a hundred and twenty done 'n' dusted – when we received a radio message from out of the blue. It was dusk, and a Puma helicopter was flying in to pick us up. We were to return direct to Rideau Camp, but no reason was given why.

I'd enjoyed training the Gurkhas. They were disciplined, they listened well and they had proved themselves keen to learn. It was good to be in the jungle again, and I'd felt a real sense of satisfaction when a guy I'd been showing how to do something finally grasped it. It was my first training task and I'd loved it.

I was pissed off we were being pulled out.

Well, little did I know . . .

We came off the Puma at Rideau Camp, and climbed up the path towards the main base, the helipad being set on lower ground. Rideau consists of little more than a few ranks of old, Second World War era 'bean tins' – corrugated iron shelters – with an attached mess hall, briefing area and classrooms. Halfway up the climb we were met by one of the Gurkha officers, who told us the CO wanted to see us right away.

We'd been in the jungle for four weeks, neither shaving nor washing. You don't do either, for the smell of a clean-shaven and freshly scrubbed squaddie can carry for miles. You aim to blend in with your environment, taking on the smell and look of the jungle. But as a result we positively reeked, which wasn't perhaps the best of ways to appear before a man like Stanley-Price.

We were ushered into the briefing room wondering what was up. All we could think was we were being sent back to the UK, but we had zero idea why. The training had been going great, so surely it wasn't that. We left our grimy Bergens piled by the door, along with our equally shitty belt kits.

All we had were the filthy uniforms we stood up in, plus our M16s. Lieutenant-Colonel Stanley-Price strode in. He was 6' 4", skinny, with dark curly hair. I tried to read his expression, but he was giving nothing away.

'Well done, guys, and sorry to drag you out of jungle, but something's come up,' he began.

He consulted a flip-top notepad, before continuing with the briefing. A Gurkha patrol had been ambushed in an area far to the west, called Big Falls. We'd been training in the Maya Mountains, which lie to the southern central area of Belize. Big Falls is a remote, deep jungle location on Belize's western border with Guatemala.

The Gurkha patrol had been operating far from our normal area of training or patrols. Possibly they'd been undertaking some kind of joint mission with the Belize Defence Force (BDF), but that wasn't our concern, and Stanley-Price made it clear it wasn't our need to know, either.

What we did need to know was that they'd been hit by a mystery armed force, presumably one operating out of a base set across the border, in Guatemala. No one knew exactly how big a footprint the rebels had, or how blatant their operations were. But if they felt confident enough to hit a British Army patrol on Belize soil, they were clearly getting right in our faces.

'Intel suggests the rebels fund their operations from narcotics,' the lieutenant-colonel continued. 'It suggests they're moving drugs from a staging base on the Guatemalan side across into Belize. Once in Belize they're either being smuggled into Belize City and onwards by air, or they're taken east through the Maya Mountains over remote jungle tracks to the coast.

'Once at the coast the drugs are loaded aboard fast boats fitted with long-range fuel tanks, and shipped north through the Gulf of Honduras to Cuba. From there, it's another hop by fast boat to Miami and the entire USA.'

He glanced up from his notebook. 'I need you to go get eyes-on a specific location that local intelligence indicates as a suspected rebel/narco gang's base. You'll be there for no more than five days, keeping eyes-on what we suspect is the point from which the drugs are being moved cross-border into Belize.

'You are going in without the BDF, so unsupported. Needless to say, this is a highly sensitive operation. There could be any number of factions involved. You're to confirm the base's location and whether traffic is coming through from there. Gather as much intel as you can: numbers; times and dates of crossing; weaponry; what exactly is coming through. Vehicles, other means of transport – you know the score.'

He fixed us with this very direct look. 'You're to insert by helo to an LS of your choosing and infiltrate by foot to the target grid. You're to be on the ground by first light twenty-first October, and I want you to have eyes-on the rebel base by nineteen hundred hours the same day.' A pause. 'Go away, make your plan and back brief me as soon as possible.'

Fucking hell.

In a flash this had gone from a cute 'n' cuddly training task to a mission that had every possibility of going very noisy, very fast. If the rebels discovered us, there would be no calling for air support or reinforcements, or even for an emergency extraction – that much was clear.

We were going to be absolutely on our own.

25

The lieutenant-colonel's briefing was delivered to us on the evening of 20 October. We had less than twenty-four hours to get in there and get the rebel base within our grasp.

We sat there in the briefing room feeling ... gob-smacked. On the one hand we craved action. We craved live operations. It was what we'd trained exhaustively for, and we hungered to be tested. But on the other hand, the odds were clearly stacked against us.

The Gurkha patrol had been a full platoon – so thirty-five strong. They'd been ambushed some five kilometres east of the suspected rebel base. Fierce fire had been exchanged both ways, before the Gurkhas had managed to extract without anyone being killed.

But only by the skin of their teeth.

'Erm ... what are our rules of engagement, sir?' It was Andy, and it was more than a fair question.

The lieutenant-colonel glanced at him. 'Make sure you don't get compromised, and then you won't get shot at, and then you don't have to shoot anyone.'

Helpful.

Normally, all operations have very specific ROEs (rules of engagement), which inform you under what circumstances you are entitled to use lethal force. Whoever was tasking this mission – and we had absolutely no idea who was pulling the strings here – they clearly didn't think ROEs very relevant.

'Any sense of the situation on the ground?' Andy pushed. 'Enemy numbers, weapons? And what exactly are we looking for? And how do we ID the bad guys?'

The lieutenant-colonel's gaze remained inscrutable. 'There's very little available. Suffice to say a platoon-sized Gurkha patrol was engaged by an armed force in the area, and was forced to withdraw. You can draw your own conclusions.'

Doubly helpful.

'Anything else? No? Right – liaise with Captain Lars Singh for ammo, rations, mapping and anything else you may need.'

With that, he stepped out and left us to Captain Singh.

We made all the obvious asks of the Gurkha captain, drawing up a long list of RFIs (requests for information): up-to-date and detailed maps of the area; aerial photos; any recent patrol reports from anyone who'd worked in the region; plus any intelligence briefs from the area, or on the narco gang itself.

We didn't hold out any great hopes, but if any of this were available it would be like gold dust to us. It would allow us to work out the type of jungle we'd be operating in, the terrain, the ground underfoot and the likely speed of progress, potential water-sources, any high ground, plus notable tracks or features that might allow us to move more rapidly.

Plus we could get a detailed sense of the enemy and the threat.

We asked for details of any civilian presence in the region – so villages, logging camps, that kind of thing. These needed to be avoided, for nearly all human settlements in Belize keep dogs to scare away jaguars – the big cats that roam the jungle. The dogs would be as likely to bark at four sweaty Pathfinders sneaking through the bush as they would any big cats.

Captain Lars Singh went away to investigate.

We killed time sanitising ourselves – removing our Pathfinder unit flashes, marks of rank, plus any clues to our identity or what country we hailed from: photos of family, clothing brand labels, ID documents of any sort – all of it had to go.

We were just about done when Captain Lars Singh returned. 'There is nothing,' he announced, simply. 'The only maps we have are the ones you've been issued with already. There is no other intel.'

Well, at least now we knew.

Our maps were 1:50,000 scale – so giving half as much detail as your average Ordnance Survey rambler's map. Worse still, they were at least twenty years out of date. We'd have to pick an LS off the map, and hope and pray it offered us a clear place to put down, for in twenty years a lot of vegetation can grow, especially in a country like Belize.

If the LS proved unusable, the mission would quickly go to ratshit. Time spent flying around trying to find an alternative spot to put down would risk alerting the rebels to what we were up to.

Next, we turned out attention to kit. We wanted Spyglass – a hand held thermal imaging sight. Spyglass requires batteries to power it, plus compressed air bottles to keep it cool, but it is a peachy piece of kit. With a range of two and a half kilometres it can penetrate a screen of vegetation or darkness, picking up people, domestic animals or vehicle engines as distinctive heat blobs.

We needed loads of other stuff: a 50x magnification Swiftscope (a tripod-mounted spotting telescope for observation work); personal night-vision units; food rations for five days in the jungle; hand-grenades; 40mm rounds for our M203 grenade-launchers; Claymores for laying down a wall of death if the narco-loonies came after us. And we needed rakes of ammunition for our assault rifles.

We handed the list to Captain Lars Singh.

He managed to rustle up some food rations, a Spyglass sight, and a Swiftscope, plus 480 rounds of ammo for the M16s. That was it. Under the circumstances, we figured he'd done pretty well. The Gurkhas were there on a training mission. It was hardly surprising they hadn't brought with them what we were asking for, which was a ready-made war-in-a-box.

We took stock.

We had 120 rounds of 5.56mm ammo per man. We each had a knife, and of course we'd brought our machetes with us, as part of our personal gear. We figured if the narco-maniacs rumbled us, we'd have to do a classic Monty Python act – *run away!*

Water was the next issue. The only place that might offer us a vantage point to get eyes-on the bad guys was a ridgeline, lying around two kilometres east of their base. Any closer, and the dogs living with the drug-runners would no doubt smell us and raise the alarm. Trouble was, few ridges in Belize tend to have any water.

High ground is generally dry ground, and the last thing a tiny, covert, unsupported and inadequately armed force like us wanted to be doing was climbing down to the low ground, to filter water. Once we got into position we were best staying put, in an effort to remain undetected. But an average human requires six litres of water per day in the tropics, and especially when undertaking physical exertion.

With the weight of rations, observation kit, air bottles, batteries, radio kit, survival gear and weaponry we had to carry, we figured we'd have to manage on a fraction of that. Eventually we opted to carry one twenty-litre jerry-can between us – so enough for one litre of water per man per day.

We'd have our belt kits, which came complete with two one-litre bottles – but we'd never touch those. That was our emergency E & E (escape and evasion) water, which we would reserve for going on the run.

The LS we'd chosen for the drop-off was five kilometres due east of the ridgeline. It was far enough away for a Puma flying at treetop height not to be heard by the rebels, but near enough for us to make the infil to the ridge in one day – which was the schedule that Lieutenant-Colonel Stanley-Price had set us.

The twenty-litre jerry-can would fill one person's Bergen, so his kit would have to be spread around the rest. It left little room for any personal gear: we had two waterproof ponchos between the four of us, a shared lightweight survival blanket, plus one spare pare of socks each. We'd rotate between the pairs of socks, trying to keep our feet as dry as possible to avoid getting trench foot or bacteriological infections.

We'd be on 'hard routine' – so no cooking, eating only cold food, and pissing in bottles and shitting in cling film, which would enable us to take all our waste out with us when we left. That way, we would leave few traces of our presence, so no clues for anyone wanting to locate, trace and track us.

Inevitably, human waste attracts scavengers: mice, rats and wild pigs all like to dig it up and eat it. The last thing you need is for a Noah's Ark load of wildlife to converge around your covert OP, for that in turn can attract two-legged animals to your location – including narco-traffickers.

With our plan sorted, we headed to the briefing room to back brief the lieutenant-colonel. Once we were done he peered at our twenty-year-old 1:50,000 scale map. 'What'll you do if tasked to get closer than the ridgeline?'

'I'll have to see on the ground,' Andy replied. 'That's our primary OP. If it's not good enough we'll relocate, and I'll send you the new grid in our first sitrep.'

Sitrep stood for 'situation report'.

'What's your lost comms procedure?' he asked.

In other words, what would happen if our radios went down and we couldn't contact Rideau Camp – which would mean we couldn't call in the Puma to pick us up at mission's end.

Andy tried his best to answer the question, but with zero intel to hand we didn't have many options.

'Right, you'll liaise with my signaller,' the lieutenant-colonel rounded off. 'He'll run an ops room for you while you're gone, listening watch twenty-four seven. I'll see you before you board the helo. Get some food and rest in the meantime.'

'Listening watch twenty-four seven' meant we'd have someone monitoring the radio at all times, remaining alert for any calls from us.

The last thing we did before trying to get some sleep was to put together the mission file. It detailed our insertion and extraction LS, our route march into the ridgeline, alternative OP locations if the first was no good, times of morning and evening radio calls (we'd check in twice daily) and our 'comms under duress' procedures.

With comms under duress, you note down particular code-words you'd insert into an otherwise seemingly normal radio call, to alert HQ to the fact you were being forced to speak with a gun held to your head. Without such a procedure the rebels could capture one of us, force him to call in the Puma, and then stake out the LS, so as to shoot it down.

Normally, Pathfinders use top-secret radios encoded with a 'crypto fill' system. It works by translating messages into numbers, and sending them in high-frequency data bursts. So, for example, if you wanted a 'radio check' it would send the number '75'. HQ would recognise 75 as meaning 'radio check' and respond with '48', code for 'message received loud and clear'.

But if we sent the number '45' – our pre-arranged 'comms under duress' code – they'd immediately know we had been captured. Unfortunately, because we'd deployed on a training mission we had none of our specialist radios with us. Instead, we'd be operating on standard comms kit and by voice means. So we needed a word that on the surface would appear perfectly normal, but was the trigger word.

We chose 'clarify' – as in 'clarify grid of LS'. It would sound perfectly normal for one of us to use it, but as soon as we did HQ would know we had been taken captive, at which point they'd initiate whatever procedures they had in place. Hopefully, they'd send in a CSAR (combat search and rescue) force to find us and pull us out.

By the time the final briefing was done I could feel my heart-rate was heightened and the adrenaline was already starting to flow. We'd been in the jungle for four weeks, so we were well-acclimatised to the environment by now. In Andy, Beano and Johno I figured I had the God Team. No doubt about it, they were fantastic blokes to be deploying with on the Pathfinders' first ever live mission.

The First Gulf War had kicked off the previous year, but we Pathfinders had been stood down at the last minute, which had been gut-wrenching. We'd been poised to go in tasked with SCUD-hunting – seeking out Saddam's mobile launchers for his SCUD missiles – but the ground war had been all about armour versus armour, and our tanks had won.

I'd just completed a HALO course, along with a bunch of other elite forces' soldiers. Like everyone else, I saw the TV news footage of the Bravo Two Zero (B2Z) lads getting paraded by the Iraqis, following their capture. I'd spent five weeks with some of those guys on that HALO course and we'd got pretty close. It was a total shock to see them in such rag order.

As I contemplated what we were heading into here in Belize, those images flashed through my mind. The B2Z patrol had been eight guys, heavily armed and operating in open desert. We were four, we were woefully under-equipped, weapons wise, we had crap radios plus zero intel, and we were about to enter a remote jungle pretty much blind.

This was one of those moments that really did make me go *hmmmmm . . .*

While the Iraqis were no angels, they did have a government of sorts and a professional military, plus a modicum of rule of law. They had probably heard of the Geneva Convention, and they were very likely signed up to it. They might not take much notice, but there were some checks and balances, at least.

More importantly, there had been a leader – Saddam Hussein – someone our prime minister could talk to and demand the return of our captured warriors. Saddam had been able to say: 'Stop dropping bombs on us and we'll send your boys home.' And sure enough those that had survived the B2Z debacle were returned – eventually.

With narco-trafficking rebels there tended to be none of that.

In the First Gulf War Britain had formally declared war. It is within the rules of war to drop patrols behind enemy lines, as had happened with the B2Z boys. This, by contrast, was a totally grey situation.

As I contemplated all of this, I felt a shudder of trepidation. We were about to mess with the drugs trade. Big bucks were being made. The corruption went to the very top of the Central American governments – everyone knew that. The rebels had shown that they were more than happy to shoot up a British patrol in Belize, which had to make you wonder just who was protecting them?

And here we were about to drop into their backyard.

If we got compromised, who on earth would come and look for us? There were no other Pathfinders in-country, or any other elite units, and that left either the Gurkhas or the BDF. No offence intended, but the BDF were hardly about to ride to our rescue. That only left the Gurkhas, and the rebels had already routed one full platoon.

It was a sobering thought, but not much of one for a twenty-something Middlesbrough lad not long into the X Platoon.

In truth – bugger the risks – I couldn't wait to get started.

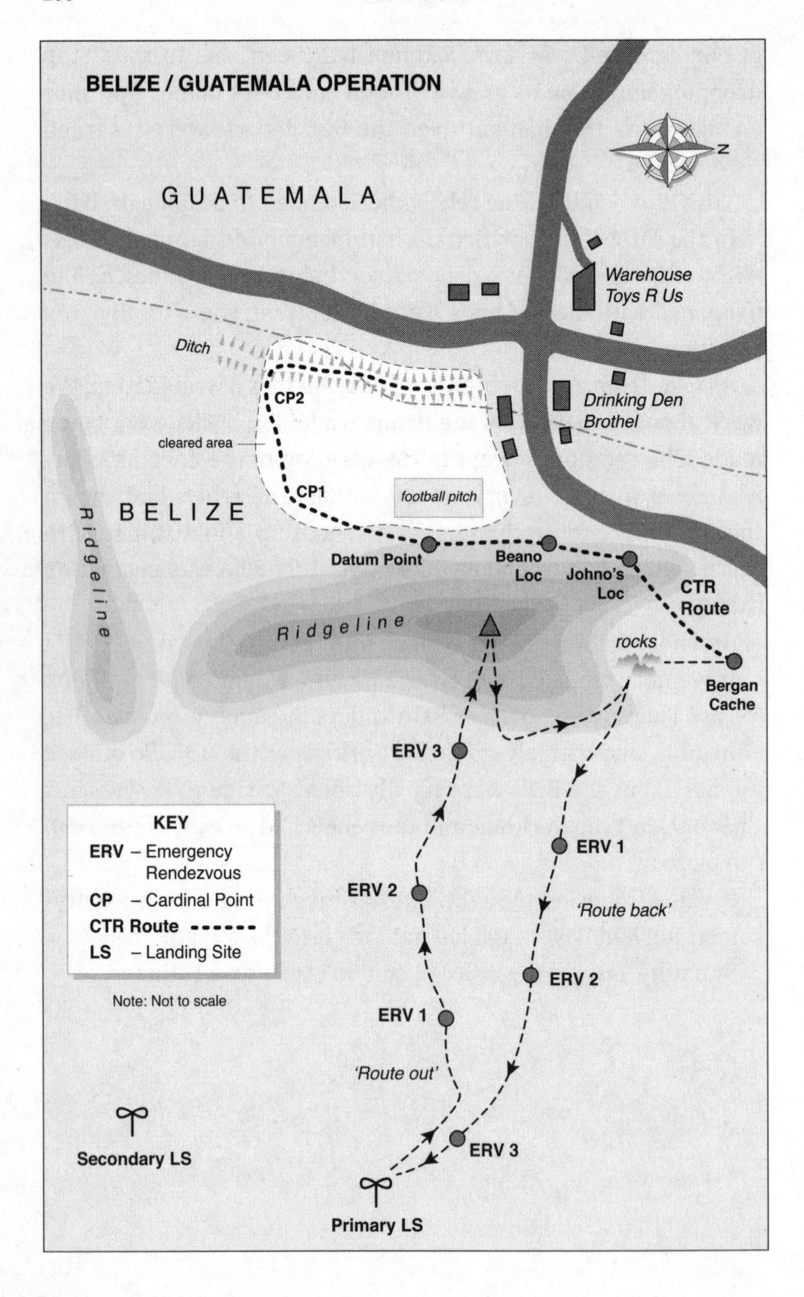
BELIZE / GUATEMALA OPERATION
GUATEMALA
N
Warehouse
Toys R Us
Ditch
Drinking Den
Brothel
CP2
cleared area
CP1
football pitch
BELIZE
Ridgeline
Datum Point
Beano
Loc
Johno's
Loc
CTR
Route
Ridgeline
rocks
Bergan
Cache
ERV 3
KEY
ERV – Emergency Rendezvous
CP – Cardinal Point
CTR Route
LS – Landing Site
Note: Not to scale
ERV 1
ERV 2
'Route back'
ERV 2
ERV 1
'Route out'
Secondary LS
ERV 3
Primary LS

26

At 0600 we were up bright-eyed and bushy-tailed.

The Gurkhas have an unusual way of doing breakfast. At 0600 they get a massive tea urn going, and drink oodles of hot, sweet milky tea. They then get a breakfast at 0900 – but it's actually a curry. They then do a repeat of the tea at 1300, and their evening meal is at 1800.

The curry gets prepared by one of the privates, using a wok over a massive fire pit. They take the contents of some British Army ration packs, do an all-in-all thrown into the one pot – and curry the lot. If they can find an animal to butcher, they curry that too – head, claws, hooves, intestines and all. They don't eat beef, because cows are sacred in their culture, but chickens and sheep beware.

We'd been living with the Gurkhas while we trained them, and it's a primary rule of hearts-and-minds work that you never refuse the locals' grub. Nothing pisses people off more than letting them know that their national dish isn't really your cup of tea. Anyway, we were all partial to curry. Sort of. But after fifty-six curries on the trot our arses were like the proverbial blood orange.

Anyhow, we sat down to a breakfast of our fifty-seventh curry, only this one was served cold in a bag. Leftovers. From the night before.

Lieutenant-Colonel Stanley-Price wandered over for a few words, brew clasped in hand. He wished us luck in the Heart of Darkness, and with finding Mr Kurtz.

Or at least, he might as well have done.

Cold curry downed, we made our way to the helipad, massive

Bergens slung over our shoulders. As we sat on our packs waiting for the Puma, I felt a mixture of emotions. On the one hand I was buzzing like a firework; on the other, I felt like we were four condemned men . . .

At 0730 the Puma landed and the pilot shut it down. Andy laid out our twenty-year-old 1:50,000 scale map on the floor of the helo, and proceeded to brief the pilot.

'We need you to take us in to here. That's the primary LS. We chose it off this map, as it's all we have. Get us in there or as close as you can. There's a secondary LS here, if the first is a no-go. Get us in, drop us off, and fuck off. That's it.'

The pilot seemed cool with that.

We climbed in. Andy took up position directly behind the cockpit, with Beano, Johno and me perched on the fold-down canvas seats in the tail section, next to our heap of Bergens. The Puma took off, swung around towards the west and picked up speed. Through the open door I could see the jungle flashing by – it felt close enough to reach out and touch the highest treetops.

The pilot was RAF, and he sure knew his stuff. If he took this thing any lower his rotors would be shaving the topmost branches. We sped across a carpet of green, the wind noise killing the chance of any chat. Now and again there was a break in the canopy, marking a river, a narrow trail, or a village. But ninety-nine per cent of what we were flying over was pure jungle.

The racket from the Puma's turbine and its rotor gear was deafening. If anything, the helo was even older than our map. The loadie – the guy who keeps the passengers and any cargo in order – kept the doors open. He kept moving from one doorway to the other and glancing upwards. We knew from previous flights what he was up to: he was checking there was no smoke or oil coming from the turbine, and that the rotors weren't about to crack or shear off.

Belize is not much more than a hundred and seventy miles long, border to border. We'd been in the air about forty minutes, when we felt the helo start to lose what little altitude it had. Moments later it flared out, the arse-end dropping towards the ground, and we sank into a clearing some seventy yards across. The loadie was hanging out as far as he could go, checking the rotors and tail were clear of the trees.

There was a jolt as the wheels made contact with the ground, and then the loadie gave us the thumbs-up. I followed Andy out of the port door – the opposite to the loadie – and Beano and Johno started chucking out the Bergens. We grabbed the packs and headed thirty yards to one side.

We went down on one knee, and made our weapons ready – so chambering a round. You never travel on a helo with a bullet up the spout, for obvious reasons: no one wants to shoot their own helicopter down. The Puma was still turning and burning, the downrush of the rotors whipping up a shit storm of dirt and blasted vegetation. As soon as Beano and Johno were with us, Andy gave a thumbs-up to the pilot. He flashed it back, the Puma rose vertically, and it was gone.

Sixty seconds ticked by, by which time the Puma was no longer audible. It was around 0900 and we were exactly where the lieutenant-colonel had asked us to be – within striking distance of the rebels' drug den.

The priority now was to get off the LS as quickly as possible. If anyone had heard or seen the helo go in, this was where they would make for. But first we needed to be dead certain we were where we thought we were.

Andy pulled out his map, compass, and GPS. He used the GPS to double check our grid and then he set the bearing we would follow on the compass, which was basically due west. Location and course set we heaved up our huge, tortoise-shell-like Bergens.

'Okay, Steve, let's go,' said Andy, glancing in my direction.

Right now I was a fresh-faced twenty-something – the youngest member of this elite unit. I'd gone from getting busted for stealing milk floats to leading off on a mission such as this one. The British

Army likes to boast it can turn 'zeros into heroes'. But I'd done nothing remotely heroic yet, and I had no idea if I had an iota of heroism within me.

But one thing was for certain: it had sure turned my life around.

I led us into the comparative cool and shade of the canopy. We pressed ahead for a hundred yards or so, until no light from the LS was visible, and then settled down to a 'listening watch'. For a good five minutes we did nothing but kneel in the shadows, listening and watching like hawks.

If anyone had got wise to our arrival, now was the time they would show themselves. But all that surrounded us were the noises of the jungle. It seemed likely that we had got in here undetected.

Listening watch done, we prepared to move out. I adjusted the straps on my monster pack, hefted it once more, and picked a distinctive tree a hundred yards ahead of me to aim for. After spending a few seconds tuning back into the environment, I led off, counting my left footfalls as I went.

Taped to my M16, adjacent to the trigger, was a tiny plastic counter that I'd spray-painted green. It was the kind that an air hostess might use to count bums on seats, prior to takeoff. It was mechanical, possessing a tiny wheel that displayed three digits, presently set to zero: 000.

I counted out ten left footfalls and hit the button. One digit clicked around: 001. From long experience I knew it would take a hundred and twenty left footfalls to cover a hundred metres of terrain, on the flat and under a heavy load. By the time my counter read 012 I knew I'd covered the first hundred metres.

To each his own for pacing and bearing.

Andy and Beano were using 'pace beads' – a length of cord ten inches long with ten beads tied along its length. Every time you did ten metres you'd pull a bead through. The pace beads were tied to their webbing at the shoulder, so within easy reach. By the time they'd pulled the ten beads through they'd covered 100 metres.

I moved deeper, clicking the counter as I went. By the time it hit 120 I knew we'd covered the first kilometre. When it hit 360 I knew we were three klicks in – time for a quick gulp from our horribly limited water supplies, and a map check. We averaged out the distances each of us had calculated and marked that point on the map.

In theory, this simple process of pacing and bearing would enable us to navigate our way along the five kilometres to that ridgeline. Whether we'd make it or not, with little water, limited ammo, bugger all heavier weaponry and just the four of us, was anyone's guess.

The Belize jungle is what we call 'dirty jungle'. It is dense and close in all directions. Everywhere there was decaying, rotting, dank, mouldy organic matter – so leaves, bark, branches, and God only knows what else. A thick layer of detritus scrunched underfoot, and to left and right of me a cloud of nasty bugs bumbled and fizzed about.

There was no cutting through this kind of jungle. To do so would leave a motorway for the bad guys to follow. Instead, everything had to be done slowly and methodically, searching for a route to weave through, and moving at a silent whisper.

We had to remain hyper-alert to any threat. To do so took massive amounts of concentration, and this was where the training really kicked in. With my gaze fixed on the next feature I was heading for, I could use my peripheral vision to scan to either side for any threat. My M16 remained in the 'patrol alert' position, ready to perform the drill we'd been banging into the Gurkha recruits: ID target; instinctive shooting – two shots; side step; unleash a barrage of aimed fire.

We'd not moved far from the LS when we hit the first rise. I led us onto the high ground, hoping for a ridge to follow, but after a couple of hundred yards we dropped back down to the level we were at before. Two hundred yards further on we hit a second rise, and climbed to another short ridge, and so on and so forth.

This was what we called 'egg-box': it was like trying to traverse a giant egg-box, and all the while remaining silent and alert for the enemy, and carrying not a great deal less than our own bodyweight.

The further west we pushed the more the terrain worsened. We hit deep ravines, choked with dense foliage and groves of 'bastard trees', each boasting a crop of vicious spines that protruded six inches or more from the trunk. We knew them well. The spikes weren't poisonous, but that didn't matter much.

I'd fallen against one once, during a jungle training exercise. The tough wooden spines had pierced my arm, the wounds turning septic. Strung between the 'bastard trees' were vines as thick as your forearm, each armed with vicious hooked thorns.

Underfoot, the ground felt slippery and treacherous. My senses were assailed by the heavy scent of dark, musty decay. The terrain was dropping away, but doubtless I'd soon hit a steep climb, and we'd be forced to scramble to the high ground, only to descend again shortly afterwards.

The jungle had an atmosphere of ominous foreboding, as if it was trying to send out some kind of a warning: *You shouldn't be here.* We all felt it. We were acutely aware of how painfully slowly we were moving. As we couldn't use machetes we had to keep boxing around patches of impenetrable vegetation, sending us further out of our way.

There was one advantage to traversing such horrendous terrain: it was unlikely that any drug gangs would be moving through here. They tended to stick to known paths and tracks, for obvious reasons: they had a cargo of narcotics to move through the jungle.

But the maximum progress we could make was 500 metres an hour. We'd hit the LS at around 0900. Last light in the jungle would be around 1900 that evening, no later.

At this rate we'd be lucky to reach the ridgeline before dark, which was less than ten hours away.

27

We kept moving.

We needed to reach the ridge in daylight and get ourselves sorted, at which point we could munch away on cold rations to our hearts' content. By the time we were nearing the point where the ridge should rear up before us, we were exhausted, and the sun was sinking below an invisible horizon.

In truth, I felt fucking horrendous. I was light-headed, piss wet through with sweat, my back was burning and sore, and I was faint with dehydration. In the early stages, dehydration causes listlessness and the lack of ability to focus. As it gets worse, you suffer a crushing lethargy, exhaustion and pounding headaches.

One of the greatest dangers is the way it degrades your ability to concentrate or remain alert – seriously impairing your chances of detecting an enemy. The heat and the humidity had been building all through the day, and I knew I was badly dehydrated before we even started the climb.

We hit what we figured had to be the base of the ridge, and dropped our Bergens. There was no time to piss about. With every minute the light was fading, and soon it would be pitch dark. Less than ten per cent of available light filters through the jungle canopy – so practically no starlight or moonlight reaches the floor.

In thick forest at night it is darker than a Neanderthal's cave.

Beano and Johno were smaller than Andy and me, so we opted to make the recce ascent, leaving them with the Bergens. We set off with only our weapons and belt kit – so each with a couple of water bottles, an emergency ration pack, compass, counter and GPS, plus spare mags of ammo for the M16s.

Our maps displayed contour lines every fifty feet. There were a good half a dozen between us and the high-point, and all close together. With our M16s gripped in one hand, we fought our way up, scrambling over fallen trees and digging in with our boots to try to secure footholds. As we neared the summit the vegetation started to thin, just as we'd hoped it would.

We needed to be careful here. Very.

And doubly watchful.

The high ground was rocky underfoot and boulder-strewn. It was cloaked in a close, less dense kind of jungle. As we crested the ridge the low evening sunlight broke through the trees. Keeping down on our hands and knees, we crawled across a fifty-foot area of flat ground, until the ridge dropped away on the far side.

In theory, there should be nothing between us and the rebel base, except for two kilometres of open air. We wove back and forth, searching for an opening in the vegetation that would offer us the confirmatory view: sight of the drug traffickers' den.

Finally, we found a gap.

We inched forward, then lifted our heads a fraction and peered over the edge. Below us, the ridge dropped off as steeply as the slope we'd just climbed. Beyond that the terrain rolled away in 'egg-box' fashion. But then, in a clearing hacked out of the thick jungle – there was the rebel base.

Two things struck us immediately as being wrong.

One, the base was much closer to the ridge than the lieutenant-colonel's briefing had suggested it should be. By his reckoning, it should have been some two to three kilometres distant. This looked to be no more than a kilometre away. And second, it was far too large. The briefing had indicated a village-sized clearing, with a few huts scattered around and the odd narco-rebel won-dering about.

This was nothing of the sort.

The two of us exchanged glances. Below us, carved out of the pristine jungle, was what looked like a small town. We could see two main roads running through it, each a sandy highway disappearing at either end into the thick trees. Clustered around those were scores of buildings, and even from this distance some looked as large as a Toys R Us warehouse – though somehow we doubted if they contained boxes of Lego or Barbie Dolls.

Pick-ups and 4x4 vehicles buzzed up and down the dirt tracks, throwing up thick clouds of dust. If this was a narco-base, they had to be running a serious amount of drugs through here – like industrial-scale quantities.

By eye, I figured the settlement had to be about a kilometre square. On the southern edge – so on our left side as we looked at it – there was a large patch of cleared forest, and what looked like fields of crops. The trees had been cut and burned, the open ground being littered with charred stumps.

On the eastern end of that – so nearest to us – was what looked like a makeshift football field. Presumably that was where the narco-traffickers booted a ball about, when they weren't harvesting or processing their drugs, or loading them up to be shipped out to market.

We could only see snatches from our vantage point, glimpsed between the trunks of trees – but that was exactly what it looked like to Andy and to me. After we'd been eyes-on for a good five minutes, Andy slithered backwards into the cover of the bush. I did likewise.

He turned to me. 'Navs good. We're bang on.' He paused. 'But fuck me, mate, it's much bigger than I ever thought.'

'Yep.'

Andy shrugged. 'Right. Best we crack on.'

We crawled about until Andy found a spot he figured was ideal for the OP.

'It's the highest point,' he whispered. 'We'll have good line of sight into the place, plus the best chance of good comms. We'll keep two forward observers here on permanent watch, and keep the others back in a rear admin area, in cover and shade.'

'What about defences?'

'Northern end drops away sharply, so no one's going to take us from there. We'll have eyes-on west. East is the slope we just climbed: no one's coming up that very easily.' He swung his head left. 'The main threat is south. The ridge drops off, but only to a saddle, then climbs to another ridge, and keeps doing that all the way into Guatemala. A force could move along the ridge and hit us. That's the direction to watch.'

We consulted the map, double-checking our position with the GPS. It confirmed we were exactly where we intended to be. Somehow, between whoever it was gathering the intel and our arriving here, the narco-settlement had mushroomed into Guatemala's version of Dodge City.

'Something else doesn't make sense,' Andy whispered. 'The crossroads – the centre – it's maybe a click west of here. That puts it just into Guatemala. But the eastern edge – it's well inside Belize territory. The place straddles the two countries.'

'Perfect for running drugs cross-border.'

'But how's it got so big without anyone noticing?'

'Pay the right bribes, anything's possible.'

'Yeah, I guess.'

We crawled back to the eastern edge of the ridgeline, and dropped down to Beano and Johno. It was around 1900 when we rejoined them, just as the last of the light was fading into deep shadow. After giving them the good news, we heaved up our Bergens and began the climb. Johno was carrying the water jerry-can, and he just couldn't seem to make any progress. He'd take two steps upwards, then slide three down.

The steeper it became the worse it got for him. Twice he lost his footing, tumbling down-slope in a heap of flailing arms and legs. Eventually, Beano opted to carry his M16, while Andy took one of his arms and I took the other. We literally pulled Johno up the hill.

It wasn't his fault. The terrain was steep, shitty and almost pitch dark by now.

Finally we reached the summit. I led us in a crawl to the area we'd chosen for the OP. We gathered together and Andy orientated Beano and Johno to the terrain, and to the location and size of the drug-runners' operation.

'I'm nominating an ERV five hundred metres down-slope due east,' Andy added. 'If anything happens here – if we're split up or compromised – that's where we'll regroup.'

ERV stands for emergency rendezvous. It does exactly what it says on the tin. Everyone set the ERV bearing on his compass. That way, if we were hit tonight we'd all know instantly in which direction to run, and where to regroup.

That done, Andy set about the next most important task – trying to radio in a sitrep to HQ. Trouble was, we were using a HF (high-frequency) radio system, and HF signals drop out come nightfall. It's something to do with needing to bounce the signal off the ionosphere – a layer of outer atmosphere surrounding Earth – and the ionosphere cooling at night and so becoming less 'bouncy'.

Andy put together a half-wave dipole antenna. The perfect antenna length for the frequency we were using was 60 metres. We had about as much chance of stringing up a 60-metre aerial as we had of weaning the Gurkhas off curry. Andy figured we could just about manage half that length – a 'half-wave' – corresponding to half the wavelength of the frequency we were using.

It's called a 'dipole', because the antenna consists of a length of insulated copper wire with a 'balun' – a junction box – set halfway along it, splitting it in two. Andy needed to get the ends of the dipole suspended around ten metres off the ground, and the only way to do so was to hurl them up and try to snag a tree branch. Basically, you tie a rock onto the end of the wire and give it a whirl.

Andy had to do all of that without standing up, because the last thing he wanted was to be silhouetted on the ridge in the setting sun. Not only that, but with the HQ at Camp Rideau being some ninety kilometres southeast of us, he had to get the antenna orientated side-on to that – so in a southwest to northeast direction.

Needless to say, it was a nightmare getting it all set up. By the time he was done, it was dark. It was horrendous trying to establish contact, and all Andy was able to transmit was the following.

'Sitrep. In position. Grid: two two four eight one seven. Nothing further to report.'

Even then, Andy wasn't sure he'd got the message through. But hell, at least he'd tried.

He couldn't risk keeping on-air for too long. The Pathfinders' specialist radios send data-burst messages, which are pretty much instantaneous. But with the HF system we were using, you had to tune the frequency in to the antenna length, at which stage an arrow on a dial would swing as far right as possible, meaning: *ready to transmit.*

It took an age to do this, and all that time the radio was basically live. Any half-decent military force, or rebel outfit for that matter, could operate a basic direction-finding (DF) unit. It takes very little time to detect a radio frequency, triangulate the signal and home in on the position of the call. That was why we normally used data-burst systems, to send short, untraceable pulses.

While Andy was trying to make his radio call, I crawled forward with Beano to the OP itself. We'd reasoned that the rebel location was too big to go dark come nightfall, so it was bound to have some kind of lighting. In which case, we should be able to gather good intel all through the night hours.

Sure enough, as darkness fell so the lights came on in the settlement below. Light bulbs were strung from wire, which looped around the place suspended from makeshift telegraph poles. It was so well lit that we could count the number of people wandering around the dirt streets, and we could also hear the faint buzzing of what we presumed were generators.

Dodge City was pretty quiet up until 10 o'clock, at which point it seemed to explode into life. This dodgy, distorted Mexican-style music drifted up to us, as crowds of people gathered at the crossroads. More and more flooded in, and nearly all of them were men. Soon, there were so many milling about we couldn't count them all, let alone keep track. We figured there were more than fifty, but less than a hundred.

The focus of activity seemed to be a makeshift drinking den, positioned just this side of the main crossroads. The action around Dodge City's main bar was chaotic and wild. Now and then a pick-up would go tearing up the main drag, with a bunch of drunken blokes packed in the rear. I guessed there weren't many traffic cops in Dodge.

No doubt about it, the place was utterly brazen.

They weren't making the slightest effort to hide.

The question buzzing through my mind was – why?

28

We completed that first, six-hour watch. It was past midnight by the time Andy and Johno came to relieve us. I crawled back to the rear area, got my head down on the poncho that doubled as a groundsheet, pulled the one thin blanket over me and crashed into an utterly exhausted sleep – my weapon at my side, fully clothed, with belt kit and boots on.

The one thing I had remembered to do, in spite of my exhaustion, was to pull on a totally vital piece of kit. I reckon the nearest thing to it in the civvie world is a beekeeper's helmet. It's basically a head-and-neck mozzie net. You pull it on like a giant sock, the fine-mesh netting bagging out around the face and fastening around the shoulders.

We'd each of us slapped insect repellent on any exposed skin, plus our combat trousers were tucked into jungle boots, to stop leeches, ants or other nasties crawling up our legs, but none of that could stop the mozzies from getting lock-on. It wasn't as if we could keep swatting whenever we felt a bite, either, for the key to such OP work was to keep still and remain undetected.

I was desperate for sleep, and at least the head net should keep my face bite-free. I rolled onto my back, thrust my hands deep into my pockets, to try to keep the mozzies off them, and within seconds I was dead to the world.

After a cold and gloopy meatballs and pasta breakfast – spooned from its tinfoil boil-in-the-bag – I was back on watch with Beano by 0700. We'd got the 50x magnification Swiftscope set up by now, the tripod and body hidden behind a screen of vegetation, and the lens itself shielded by a length of scrim – scrim being a perforated camouflage material.

Because the scope was focused on a point a good kilometre away, it didn't register the scrim and could see right through it. The material would stop the glass lens flashing and glinting in the sunlight, which would be a dead giveaway. We'd also taped up the entire scope with green gaffer tape, smearing camo cream into it to make a DIY DPM (disruptive pattern material) cover.

The scope sat twelve inches off the ground on its stubby tripod, and it was pretty much invisible. Beano worked it – acting as the observer – while I took notes, which made me the logger or scribe. The reason we split the tasks was so that the observer could keep his eye glued to the lens, and so wouldn't miss a thing. In this way we drew up a detailed sketch map of the place, including where it dog-legged northwest at the far end, disappearing into the jungle.

We then switched to logging human and vehicle movements.

'There's the blue truck again, heading north on the south–north drag,' Beano muttered.

I repeated it back to him, as I wrote it down.

'There's the open-backed yellow pick-up, moving east towards the warehouse at the crossroads.'

I confirmed it and noted it down.

'That's three vehicles on the move now, what with the black SUV.'

Having noted everything Beano had reported, I crawled away to the rear area. It was 1300 and watch changeover time.

'Lads, change of shift,' I whispered. 'Crawl forward to Beano and he'll brief you in.'

I proceeded to curl up and sleep through my allotted time, while Beano took up our rear sentry position. Then we swopped over, me crawling beyond the admin area to the rear sentry point while Beano got his head down for a few hours. I kept watch south and east, in case we had any unwanted visitors coming at us the back way.

As I sat staring into the jungle, for a moment I wondered what someone who knew me from back home might think, if they stumbled upon me now. During our brief stopover in Rideau Camp we hadn't shaved or washed. To do so would have gone against how we approach such missions. But as a result we were coated in approaching five weeks' of stubble, sweat and shit, plus jungle detritus and grime.

Our faces were caked in thick layers of congealed camo cream mixed with mozzie repellent, our eyes staring out of them red-rimmed and more than a little crazed. I figured if Mum or Dad or Neil or even Grandma Doris Dring climbed up this hill, they'd most likely take one look at yours truly and run a mile. I just hoped the same could be said for any marauding narco-traffickers.

The sun set.

Darkness descended along the ridge.

A light wind got up and whipped away the sweat from my skin, leaving me freezing. I sat cross-legged, my weapon across my lap, still as a rock and staring into a wall of darkness. And I listened. At night, your vision becomes next to redundant. All that will warn you of approaching danger is your hearing, and strangely that sense becomes heightened, as if to compensate.

Above me a faint burst of starlight broke through the thinner bits of canopy, while beneath the trees there was just the slightest suggestion of the shimmer of the moon. Here and there a firefly flittered through the darkness, its fluorescent blue-green glow seeming to hang in mid-air, as if by magic.

From behind me the shitty, warped Mexico-beat drifted up from the settlement. The whole effect was utterly bizarre. I was staring into the pristine jungle, with its wild serenity and beauty, yet the soundtrack that bled through to my senses was Latino dance music played at the wrong speed, plus the odd snarl of a revving motorbike engine – for there were plenty of those beetling around Dodge.

An odd thought struck me as I stared into the emptiness. I'd heard the phrase 'hiding in plain sight'. In other words, not hiding, so people think you have nothing to hide. But Dodge was just so utterly in your face. So deliberate and blatant. So maybe – just maybe – the lieutenant-colonel's briefing had got Dodge totally wrong.

Maybe it wasn't a Central American drugs-runners' megastore, after all, and it wasn't populated by narco-rebels. Maybe it was just some odd kind of town that had spontaneously sprung up in the middle of nowhere, like a giant errant mushroom? Maybe the inhabitants of Dodge were all farmers or loggers or fishermen, or something, who had nothing to do with the drugs trade?

After all, so far we'd seen nothing that proved they were drug-runners.

Sure, the Gurkha patrol had got hit just a spitting distance away from here. And sure, the town didn't seem to give a damn about territorial integrity – spanning an international border as it did. And sure, you had to wonder how they made their money, if not via drugs.

But we couldn't discount it as a possibility – not until we had absolute proof that the inhabitants of Dodge really were up to their armpits in narco-dollars, and all the nasty shit that goes with it.

The following morning Andy managed to radio through a second sitrep: '*Zero, Three-Three*. Sitrep: current location OP situated at grid two two four eight one seven. Target details – grid two two four eight one eight. Activity: village active but no sign of narcotic movements. Continuing on task.'

Zero was the Gurkha commander's call-sign; *Three-Three* was us.

That done, we gathered for a communal heads-up. Overnight we'd secured more intel. The bar was more than just a bar: there were a dozen women working the place who appeared to be 'night fighters'. In other words, it doubled as a brothel. We'd all seen enough of them in our time to know what they looked like.

The rest of the inhabitants of Dodge were nearly all men. Young men, Latinos, wearing long pants and football shirts and with a good few sporting Stetson-style hats. There was a distinct lack of women – apart from the hookers – or kids, toddlers, babies in prams, or anything else that spoke of normal town life, or of domesticity.

In fact, the distinct impression was that Dodge was not a place where people settled or raised families, nor was it any kind of community at all. Somehow, it gave off this sense of being a place of work; of being all about money – of making large amounts of cash. But the million-dollar question remained – just what work were people doing here, and how was the money being made?

We'd drawn up several detailed sketch maps of the place, locating most of the significant buildings and their approximate dimensions – including the Toys R Us warehouse where the males tended to congregate and gather. And we'd recorded the routes driven by the vehicles, and the main points of ingress and exit to the settlement.

Subconsciously, we were doing so with a view to a force coming in at some time in the near future and prosecuting the target – though what that force might be was anyone's guess. Most likely, we were here doing a favour for an American agency; most likely, an anti-narcotics outfit; so maybe the DEA – the US Drugs Enforcement Agency.

In due course we'd probably be handing over the mission file to whoever was the force commander of that unit, and that meant we had to 'do our job and be the best', as Jon H would have put it. That was our priority right now.

We were building up a very good picture of what Dodge was about – we just didn't have any hard evidence or proof right now. Four days and counting to secure that evidence, and to complete our mission file and target briefings. If we failed, we'd get pulled out with our mission very much not-accomplished.

The unspoken question pinging around everyone's mind was this: *How far would we go to secure that evidence?* Back at Rideau Camp the lieutenant-colonel had asked us what we'd do if we needed to get closer. Closer to Dodge. We hadn't given an answer.

But as Pathfinders, failure to accomplish the mission really wasn't an option.

29

The three days that followed mushed into one dehydrated, sleep-deprived, sweat-soaked soup. It was pretty much déjà vu: observing, logging, reporting. Burning heat, voracious mozzies, flies as big as mice, rats as big as pigs and vicious stinging ants – it all took its toll. But nothing hurt or hampered us as much as the dehydration.

By the end of day three I had no fluid left in me to sweat out. I had a permanent splitting headache and I'd sweated myself dry. Even lying still and keeping movement to a minimum the heat was still oppressive, the thirst unbearable.

I craved water. We had one litre per person per day. Somehow we still had to retrace our steps through the jungle to the extraction LS, and we'd be starting out hopelessly dehydrated.

It didn't bear thinking about.

The one significant development was that we were seriously starting to worry whether Dodge was a valid target. Sure, the place was seedy, creepy and decidedly odd, but we'd yet to see one parcel of drugs getting shipped through. What if it was a duff tasking? If so, it was crucial that was reflected in our mission report: *Dodge City is not a valid target.*

But there were parts of Dodge we just couldn't see from our vantage point atop the ridge. In particular the far end where the settlement kinked hard right was out of our field of view. Maybe the answer lay there? Maybe if we got sight of that hidden area the purpose of Dodge would suddenly be revealed, in all its dark and menacing glory?

The night of day three I was in the admin position, with Andy sleeping and me on rear watch. All of a sudden three clear shots tore the night apart: Pthew! Pthew! Pthew! Andy came instantly awake and I was hyper-alert. The gunfire had come from the Dodge direction, but what did it signify exactly?

Andy eyed me in the darkness. 'What the fuck?'

I shrugged. If the shots had been aimed at our ridge-top position, Beano and Johno would have crawled back to warn us, so we could prepare to bug out. Instead, they'd stayed in their positions. We just didn't know what to make of it.

We stood-to – so with our weapons in the aim and covering our arcs. The shots had sounded like a series of crisp slaps – so most likely a 5.56mm Colt family rifle. Of course, our M16s were also Colts, and we hadn't exactly expected to hear that kind of weaponry being used in and around Dodge. Generally, the Colt was the weapon of the good guys. A 7.62mm chambered A47 would have been much more in keeping with what we were expecting.

A while later Beano crawled back to join us and we got a heads-up. 'Right, we were watching a normal Dodge scene. Same old same old. Just after midnight a large group of blokes came piling out of the whorehouse. Massive ruckus – a bar brawl spilling onto the streets. Then came the shots. No idea where they came from. As far as we could tell no one was dragged away dead or wounded. Gradually it all went back to normal. Or least, what passes as normal for Dodge.'

'One thing's for sure,' Andy whispered, 'we know they've got longs now.'

'Longs' was Army-speak for any weapon longer than a pistol or a machine pistol.

'Yeah,' I nodded. 'And another thing: no one ever plays football on the "football field". So maybe it isn't one. Maybe it's a parade ground?'

Andy eyed me for a second. 'Maybe. And those ditches that run down either side – maybe they aren't for drainage? Maybe they're defensive trenches. Battle trenches – just like we'd dig?'

The point was that we just didn't know. Tomorrow was day four – our last with eyes-on the target. We'd already received confirmation via radio that they were pulling us out on the afternoon of day five – most of which we'd spend collapsing the OP and trekking back to the LS. It looked as if Dodge was going to end up a duff tasking, even if by default.

We returned to our positions and drifted back to a troubled sleep or an equally troubled watch, as the night wore on.

The first morning watch of day four was mine and Andy's. We crawled across to the forward position. It was my turn on the scope though I wasn't expecting to see much.

It was around nine o'clock in the morning when the first of the mules hove into view. The animal nosed its way out of the hidden part of the town, towards the far northwest, and wandered its way down the main drag. It hit the crossroads, where the Toys R Us warehouse was situated, and I twirled the Swiftscope's focus ring and pulled it into crystal-clear clarity.

The donkey or mule – they didn't teach us packhorse identification in the Pathfinders – was a dirty off-white colour. At first I kept losing it as it plodded between the screen of trees or behind buildings, but not before I'd realised there were more of them coming on behind it.

I felt a kick of excitement to the guts: it looked like what we had here was a mule train. Andy scribbled furiously in his notebook while I kept mouthing commentary.

'Okay, that's nine mules now and counting . . . A column of 'em, either singly or in twos and three abreast . . . Plus there are escorts . . . I see three guys at least with the animals . . . Now there's six. Six escorts . . . They're dressed in combat fatigues, with wide-brimmed hats . . . I see twelve mules now . . . I keep losing 'em and finding 'em again . . . Each has got a wooden frame type thing on its back, with a blanket underneath to cushion it. Got to be for carrying loads . . .'

Finally, I lost track of them.

'Lost 'em,' I whispered to Andy, but the raw excitement in my voice was clear. 'They didn't reach the crossroads and they didn't go back into the jungle, so there's only one place they can be. They've gone to ground at the Toys R Us warehouse.'

'Okay, keep a close watch,' Andy replied. 'If a mule so much as farts in there I want to know about it.'

I kept my eye glued to the scope. For a good hour nothing more happened, but I felt convinced the appearance of the mules was a total game-changer. Of course, in theory the mules could be there to carry anything.

But in my heart I knew we had us a drugs caravan.

Around 12 o'clock midday I detected movement. The warehouse had a corrugated tin roof and sides, and around the corner nearest to the main drag appeared the first mule.

'Mule one spotted,' I whispered to Andy. 'At the warehouse. There's a large white sack slung over its back. Correction, two white sacks, kind of hung over the wooden saddle-frame.'

'Mule two – likewise. Mule three . . . Mule four . . .' I counted out the twelve animals, each of which was loaded up with white sacks. Now, it could in theory have been self-raising flour, for baking a load of Dodge City bread, but I really didn't think so.

I guess Andy could sense my burning excitement. 'Keep it calm, Steve, keep watching and keep giving me the commentary.'

'Okay, I've got their escort appearing now . . . That's one, two, three, six guys . . . More like a dozen now . . . Plus weaponry. Mostly I can see AR15s, but there's a couple of long-barrelled pieces and some shorter machine-pistol-type weapons . . .'

The Colt AR15 is the predecessor to the M16, and a fine assault rifle. If they were mostly armed with AR15s that would account for the shots we'd heard the other night.

'Okay, a lot of milling about now . . . Lot of blokes smoking . . . Bad for the health, that . . . Shouting instructions . . . Gesticulating . . . I'd say they're making their final plans before getting under way . . .'

The road was also getting busy now. Pick-ups and 4x4s buzzed about, carrying more blokes to and from the warehouse. But eventually, the main party with the mules formed up in a line – animals and escorts – and moved off, heading back the way they had come.

'I see sixteen mules now, all heavily loaded . . .' I commented to Andy. 'Donkeys aren't tied together, but ordered, walking single file . . . Plus I count maybe eighteen escorts now, all armed . . . Each walking with a weapon slung over their shoulder . . . All wearing DPM combats with those wide-brimmed hats . . . Okay, they're moving west on the main drag and more blokes are joining them . . . I count twenty now. At least twenty escorts . . .'

It was 2.30 in the afternoon by the time the mule train meandered out of sight, heading northwest into the jungle. I kept my eye glued to the scope for another twenty minutes, but Dodge had gone back to doing what Dodge did best – trying to look like a 'normal' jungle settlement.

No more mules.

No more white sacks.

No more weapons visible.

I turned to Andy. 'They loaded up their donkey train and fucked off. What else could it be if it isn't drugs?'

Andy nodded. 'If it's not drugs why all the guns? That's a fair amount of firepower they've got there.'

'Yeah. Like enough to mess with a Gurkha patrol.'

'Exactly.'

'But why so relaxed looking? They looked like they're untouchable. Like there's no threat. That's how they looked.'

'They left the place with twenty armed blokes. They may pick up more along the way. How would you be feeling, with that kind of firepower to hand?'

'Fair point. So where are they heading? They headed northwest – that's back into Guatemala.'

Andy shrugged. 'Don't know.'

'Who's in the warehouse? What're they using it for? Does it double as the armoury? Is that where the weapons are stored? Is that how they keep the village looking "normal"?'

'No idea. Lot of unanswered questions.' Andy paused. 'I think we need to get in closer. I'd like a closer look.'

'What're you thinking?'

'Extraction's tomorrow evening. Let's work on the assumption it'll take us the same time to get out as getting in. We'll have lighter loads, but that doesn't necessarily mean we'll be quicker. Presumption is the mother of all fuck-ups. So, we've got the remainder of today and tonight to build up a better picture.

'Think about it: all we've seen is some armed guys and some mules enter and exit the warehouse, carrying some kind of a load. If it is a drugs operation, we need to get a much closer look: we need a sense of entryways and exits; numbers of armed men; guards and guards shifts; defences.'

Andy glanced at me. 'I think we need to do a CTR.'

CTR stands for close target recce – in other words, getting as close as possible without getting killed, injured or worse still ... captured.

'Right. Yep. Okay, mate. Agreed.' I figured Andy was right. 'But, bear in mind, mate, to get close to Dodge means crossing the border from Belize into Guatemala, and everything that comes with that ... If we get seen, chased, shot-up, or worse still caught, it's cross-border, which is far heavier shit.'

Andy was silent for a second. I was the baby on the patrol, but that didn't mean for one moment he would discount what I'd said. 'Fair point. Right, I'll go get some feedback from the others. Stay here, and keep a bloody close eye.'

Andy wormed his way back into the undergrowth and was gone.

30

I kept my eyes glued to Dodge, but there was nothing. The place seemed to have sunk into its normal mid-afternoon torpor. Drug-running or no drug-running, this was siesta time, and the inhabitants of Dodge were taking it slow and easy.

Andy signalled me back for what we in the Pathfinders term 'calling prayers'. When a major decision such as this was needed, it was down to all on the patrol to have their say. Prayers gave everyone the opportunity to do so, regardless of their rank or role.

We gathered in a circle, kneeling, the four of us facing inwards, heads almost touching. More or less immediately Beano made it clear he was dead against what Andy was suggesting. His objections were all very reasonable if you took the emotion and the adrenaline out of the situation.

'The risks are too severe. We'll be on our own, with fuck-all firepower, no machine guns, no grenades – and up against who knows what if it all goes to ratshit. If we get caught, we'll be four blokes on the very nasty end of a very nasty load of shit – in a corrupt, criminal settlement that doesn't officially exist. We'll face torture, abuse and ransom – and that's if we're lucky.'

Beano eyed the three of us. What was there to say? He was dead right and we knew it.

'Technically, we'll be crossing the border into another sovereign nation,' Beano continued. 'Who the fuck ever gave us permission to do that? We'll be an embarrassment to our own government. They'll have to deny us. Say we went rogue. Plus we've got zero

ROEs. None.' A pause. 'Guys, we are not trained to wound, and if it does go tits-up – which it more than likely will – there's going to be a load of blood and body parts spread across the jungle, most likely ours and theirs.'

There was nothing much we could say to argue. Trouble was, despite all that I still wanted to go.

I turned to Andy. 'Mate, if a CTR's what you want to do I'll back you. I'm game.'

Beano shook his head. 'Look, the risks far outweigh any potential benefits.'

All eyes turned on Johno the Joker. If Johno sided with Beano it would be a hung vote, and caution would have to prevail. He rubbed one grimy, filthy hand across his shaven head.

His eyes narrowed. 'Fuck it, I'm up for it.'

It was three to one, which gave Andy the mandate he needed. 'It's decided, then: we'll do the CTR.'

'Well, you know my feelings on it,' Beano objected. 'You know how I feel.'

'Yeah, Beano, I know your feelings,' Andy countered. 'But a vote's been taken and we're gonna do it.'

'Right. I hear you. Okay.' Beano shrugged. 'If the decision's final, I'll get behind it.'

That was why at the end of the day I liked Beano. It was the mark of the man that against all his better judgement he'd come onside. It was typical Beano. He'd said exactly what he thought. Aired his views. But then he'd rallied behind the group decision, because that was what was needed right now.

And in truth, of course, we all knew that Beano was right. He was bang on. What we were about to do was insane. But votes cast, that wasn't going to stop us.

'Right, we're gonna pull back from here, do the CTR overnight, then move out for the helo pick-up,' Andy began. 'We'll collapse this position, put in a deception bearing, then swing north and make our way around the base of the ridge to a Bergen cache.

We'll ditch the packs and go to belt kit and grab bags. And from there we'll move around to the eastern edge of the clearing.'

The 'deception bearing' meant heading off in the opposite direction to the one we intended to take. We'd do it in case anyone picked up our trail, to lead them away from where we were actually heading. Early on, we'd leave the Bergens in a cache – a hide – so that we could move light and fast. That way, if the bad guys hit us we could make a run for the helicopter pick-up point as swiftly as possible.

'At the point where the canopy starts to thin we'll deposit Johno, a hundred yards back from the edge of the clearing,' Andy continued. 'We'll be moving in the dark, so we'll roll out a length of comms cord from Johno onwards. Where the cord meets the clearing we'll position Beano, as backup and fire support.'

The comms cord would serve several purposes. One, a tug on it from either end would signal 'enemy coming'. Two, it would serve to guide us from the clearing back to Johno, moving by feel alone. Plus Beano would be there to signal Andy and me back to our entry/exit point, and to draw any fire if it all went noisy.

'CTR team will be me and Steve,' Andy continued. 'If it all goes tits-up we RV with Beano, and trace the comms cord back to Johno, at which point we'll have vanished, as far as the bad guys are concerned. We'll go silent. It'll be impossible for anyone to track or trace us; we'll be dark, silent and invisible. We'll stay there until it's light enough to effectively E & E.'

'Right.'

'Great.'

'Sounds like a plan.'

Before collapsing our ridge-top position there was one thing we had to do: report in by radio to HQ.

Andy made the call. '*Zero, Three-Three.* Sitrep: current location OP. Update: seen mule train, unidentified cargo, plus escorts with guns. Continuing on task.'

'Roger. Out.'

That was all we ever got – 'roger, out' – so there didn't seem much point in mentioning the coming CTR.

Sitrep done we collapsed the Swiftscope, stuffed all our gear into the Bergens – including our cling film-wrapped parcels of four days' worth of poop – and prepared to move out.

'One more thing,' said Andy, as we heaved up our packs. 'With no ROEs, the default setting obviously is fire if fired upon. Use lethal force. But we're moving cross-border, into Guatemala, so I figure we need to prioritise.'

He glanced around the three of us. 'If we're compromised and fired upon the priority is to get back across the border, fast. Only return fire if pinned down and surrounded, and there's no other way. Otherwise, we make a run for Belize.

'Beano, unless me and Steve are taking horrendous amounts of fire, or I shout for you to engage, hold fire. The priority is to remain covert, disengage and bug out. Lads, the last thing we want to do is start slotting people the wrong side of the border.'

It was mid-afternoon by now. We turned east, dropped off the high ground, scrambled down the slope and put in a five-hundred-metre dash due east – our deception bearing. That done, we turned northwest, and trekked through the jungle to a point due north of our former ridge-top position.

We cast around in the jungle, settling upon two distinctive boulders about three feet high as a marker for the Bergen cache. Then we moved fifty metres due north of that feature, and that was where we dumped the packs. You'd never cache them on top of the distinctive feature itself, because that was too obvious a search point for any hostile force.

We piled the Bergens together and covered them in vegetation, until they were all but invisible. From here we'd move in 'light order' – so with belt kit, 'grab bag' and weaponry only. The grab bag is a small daypack that normally travels in the top of your Bergen. It's called a grab bag because if you do have to go on the run it contains your grab 'n' go emergency kit: medical pack, radio, batteries.

Normally, your grab bag would also be stuffed with spare ammo and grenades, but with only 120 rounds per man we had all of that on our person, where it was well accessible.

Bergens cached, we settled down to what the British Army does best – the hurry up and wait. We'd only start the final approach at last light – so when the jungle was still bright enough to navigate, but dark enough to conceal our movement.

We killed time with preparations – caking ourselves in a fresh layer of camo cream, covering every possible exposed piece of flesh. That done, we smeared more of the stuff over every piece of kit that might conceivably give off the slightest glimmer under the lights of Dodge City.

We checked each other from head to toe, just to ensure we'd not missed anything. We checked over all our gear to make sure nothing would jingle or clatter about as we moved. Anything that made the slightest sound was muffled with a fresh application of khaki green gaffer tape. By the time we were done, we could move utterly silently and we were completely blacked out.

Finally, we checked that we had a round up the spout of our M16s, so we could return fire instantly if we were set upon by the bad guys. As we went through these procedures, a part of me still could not believe we were about to do this: to move as a two-man team and penetrate into the very heart of Dodge.

The forest shadows lengthened.

The light was fading fast.

Andy gave the signal to move out. As far as possible, not a word would be spoken between us now: it would all be done with hand signals.

We flitted through the darkening jungle as silent as wraiths. When we reached the drop-off point for Johno, we took the comms cord off him and started to play it out through the trees, every footfall taking us closer to where the cover ended and the real danger began.

By the time we got close to the clearing we'd dropped to a hunch, here and there slivers of man-made light marking where the protective screen of vegetation petered out. The sounds of Dodge City – previously deadened by the jungle – began to filter through: the rhythmic put-put-put of the generators; the incessant Latino beat; a vehicle engine echoing through the trees; the odd human cry.

Close now.

We reached the edge of the clearing.

Beano took up position just inside the trees.

I moved ahead at a crouch, Andy sticking some five metres behind me.

We hit the open and I went down on one knee, Andy doing likewise. It would be a good few seconds before our eyes got accustomed to the light level here. From the darkness of the forest we were now in a zone where the lights of Dodge bled out into the city limits.

As our eyes adjusted, more and more detail became clear. Before us lay an expanse of cleared ground that had been hacked and burnt out of the jungle. The terrain was a mixture of charred, blackened tree stumps, a fresh knee-high growth of weeds, plus what appeared to be crude ridges of old vegetation, heaped as if ready to burn.

Vision adjusted, I turned left and moved along the fringe of the jungle, counting my paces, my eyes alert for what we needed to locate next. I found it after 120 left footfalls, and went down on one knee. Andy came up on my shoulder.

Nodding at an odd-shaped stump lying to my left, I said: 'Okay, mate, V-shaped tree-stump: that's our datum point.'

'Okay,' Andy confirmed, his voice barely above a whisper. 'How many paces you done from Beano?'

'A hundred and twenty.'

'Me too. We reach the datum point we know it's a hundred and twenty paces north along the tree-line, and that gets us back to Beano.'

'You got it.'

The reason we needed the datum point was that we'd never find Beano otherwise. He was a black form amidst a black wall of vegetation, so basically invisible. The V-shaped stump was very distinctive; it stood out like the proverbial dog's bollocks. It was our marker to lead us back to our fire-support man, and from there we could trace the cord back to escape and to safety.

Datum point established, we planned to do a 360-degree scan of the target. We'd follow the wall of jungle, stopping at the four cardinal points – due east, south, west and north. At each we'd sit or lie completely still and observe, noting down all we could see. At the end of the 360 we should have a full picture of Dodge, and hopefully have found a master probe position – the point from which we could do the unthinkable, and push right into the very centre of the place.

We needed to discover some means via which we could sneak in, getting close to the warehouse in particular, and without being detected. We had no idea how we might do that yet – but methodically executing the 360 scan was the only way to find out.

Moving off from our V-shaped tree, we pushed into more open terrain. To our right the glow of the town threw a halo of orange into the overarching darkness. From that direction we could hear shouts drifting across to us, plus screams, and snatches of raucous laughter. It was getting towards the witching hour in Dodge, when the wild partying would begin.

Being lead scout my senses felt incredibly heightened; honed as sharp as a razor blade. I was acutely aware of how real was the threat. A horrendous feeling gripped me – the fear of impending capture. Dead would be okay. Getting home safe and sound would be better. But getting taken captive in Dodge – I'd rather boil and eat my own head.

Tension crackled back and forth through the shadows. The adrenaline was pumping. We were two, pitting ourselves against dozens – *scores* – of the bad guys. And these were a drugs mafia in a lawless no man's land. As bad guys went, they didn't get a great deal worse.

Andy and I were living the task now. We were a hundred per cent absorbed in what we were doing. This was the point when Jon H's immortal phrase really had to mean something: *Do your job and be the best.* After all the exhaustive training we'd undertaken, this was where the rubber hit the road.

For a fleeting moment I remembered Beano's warning: *The risks far outweigh any potential benefits.*

For our sakes, I hoped we were about to prove him very fucking wrong.

31

We reached the first cardinal: time for a ten-minute pause to observe. It was so hot and humid my combat trousers were soaking wet, and sticking to my legs. For a moment we turned to face each other, automatically giving each other the once over and checking we hadn't sweated off any camo cream.

That done, we focused in on Dodge. At first we tried looking through the CWS (common weapon sight) night-vision scopes attached to our M16s, but they were pretty useless. When trying to observe a human settlement lit up by artificial light, the illumination is too strong for such night-vision equipment. The lights at the target bleed into one blinding, confused mass.

We lowered the scopes and settled in to watch using nothing more sophisticated than the human eyeball. Everything we did right now had to be slow, methodical and unhurried. I sat shoulder-to-shoulder with Andy, dead still, and we watched silently.

Up on the ridgeline we'd had a couple of massive spiders rampage through the OP, plus we'd had enormous hornets buzzing around. But the real issue had been the flies. They'd settled on the parts of our sweat-soaked bodies we couldn't easily reach – the back, around the ears, the head – and chomped away. They were after the salt we were sweating out, and the resulting itchiness would drive you stir crazy.

Here, sat some two hundred metres out from the fringe of jungle, the trouble was the mozzies. They buzzed and whined around our heads in a thick and ravenous cloud. There was nothing we could do about it but sit and get bitten. Silence and stillness was everything. One rapid movement – one little swat – could give the entire game away.

'Did you see that?' Andy whispered.

I'd seen it.

A car had barrelled down the main drag, its lights flashing away. Did that signify something? What did it mean? Was the driver warning that a hostile force had been detected, and for the gunmen to stand-to? Or was it just a bloke heading to the bar-cum-brothel, and signalling in advance the number of ladies-of-the-night he was after?

Then silence for what seemed like forever. It was probably only a minute, but it felt like an age.

'See that?' Andy prompted again. 'That crowd?'

No doubt about it, downtown Dodge was getting busy. It looked as if a good sixty people had converged on the central crossroads, around the warehouse-cum-bar area. Question was, were they there for their nightly piss-up or to break out the guns?

We moved off.

We hit a further cardinal and did the watch again. Still there was no obvious master probe position – a point from which there was a clear route to take us into the target unseen. It was when we were moving from cardinal number two to number three that I stumbled upon something.

Or rather, I all but fell into it.

I set my right foot down carefully, only to feel a distinct lack of ground beneath it. I'd been so concentrated on the threat emanating from Dodge that I'd missed what lay right before me, and practically tumbled in. Catching myself, I teetered on one leg, then managed to pull back onto terra firma.

I stared.

Before me lay a wide ditch filled with water.

I signalled Andy to a halt, and he came up close on my shoulder.

Nodding towards the feature, I ran my eyes down its length. Andy did likewise. My intention was clear. While we didn't have a clue how deep the water was, we could see the ditch stretching off more or less dead straight and leading into the heart of the hidden city. The light from downtown Dodge glimmered on its stagnant, gunky surface, like a mermaid beckoning us in.

We stared at each other, before Andy put it into words. 'Right, mate, in we go . . . Let's use the ditch.'

No point hanging around. I turned and lowered myself in, feeling for something solid with my boots. My feet came to rest in the gloopy shit at the bottom, the water around my waist level. The side of the ditch stretched a yard above me, shielding most of me from view.

In short it was perfect, all apart from . . . the smell, plus the identity of whatever else it was that shared the ditch with us. To left and right nameless, shapeless things slithered and plopped about in the darkness. There wasn't the slightest current to the water, because it wasn't flowing anywhere.

It was a filthy, thick, stagnant, swampy shithole of a place.

Andy joined me. For a moment we exchanged whispers, trying to fathom out the ditch's purpose. Was it an open sewer? It smelled bad, but maybe not that bad – plus there were no obvious turds or flecks of bog-roll floating about on the surface. Was it a drainage ditch? Hardly likely, with the water flowing nowhere.

Was it defensive? We didn't think so, as it ran in entirely the wrong direction. It didn't run moat-like around the edge of Dodge; it arrowed into the heart of the place. In any case, who ever would want to sit in a ditch full of water to carry out their watch? Only fruit-cases and lunatics – *and Pathfinders* – would choose to spend a stint in here.

Maybe it was something to do with the drugs? Maybe they processed the drugs here in Dodge? Maybe the warehouse was a factory – a refinery – and they needed the water as part of that process. Maybe we were wading through a cocaine infusion: one gulp and we'd be off our faces?

Who fucking knows?

All we did know was that it was perfect terrain for us.

Pathfinders are taught to operate in a different reality, to embrace what others fear. We're taught to own the night; to inhabit the darkness. We're trained to be totally at home under moonlight, in starlight and deep black. Darkness is the cloak in which to hide. We learn to love it, and to make of it our own.

We're taught to seek out the kind of terrain – horrendous swamplands, burning desert and remote and inhospitable bush – which is largely abandoned by sane human populations, because those are the kinds of places within which covert operators like us can thrive. No other right-minded people should be there, which means we can move through them undetected and prosecute our mission.

Just like this shitty little ditch, right now. Only a head-case would want to join us in here, and that's why – despite everything – it was pretty much perfect.

I turned to Andy. 'Happy?'

'Happy,' he confirmed.

Turning to face the way ahead, I slipped down until I was kind of on my hands and knees, my head just out of the water, my right hand gripping the pistol grip of my weapon. Like this I figured we could half-crawl and half doggie-paddle ahead, while maintaining the lowest possible profile.

The tips of my fingers gripped the muddy bottom as my boots shoved me into motion from behind. Underfoot – *beneath my fingers* – was a mass of decayed, rotting vegetation, thick mud, and God only knew what else. My left hand sank up to my wrist, as I used it to drag my way ahead.

Nice.

I kept the M16's barrel and its working parts held out of the water, the butt supported on my forearm.

I did this for five minutes or so, trying to count the push-offs with my legs and translate it into distance covered. When I figured we'd gone around fifty yards I stopped. Sliding up to the right bank, to maximise cover, I raised my head ever so, ever so slowly.

I felt Andy appear beside me, his chin practically on my right shoulder, up tight against my back. Together, our two heads emerged, plus the gaping barrel of each of our M16s.

We each chose an arc within which to search, keeping the other briefed on whatever we'd detected. That way, you try to build up as detailed a picture of the terrain and the threat in the shortest time possible.

'I see a wagon,' I whispered. 'Crammed. Maybe a dozen guys in the rear.'

'Direction of travel?'

'Lights on moving east on the main drag, so away from us.'

'Weapons?'

'None that I can see.'

Andy swivelled his eyes around, scanning the terrain. 'I see pedestrians. A group of eight, maybe more. Moving away from the main crossroads, towards us.'

'Weapons?'

'None visible.'

'It's gone back to being Undercover Dodge.'

'Looks like.'

We were both acutely aware of the time. It had taken us three hours from leaving Beano to dropping into the ditch, in which time we'd covered no more than a few hundred metres. Any faster and a CTR gets rushed, and that can prove fatal. It was now just past 10 p.m. Here in the open, first light would be around 6 a.m. – so eight hours away.

Time was running out.

On a CTR the exfil – getting out again – is arguably the most dangerous part. There's a big temptation to hurry. You have the intel and you want to get out and get it radioed back to HQ. The adrenaline is burning off and fatigue is settling in. We knew Dodge would start to settle down around 3 a.m. if it followed its normal nightly pattern. Fewer people around would mean less chance of getting seen.

But it was crucial we left ourselves enough time for the exfil. We had to be back in the cover of the jungle by first light. If not, we were done for.

'Right, Steve, crack on, mate. Push on.'

I slid into the belly down position and paddled onwards through the mire. As I pushed ahead I could hear the plop and splash and thrashing of whatever critters were moving through the water. My face was about level with the surface, and there seemed to be movement on every side.

Worse still, I could feel the odd creature working its way in. On my back, my inner thighs – even around my neck – I'd felt that familiar, faintly stinging bite sensation, as a leech attached itself. Jaws inserted, they would now be merrily sucking away, ingesting a gut-load of my blood.

It was horrible.

But there was jack I could do about it.

For some reason – maybe the sheer, razor-edged fear and the buzz – I'd been dying for a piss ever since we'd left the cover of the jungle. The nearer we got to the centre of Dodge the worse it seemed to get. I was close to bursting.

I turned to Andy. 'Mate, I'm busting for a piss.'

All I could make out against the dark of the water were the whites of his eyes. They twitched back and forth. 'Can't do it, mate. Don't do it.'

Andy was right. The golden rule of crossing jungle water is never take a piss. If you do, you open up your urethra and all kinds of bacteria and parasites can swim up your urine stream and take up residence in your bladder. There is even a fish in the jungle that allegedly likes to do so. It's called the candiru fish – or the 'toothpick fish' – and it extends its spines so you can't pull it back out again.

I thought momentarily about the candiru fish and decided I wouldn't have a pee. Either I held it until we were out of this stinking ditch and safely back in the jungle, or until the narco gang grabbed hold of us.

That would be my condemned man's last wish: I want to take a piss.

32

We'd completed ten silent watching stints from the cover of the ditch. The noise, the sights and the smells of Dodge were all around us now – to front, right, left and rear. It had taken two hours to complete the crawl, it was midnight in downtown Dodge, and boy was it ever getting lively.

We could hear loud shouting and drunken laughter from the direction of where we figured the bar-cum-whorehouse had to lie. By my calculations it was a hundred yards to our front right. Then there was the noise of what sounded like a street brawl, the thud of fists pounding flesh interspersed with angry yells and cries.

The Toys R Us warehouse should be just to our left, on the opposite side of the crossroads, and that was where we figured the greatest threat would emanate from. We moved to that side of the ditch, in preparation for lifting our heads and our gun barrels above ground level.

My heart was beating like a fucking machine gun as we inched out of the foetid water and raised ourselves higher, to the point where we'd get a real eyeful of Dodge.

I was about to ease myself over the very lip when: PCHTHEW! PCHTHEW! PCHTHEW! PCHTHEW!

I froze, as did Andy, our faces pressed tight into the mud. That was three shots from a Colt AR15, and they'd sounded up-close and personal. All we could do was keep utterly still and silent, and try to use our sense of hearing to work out what the fuck was going on.

A series of irate yells were exchanged across the road junction.

On one side it sounded like the blokes from the bar brawl kicking up hell. On the other, it sounded as if someone was shouting angrily from the direction of the warehouse. Whoever it was on the warehouse side seemed to win the shouting match, for the noise from the bar gradually died down again.

'Warning shots,' Andy mouthed at me.

'Sounds like.'

We both figured the same thing. That was Dodge's equivalent of a bunch of RMPs on horseback, getting a load of drunken PARAs to wind their necks in.

Gunshots or no, it was time to get this done.

I eased my head above the edge of the ditch. As soon as I did so the sights and sounds assaulted me. The ditch had kept us somewhat sheltered. Badly distorted Latino beat pulsed out of speakers bolted to the roof of the nearest building, and all around us people were milling about in wild confusion.

It was like Aldershot on a Friday night, only this place wasn't supposed to exist, and it was bereft of even the vaguest modicum of the rule of law. We were right in the heart of Dodge now – spitting distance close – and still no one seemed to have seen us, or got wise to our presence.

Just then I felt a tap on the shoulder. 'There's too much going on,' Andy hissed. 'Divide forces. You take the buildings; I'll do the people.'

What he meant was that I was to note down all the building details, and he'd do likewise with the human occupants.

I nodded.

I started with the bar. It lay a hundred yards to my left, a rickety-looking wooden construction with a series of bright neons bolted to the roof. I couldn't understand the Spanish wording. Probably 'Best Beer & Girls This Side of Texas'. But the neon beer bottle signs needed no translating.

A crowd swayed back and forth in front of the bar's open doors. It was ninety-nine per cent male, and not a man among them was without a beer bottle clutched in one hand. A good number had weapons – mostly pistols – clenched in the other, or strapped into holsters slung on their belts.

Just a normal night in Dodge, by the looks of things.

Two women in extremely short skirts were catcalling from the bar's steps, trying to entice the nearest drunken bandido into their arms. I couldn't understand the words, but I got the meaning nonetheless. *Come on, you pigs! Which of you is sober enough to prove your manhood with one of our lovely girls?*

I was about to volunteer, but figured I'd get a rocket from Andy.

I looked beyond the bar. The dirt road snaked off into the jungle, its path lit up by these crazy strings of light bulbs hanging from tree trunks driven into the ground. The whole place gave off the impression of having sprung from the jungle like a rash, practically overnight. And there was a sense that the jungle could just as quickly suck it all back in again.

Swivelling my eyes left, I brought my gaze to rest on the warehouse. It looked to be some forty metres wide by sixty long, and both the sides and the roof were of 'wriggle-tin'. The galvanised iron looked shiny and new, as if the place had only recently been thrown up. I estimated it to be around one and a half stories – twenty feet – high.

There were no neons on the building's roof. No Toys R Us sign. It was set back from the road a good twenty yards and it was half-screened by vegetation on all sides. Whatever went on down at the warehouse, there was a dark sense about the place – as if it didn't want to advertise its wares.

The roof was of a low-ridge construction, and there was a window in the end nearest to us. A light was burning inside. The window was large enough and at the right height for an assault force to smash their way through and gain entry. On the long side visible to us there was a large sliding door, which right now was set slightly ajar. Two guys were hanging around the crack in the door: *sentries.*

I took a moment to wipe away the gunk that had dripped off my hair into my eyes. Every movement I made was very, very slow and very, very deliberate. I couldn't see with shit in my eyes, hence the movement couldn't be avoided. Just as I'd cleared my vision a vehicle pulled up at the warehouse.

A pick-up, with four men in the rear.

They jumped down and headed inside. A couple of narco-rebel types came out and climbed aboard, and the pick-up pulled away, nosing through the bar crowd and speeding off to the far end of the village.

Change of sentry. Had to be.

Moments later shots rang out: *Chthudd! Chthudd! Chthudd!*

I hit the dirt instinctively, but even as my adrenaline spiked my mind was processing the sound. Low velocity 9mm pistol rounds, for sure. Which meant trouble at the bar-cum-whorehouse. *Got to be.*

I glanced at Andy, who confirmed what I'd just been thinking.

'Bar fight,' he mouthed at me.

I levered my face out of the slimy gunk at the edge of the ditch and chanced a look in the direction of the town's watering hole. High spirits, whoring, beer and bravado, plus a good bit of gun-slinging: without it, you just couldn't have a proper night out in Dodge.

There was a very marked difference between the activity I was witnessing here and that over at the warehouse. The bar was packed with wild party people. By contrast, everything about the warehouse was quiet, serious and darkly businesslike.

I lay still and surveyed the place some more. I was checking for any guard dogs, for any roving patrols, and for any electronic surveillance or other security measures they might have in place. Basically, anything that might hinder an assault force from prosecuting the target.

From what I could see now, the process of loading the mule train seemed a lot, lot clearer. I could see the point at which we must have lost sight of them: there was a small track branching off the dirt road, leading into the rear yard of the warehouse. That was how the mules must have been taken in.

They'd been loaded up with their sacks of dope, marshalled in the yard once more, then led onto the road and into the jungle.

The centre of gravity for any coming raid had to be this warehouse, that much was clear. It had to be hit hard, locked down and neutralised, before the wider inhabitants of Dodge could manage to muster any collective resistance.

By the numbers we'd seen, we figured there had to be several hundred men here in Dodge. We reckoned there were the growers, the croppers, those processing the shit in the warehouse, and those tasked with shipping it out by mule train. It was a big old operation, and any assault force would have to hit the place by utter surprise – with such a shock and awe factor – to deter any resistance.

Fortunately, we had just worked out their means of doing so. If the two of us could crawl several hundred metres through this ditch and get to within striking distance of the target, so could a bunch of Delta Force operators, or Navy SEALs. Rather than flying in gung-ho and all guns blazing, they could sneak in silent and unseen, and strike without warning.

And that was the kind of intel that made the present risk more than worthwhile. I thought back to Beano's words: *The risks far outweigh any potential benefits.* If we got out of this alive, we'd have vindicated the decision to conduct the CTR.

We figured it was time to start the long crawl out. As we moved off, we traded hushed whispers, swopping all the intel that we'd learned. It was crucial to do so, in case one or other of us got hit or taken captive.

For if that happened and we'd kept vital intel to ourselves, it would die with us.

33

It was 2.30 a.m. when we turned around and started the long crawl back. There were four hours until first light, and we needed to be back in the jungle by then. Of necessity, we made better progress than before.

By the time we crawled out of Dodge's cocaine sewer it was already 4.40 a.m. I led off, reversing our bearings, until I picked out the V-shaped tree stump. Datum point found, I moved to the north of that, counting out my paces. When I hit 'one hundred and fifteen', I called out softly into the darkness.

'Beano!'

'Yep.'

There he was in his fire position on the fringes of the canopy. It was 0545 by now, and we'd just completed an eleven-hour CTR. Towards the east the horizon was shooting up with track marks of red and pink, as the jungle awoke to a new dawn.

We'd made it just in time.

Grabbing the comms cord, we traced it into the jungle shadows. Soon, all was darkness again, and it felt good. Mighty good. I was leading, and Beano was taking up the rear, coiling up the comms cord as he went.

As we neared Johno's position I could just make him out in the gloom, kneeling with his weapon at the ready. If I could see him I figured he could see me, so no need to make a call announcing our arrival.

All four of us knelt, facing inwards, bare inches separating our faces.

'We did the three sixty, found a ditch, moved through that into the centre of the place and . . .' Andy began, as he briefed the others in.

Intel disseminated as best we could, it was time to move. With every second the forest was brightening imperceptibly and we needed to get ourselves gone.

'Okay, Steve, quick as you can – back to the Bergen cache.'

I needed no second urging. After taking a few seconds to empty my bladder – it was now or never – I set off, counting my footfalls as I went. I navigated back to the two distinctive boulders, located the Bergens, peeled off my sweat-soaked daysack, stuffed it inside, strapped down the top and hauled it on.

Andy pulled his map out. 'Okay, we're here. Put a southeast bearing on your compasses. Head five hundred metres southeast, as the deception bearing. Once that's done, turn due east and head for the helo pick-up point. Steve, stop once we're an hour and a half in, so we can send a sitrep and get some breakfast.'

Ninety minutes later we'd put a good two kilometres between us and the narco-rebels' location. We stopped. I stood watch with Johno, while Beano and Andy got the radio working. It was vital we got a message through, just to check there were no changes to the helicopter pick-up plan.

That confirmed, we set about the next priority: de-leeching.

With Johno and Beano on stag, I got together with Andy and we arranged our Bergens facing inwards. Then we went to it. First off – trousers down, to check the leeches' favourite place: around and on your manhood. Sure enough, my groin was a mass of writhing, glistening bodies. It looked like a mini version of Medusa's head.

Leeches.

God how I hated them.

Black bodies, each by now engorged to five times its normal length. When the first leech had slithered up my trouser leg, searching for somewhere warm and snug to attach itself, it had been the size of a small pen cap. Now, after six hours' feeding it was swollen to the size of a marker pen.

'Lighter?' Andy offered.

The most satisfying way to get rid of them is to burn the bastards off. The second most satisfying method is to douse them in insect repellent, and watch them twist and worm.

I grabbed Andy's lighter but I knew I really shouldn't have. Leeches secrete an anaesthetic in their saliva, so the victim doesn't feel much pain when they bite. Once attached, they pump hirudin, a powerful enzyme, into your veins, to stop the blood from clotting. That enables them to feed and feed and feed.

If you put a naked flame to one it immediately contracts, withdraws its teeth and drops off – but in the process it voids a big chunk of its stomach contents into your bloodstream. In other words, it vomits all the blood back into your veins, including any diseases the leech might be carrying.

But I hated leeches, and I was dying to see the bastards burn. I flicked the lighter, lowered the flame and watched the first one hiss, writhe and sizzle. After a few seconds it dropped off, leaving a stream of blood pouring down my leg. The anti-coagulant would make the wound bleed for some time, but I'd just have to live with that.

I pulled up my shirt and did a repeat performance, using British Army mozzie repellent on those I couldn't reach with the naked flame. That done, I got a cold bag of food down my neck, plus a swig or two of water – pretty much all I had left. Then I got my weapon ready to take over stag, while Beano and Johno did the same as we'd done.

The remainder of the day was one hard slog. All my food was eaten now, and had been replaced with two plastic bottles of piss and a cling film wrap of turds. I was so hungry and thirsty I was actually looking forward to a Gurkha classic – a mess-tin of curried aardvark, all washed down with gallons of sweet, milky, spicy tea.

We reached the helo pick-up point after a six-hour beast. Leaving Johno and Beano with the Bergens, I went with Andy to a point at the canopy's edge where we could get eyes-on the clearing. We checked its suitability for a landing, and made sure there was no evidence of any hostile presence. That done, we settled down to wait.

At just prior to 1530 we heard the faint beat of helo rotors. All four of us moved into the centre of the LS, in preparation to board. I stood with my back to the wind holding an orange air marker panel (AMP) above my head. An AMP is a foldable piece of fluorescent vinyl that collapses to the size of a deck of cards. It serves a dual function: it helps identify us as friendly forces, and provides an obvious visual marker for the pilot to home in on.

As the Puma appeared over the ragged fringe of jungle, I saw the pilot spot me and my AMP and adjust his line of approach, and then he was flaring out to land. He came down nose-on to me, fifteen metres in front. I gave the thumbs-up to the pilot, signalling they were down safely, and got the same in return.

We crabbed around to the side door, and threw the Bergens up to the loadie, who stacked them in the rear. I couldn't help but notice the look on his face, as he clocked the state of us. Probably the smell, too. Moments later we clambered aboard and the Puma was airborne, streaking east just a few feet above the trees.

I sat there in the noise and the slipstream, the heady smell of avgas – aviation fuel – thick in my nostrils, and relived the mission in my mind. The five days we'd spent in the jungle felt like as many months. I still could not believe that we'd been right in the very midst of the bad guys, and got away with it.

The noise made talk impossible, but as I glanced at the others – Andy, Beano and Johno – I could see by the smiles on their dirt and shit-streaked faces that they were feeling exactly the same as I was.

We'd done it.

Against all the odds we'd pulled it off.

We'd done the job and been the best – or at least as good as it gets.

We'd got in and out again without a single shot being fired and more than completed our task. *Do your job; be the best.*

The Puma dropped towards the LS at Rideau Camp. Through the open side door I could see a tall, wiry figure waiting for us. Lieutenant-Colonel Nick Stanley-Price, if I wasn't mistaken.

We piled out, grabbed our Bergens and made our way over to him.

'Morning, boss.'

'Good morning.' He smiled. A rare thing with the lieutenant-colonel. Next thing he went from man to man, shaking us all by the hand.

He paused at Andy. 'I hear a well done is in order. When will you be ready to back brief me?'

'Just as long as it'll take us to put a report together.'

'Good. As soon as you're ready then.'

He turned and began the climb up to the camp proper. We heaved up our Bergens and followed, heading for the bean-tin hut where we'd been billeted. We left everything we could outside in a stinking, fly-blown heap. Then we broke out our reporting files: every Pathfinder carries a waterproof fiche containing half a dozen pieces of lined paper, blank paper for sketching, graph paper for grids, plus coloured pens and pencils.

Andy gave Beano the job of writing up our notes from the moment the Puma dropped us to the moment we left our OP on the ridge. He gave Johno the job of putting together all the sketches that we'd made from the high ground – the panoramics. That left me and Andy to write up a report on our CTR, including plotting the exact location of Dodge vis-à-vis the border.

An hour or so later we joined the lieutenant-colonel in the briefing room. Andy talked him through the entire mission, culminating in us crossing the border and doing the CTR. I noticed that Lieutenant-Colonel Stanley-Price had a distinctly raised-eyebrows expression on his face – *You did what?*

Andy shrugged. 'We weren't in a position to give you the accuracy you needed, so we took a calculated risk. It paid off. It means I'm one hundred per cent confident in the information I'm giving you now,' Andy added.

He handed over the written reports. Lieutenant-Colonel Stanley-Price eyed them for a second, then glanced at the four of us. 'Job well done. I have someone I need to get this to, pronto. In the meantime, get yourself squared away, ammo handed in, and go get a feed on.'

We thanked him and returned to our billet. After we'd debombed our mags, cleaned our M16s, and scrubbed our kit, we went for a shower – which was sheer and total bliss. It was midnight by the time we sat down to a bucket-load of curry and a pint of tea, all courtesy of Captain Lars Singh.

In the circumstances, what could be better?

That night we slept the sleep of the dead. We'd been on the go for thirty-six hours solid, with prior to that four days of snatching sleep here and there between watch duties. We were beyond exhausted. Over breakfast the following morning we got a more detailed heads-up from the lieutenant-colonel.

'Fantastic job, guys,' he enthused. 'Bloody well done. Hope you're well rested? Look, I figure you need a bit of down time, after all that . . . So, I've sorted out a Puma to fly you out, so you can have four days R&R in Ambergris Caye. I figure you've earned it.'

Ambergris Caye is an island resort located some thirty kilometres off the coast of Belize. Rumour had it that it was very nice indeed.

'Good stuff.'

'Cheers, boss.'

'Thank you very much.'

He smiled. 'Ten o'clock – the Puma will be in for you.'

We flew out of Rideau Camp heading for sun, sea and beer, and we couldn't have been happier. But of course, in the back of our minds – Andy's, Beano's, Johno's and my own – was always the hope: the hope that we would be the ones who'd get to prosecute the target; that we would get to wreak righteous vengeance on Dodge.

But even with a full complement of Pathfinders – we were a twenty-nine-strong unit by then – there was no way we were going to take out Dodge on our own. We could guide the main force in, which is a classic Pathfinder role. We could be the pointy tip of the spear. But it would take real grunt, muscle and firepower to put an end to a place the size and strength of Dodge, once and for all.

As we flew out of Rideau Camp we nurtured a quiet hope. We'd had eyes-on the place. We'd been right in there. Who better to lead the assault force to smash the narco-rebels?

And so we crossed our fingers and said a prayer that we'd be back, even as we jetted into Ambergris Caye.

34

For some unknowable reason Beano decided to break the habit of a lifetime, the day we hit Ambergris Caye. Maybe it was all the stress of the mission, especially the CTR: *The risks far outweigh any potential benefits*. Who knows?

Either way, just as soon as we checked into our beachside resort Beano decided to start drinking. *Alcohol.* I'd expected him to go mad for the chocolate. Instead, he went loony for the Jamaican rum punch. The rum is 40 per cent proof, and it's mixed with tropical fruit juices and served in a coconut, with a paper umbrella and a straw to drink it through.

We ended up taking an evening walk down the beach road, which was lined with car and truck tyres cut in half, forming a kind of fence. Beano decided to rugby tackle every one and knock them out of the sand.

'Go on, Beano,' we urged him, even after he'd dislocated his shoulder. 'Get the next one. Smash it!'

Beano was what you would call a two-pint psycho. He spent the rest of our time on Ambergris Caye nursing the mother of all hangovers. But hell, no one had forced him. He only had himself to blame. After he'd dipped into the evil brew he decided he really did not like it, so he went back to fizzy pop and chocolate bars, leaving the three of us to enjoy the beer.

On our third day we decided it was time to pay a visit to the world-famous San Pedro Shark Bar. The bar stands a good hundred yards out to sea and is accessed via a rickety pier. It's a circular construction with a pool in the middle, so a bit like a wooden doughnut on stilts.

You walk in the door, and the centre is open to the sea. Below is a circular pool, thirty feet wide, with chairs and tables set around it. In the pool are a shedload of sharks. They can't get away, because around the base of the structure is a strong metal cage. So they have to swim around looking at the people above them, wondering how they can get to have a chomp on one of their legs.

We ordered some beers and leaned on the railing surrounding the pool, gawping at the sharks. There was a big hammerhead, a tiger shark, a couple of lemon sharks, some nurse sharks and two massive rays. They were circling around and around looking trapped, angry and menacing. We decided we liked the place and would stay for a while.

By the evening we'd run out of cash. This was serious. No more money meant no more beer, which was just not acceptable.

'Anyone got any more money?' I asked, for the umpteenth time.

'No.'

'Nope.'

'Me neither,' I said. 'I'm skint.'

All eyes turned to Beano. We knew he had money, because he'd not been drinking and so had missed out on any number of rounds.

He glared at us. 'I told you: I am never ever buying another drop of alcohol.'

I glanced over at a group of middle-aged American tourists, leaning against the railing running around the shark pool. 'Okay, right, here we go: I've got an idea.'

I wandered over. They were all goofing off about the fish. 'Hey, man – sharks. Look at those sharks.'

'Excuse me.'

They glanced my way, They didn't look entirely overjoyed at my interruption. I guess I was a bit the worse for wear: I had a three-day growth and a belly full of beer.

I nodded at the water. 'You've seen the sharks?'

'Seen the sharks? How could we miss 'em!'

'Right. How much would you pay to see someone swim with the sharks?'

'Ha-ha, buddy. Yeah, good one.'

'No, seriously. How much would you pay to see someone swim with them?'

The nearest guy's eyes bulged. 'You serious?'

'Yep.'

They exchanged glances. They were clearly interested, but for all they knew I might just take their money and run. It didn't exactly look as if they were built for speed.

'Would you pay me a hundred dollars?'

They stared at me, as if they were waiting for me to burst out laughing, and inform them it was all a big joke. Which, of course, it wasn't.

'Would you pay me a hundred dollars?' I repeated.

'Hell, man, I'd pay you a hundred dollars. Sure I would.'

'Right,' I told the money-man. 'Get your cash out.'

He pulled out a fat wallet and waved a hundred-dollar bill around.

'Right,' I said. 'I'll be back.'

I walked over to Andy. 'Right, mate, we're gonna make some money here. I've got these Yanks and they're gonna pay a hundred bucks to see someone swim with the sharks. I'll do it – you make sure you get the money.'

Andy was onside immediately. 'Right, okay, mate, go for it.'

The bar was packed by now and getting well into the evening swing. There must have been a hundred people packed round the central pool. The Jamaican reggae beat was pumping, and figures were gyrating around each other as I made my way to the railing, dressed in shorts, T-shirt and flip-flops. I climbed over the railing, and stood on the inner planking that ran around the crater rim, hands gripping the wooden bar behind me.

Don't look down.

All of a sudden the bar seemed to freeze, like someone had pressed the pause button. All heads turned towards me in slow motion. Then someone – Andy, most likely – let out a deafening roar. 'JUUUUUMP!'

In an instant everyone knew what was coming. The place erupted: 'JUMP! JUMP! JUMP! JUMP!'

People were pounding the railing in time to the chant.

No bottling now.

I reminded myself that we were skint, that there was no money in the beer kitty, and therefore it stood to reason I should take one for the team. I let go and felt myself fall. It was a fifteen-foot drop, before my flip-flops ploughed into the water. I'd built up enough momentum so that I plummeted down a good twenty feet, and then I touched bottom.

There I was in the shark cage, with the sharks. I came back up, broke through the surface, and moments later I was treading water, with all around me the pointy shapes of fins. Above me was a row of faces wild with glee and bloodlust, leaning out as far as they could go and cheering like lunatics.

My legs started going like a motorboat's propeller on speed, and my arms were churning like a pair of paddle-steamer's wheels on acid. But with every stroke the side of the cage didn't appear to be coming a great deal closer, and a voice inside my head was going: *fuck, fuck, fuck . . .*

I felt something big and cold brush against me. *Oh fuck, I'm going to get bit!*

My arms stretched out, I lunged for the wooden walkway running around the edge of the shark cage, and in one swift and terrified movement I hauled my body out, sensing massive jaws chomping at the legs dangling behind me. With a final, desperate kick I swung myself around and sat down on the platform, staring back at some very pissed-off-looking fish.

Above me, the crowd was going ape. They were clapping and screaming and hollering and waving wads of dollar bills, crying for me to do it all again. I was looking for Andy and the others, a big, silly grin on my face, when all of a sudden a door in the side of the wall above the shark pool opened, and out sprang a guy with a large machete.

He waved it at me, and started to run – heading around the walkway in my direction, with the clear intent to hurt, maim or kill. I recognised him. It was the bar owner. Earlier, when serving us copious amounts of beer, he'd seemed more than friendly.

Not any more.

He started screaming. It was so loud I could even hear him above the crowd. 'OUT! GET OUT! GET OUT!'

I ran. I bolted out the back way, hit the jetty and sprinted for the beach. Machete man was still in pursuit, but halfway down the gangway he seemed to run out of puff. He stood there for a good few seconds, hurling insults after me and waving the blade, and then he turned back towards his bar and disappeared inside.

He disappeared inside, and almost instantly, Andy, Beano and Johno appeared. I realised that amidst all the terror and confusion I'd managed to lose my flip-flops. But as the lads walked towards me, at least Andy was brandishing a fist full of dollars.

'Anyone seen my flip-flops?' I asked.

'Yeah. They're being chomped on by a tiger shark.'

'Oh. Right.' I turned back to the bar. 'I'll just go back and fetch 'em.'

There were groans from the others, but I couldn't keep the bluff going. I dissolved into a fit of giggles. 'Only joking.'

All's well that ends well, I told myself. We wouldn't be frequenting the Shark Bar any time soon, but there were plenty of other watering holes along the beach. I could score myself a new pair of flip-flops, leaving plenty of cash to spare for the beer.

A skinful, by the looks of what Andy had managed to whip up.

*

We arrived back in the UK a few days later, and Jon H invited us to the bar. Lieutenant-Colonel Stanley-Price had been in touch, he explained.

'I understand it's a job well done in Belize. I've had good reports, lads. Very good reports.' He eyed the four of us. 'Only to be expected.'

That night, the drinks were on him.

It was praise indeed from a guy like Jon H.

35

Post Belize, life became one long round of specialist training, interspersed with putting other units through their paces, just as we'd done with the Gurkhas.

We deployed to Malaysia on Nelson's Glory, a joint training exercise with other elite forces' units. I learned how to parachute into the open ocean in pitch darkness, and from there to RV with a RIB (rigid inflatable boat) to do a NAVEX (navigation exercise), moving from point to point at night through the Malacca Straits – the world's busiest shipping lane – unseen and undetected.

I learned how to HALO into the deep jungle of Sarawak – a remote part of Malaysia – and how to launch a live-firing direct-action attack against an 'enemy' position. I learned how to receive parachute drops of resupply kit in the deep jungle; how to cache such equipment; and how to use it as supplies to live off and re-arm from over extended periods of time.

We deployed to East Africa to train the Zimbabwean Special Forces – 'SAS'. They wear the same beige beret and winged dagger badge and belt as the British unit – a throwback to when Zimbabwe was a British colony. Zimbabwe was about to host the African National Games – their regional equivalent to the Olympics – and they were worried about a terrorist attack from rebels based in neighbouring Mozambique.

We were there to train up a specialist Pathfinder unit within the Zimbabwe SAS, teaching them how to jump out of aeroplanes and insert into the bad guy's backyard. That meant getting them up to 12,000 feet on their HALO jumps, and teaching them how to do the even more specialist HAHO – high-altitude high-opening – insertions.

With HAHO we got them to bale out at altitude and pull their chutes immediately, whereupon they could glide between fifteen and eighteen kilometres across the savannah, depending on wind direction and speed. HAHO is a fantastic insertion technique, because it allows a patrol to fly across a border without the aircraft carrying them ever having entered hostile airspace. As such, it's perhaps the most secretive way to penetrate into enemy terrain.

We got to teach them TLZ (tactical landing zone) insertion techniques, whereby a Hercules transport aircraft puts down on a rough airstrip hacked out of the bush – the force aboard debussing on foot and in vehicles – and gets airborne again without ever having stopped rolling. Such TLZ insertions get a large body of men and machines on – or off – the ground rapidly, and without the danger of parachutists losing each other in the air.

But the real highlight for me proved to be Exercise Purple Star – the single largest NATO airdrop since the Second World War. It was 1996, I'd been promoted to corporal, and I had my own patrol to command.

Johno was still with us, but he was off on another training job when Purple Star went down. Andy had left the Pathfinders, and had gone into JATE – the innocuously-named Joint Air Transport Establishment, which is in reality a highly secretive body based at RAF Brize Norton, overseeing cutting-edge James-Bond-type military air-insertion techniques.

Andy's absence was only temporary. He had to spend two years at the JATE, so as to earn his promotion, at which point he would return to the fold. Beano had also left, having been posted to 3 PARA – also necessary to receiving his promotion.

One of the big downsides of being a black economy outfit was that you couldn't significantly advance your rank within the Pathfinders. I never fully understood why and it bugged the shit out of all of us in the unit. But in short, we had to

Kenya, 1996, during PF jungle training. I am a part of the training team delivering a brief on the upcoming day's activities. The PF will often travel overseas to conduct their own internal training whether it is in the Arctic, jungle, desert or contemporary operating environment.

Kenya, 1996, armed with my trusty M16A2, standing near the top of a waterfall getting a look over the canopy top.

Egypt, 1996. I commanded an eight-man PF team during a coalition Mission Readiness Exercise. Navigating the desert terrain can be extremely dangerous at times: the loose sand, often referred to as 'sugar', can flip a 'Pinkie' Land Rover very easily, resulting in the crew being thrown from the vehicle.

Egypt, 1996. An eight-man PF patrol takes the opportunity to 'get a brew on' deep inside the western desert on the Libyan border.

Egypt, 1996. An eight-man PF team moves west across the vast desert towards the Libyan border. Motorbike outriders are used to prove the route ahead and pass messages between the 'Pinkie' Land Rovers when operating on radio silence.

D-Day as KFOR troops spearheaded by 1 PARA battlegroup are flown across the border from Macedonia into Kosovo. RAF Puma helicopters deposit troops and equipment along the Kacanik Defile in preparation for the move into the capital Pristina. (EPO/Antonio Bat)

Russian main battle tanks protected with explosive reactive armour (ERA) thunder into Kosovo making their way to secure Pristina airport. My patrol was sent ahead of the main battlegroup to report on their progress hoping I didn't have to call in an artillery bombardment to stop them.

Final words to my patrol as we prepare to board the helicopters to fly into Pristina airport to confront the Russians and possibly begin World War Three. I am standing far left pointing to the helicopters; on my left is Ginge, and then Hendo, followed by the man-mountain Taff on the far right.

Troops from 1 PARA are blown around as RAF Puma helicopters land in numbers to move them across the border to face the oncoming Russians. Nearly every man is carrying a LAW 80 missile launcher, our only anti-tank weapon system with which to engage the Russian tanks. We all knew the missiles would just bounce off the ERA fitted to their tanks – we might as well have been throwing stones at them. (Kevin Capon)

By April 1999 over 375,000 Kosovars had moved south into the neighbouring country of Albania. Slobodan Milosevic, the then president of Yugoslavia, had vowed to ethnically cleanse Kosovo under the codename of Operation Horseshoe, attempting to wipe away any record of their very existence. (Eric Feferberg/AFP/Getty Images)

World War Three begins as 850 men from 1 PARA battlegroup are ordered by US General Wesley Clark, then Supreme Allied Commander Europe (SACEUR), to mount RAF helicopters and fly to Pristina Airport and hold it against the oncoming Russian troops at all costs. Luckily at the last moment that order was rescinded. Interesting to note that although this was a NATO operation, only British troops would have done the fighting. (Russell Boyce)

During the Kosovo operation my patrol was sent ahead of the battlegroup crossing the border from Macedonia into Kosovo first, with the task of observing the movement of Russian and Serb forces. Our only support would have been provided by the 105mm Light Guns of 7 RHA, capable of delivering a devastating bombardment with pinpoint accuracy at a range of over 17 kilometres. (Crown Copyright)

Pathfinders are trained to operate across all environments, the Arctic being one of them. Working alongside the Swedish Special Forces inside the Arctic Circle we developed our winter warfare techniques, tactics and procedures including parachuting onto frozen lakebeds. (POA(Phot) Sean Clee/Crown Copyright)

Snowbound. Whiteout. We were dropped in the wildnerness by a Swedish Special Forces helicopter and told to find our way out on skis, towing a pulk – a massive sledge of supplies – and with a hunter force on our tail.

return to our parent units to get officially promoted.

My patrol for Purple Star consisted of Neil 'Tricky' Dick, Steve 'Harry The Dog' Harris, James 'Tomo' Thompson and Pete 'Dino' Dunellen. If I had a problem child in my patrol Dino was it, as Exercise Purple Star was about to prove.

For Purple Star my patrol had to HALO in from 16,000 feet, with a unit of Force Recon Marines – an American 'pathfinding' unit similar to our own – attached to us. We'd HALO into North Carolina, trek through a heavily-forested region – one thick with bears, moose and other big, grouchy animals – and recce and mark a series of DZs, onto which 16,000 British and American paratroopers would converge, complete with armoured transport and weaponry.

Needless to say, the eyes of the world – not to mention the British and American high command – would be on us.

To add a little extra to the mix, we had twenty-four hours from getting boots on the ground to making the mother of all airdrops happen. It wasn't just British face that we had to save here. It was lives. A badly-marked or situated DZ; a misreading of the weather conditions; a mess-up in the split-second timing: it could so easily end up costing many good men's lives.

At first all went swimmingly. The HALO was a blast, we cached our chutes, hauled on our Bergens and set off – counting our left footfalls as we went. We were moving at night on sandy tracks that snaked through a high coniferous forest, operating on NVG (night-vision goggles). Unlike jungle, northern pine woodland is often thin enough to let enough ambient light through for NVG to work.

After we'd been on the go for a good few hours, I signalled for a map stop. We were moving in a linear formation, and I was acutely conscious of how the largest air drop since the Second World War was just hours away, and if we made a wrong turn or fucked up we were right royally in the shit. In such gently undulating pine forest everything looks the same, so the only way to navigate was by trying to match the contours of the ground to the map.

Ahead of me I saw my lead scout come to a silent halt.

He dropped onto one knee, his assault rifle covering the arc of fire to his front. I went down in a similar stance on his right shoulder, my weapon covering the arc of fire from there through 180 degrees to the operator at my rear. He in turn did likewise, covering the arc on the opposite side of the patrol, and so it cascaded down the line, such that all areas to either side of us were being watched by a pair of unblinking eyes and menaced by a weapon's barrel.

Like that we remained still and silent for a good five minutes, doing a listening watch – so checking if we had followers, or if there was any threat up ahead. That done, we removed our packs, and placed them in a circle, with the guys sat on those facing outwards, and very much on watch. I turned inwards, using the space in the centre to spread the map out on the ground.

I broke out a small maglight, which I'd adapted to shine only the tiniest pinprick of light. I'd done so by taping black gaffer tape over the torch lens and cutting the smallest hole possible in the tape. As a result, it emitted a thin laser beam of illumination, one that would be well shielded by the guys sat all around me.

I found our last position, and knowing we'd marched for 800 metres on 6100 mils magnetic (a highly accurate means of measuring direction) I orientated my map to my compass, measured off the equivalent of 800 metres in that direction, and located our new position.

That done, I double-checked: I searched the map for any noticeable features, then scanned the forest all around me to see if they were present and correct. Once all was clear, I identified the next map check position, set the bearing and was ready for the off.

One at a time I tapped the lads on the shoulder. One at a time they turned inwards. 'Right, we're here. We're going here. Bearing is four eight double zero mils magnetic, distance one kilometre.'

Each guy set the bearing on his compass.

'You happy?' I queried, before turning to the next.

I got to Dino the Purple Dinosaur last. I gave him the brief, then asked if he was happy.

A slight pause. 'Yeah, mate, happy. Just a quick one.'

'Yeah, go on.'

We were smeared in camo cream and our faces were so close I could feel his breath against my face. I couldn't see his expression though; it was too dark for that.

'Mate, can't find me NVGs.'

'What do you mean – they're not in your kit?'

'No. I can't find 'em. I think they've come off.'

We were all wearing our NVGs on a strap around our necks. That way, you could pull them out of your smock-top, do a quick scan, then put them back in again. You'd rarely work on NVG all the time, for you'd lose your 'natural' night vision – your eyes' ability to adjust to low light conditions.

We'd just got these new NVGs from the British company, Pilkington. They worked in conjunction with a new laser-gizmo attached to our weapons. It fired out an infrared laser, one that placed a small dot of infrared light on your target. Although it was invisible to the naked eye, it appeared as a red dot under NVG.

Losing one of these state-of-the-art NVG units was not good news. More importantly, we still had a very long way to go before we hit the DZs.

'Right, mate, when was the last time you had it?'

'I think when we landed.'

'Back at the DZ? Why didn't you say something earlier, you muppet?'

If ever there was one, this was a things-that-make-you-go-*hmmmm* moment. I'd had quite a few of them with Dino.

Dino had joined about a year earlier. He was as bright-eyed and bushy tailed as I'd been, when first into the Pathfinders. Difference was, he had a lifestyle well above his pay grade. He'd not been long with us when he purchased a brand-new

BMW. On a Pathfinder private's wage it didn't add up.

Sure enough, I got the call a few weeks afterwards. The debt-collectors were here looking for Dino. I called Dino in and asked him what was what. Apparently he was behind on the car payments. It was a case of £600 in every month; £800 out.

I told him this bullshit had to stop. If he promised me it would I'd get the bailiffs sorted. Dino promised. I headed down to the main gate and found two guys in the gatehouse. They were big units, complete with combat trousers, tight black T-shirts, gold chains, earrings, tattoos – the works. But they were well out of shape.

'So, guys, what're you here for?' I asked.

'We're here for the car.'

'You're not having the car.'

'That's what we're here for.'

'Well, you can't have it.'

Dino may have been something of a car crash, but he was *our car crash*. A Pathfinder. He'd done Selection. Made it through. That made him one of the brothers, or maybe 'ginger stepchild' would be more appropriate.

'How much does he owe?' I asked.

'Four hundred and fifty quid. But his next monthly payment's due in a few days time.'

'Right, I'll get you four hundred and fifty cash, and then you can go away. He's promised me he'll make the monthly payments from here in.'

'Not what we were sent here for. Sent here for the car.'

'You're not getting the car. It's four hundred and fifty quid or nothing.'

'Okay, we'll take the cash.'

I got the Pathfinder's 'banker' to withdraw £450 from the petty cash, after making sure we were clear that Dino would have to pay it back from source – so before his wages were given to him. Then I returned to the fat lads and gave them the £450.

They didn't even bother to say thank you. 'Okay, but if the next monthly payment's missed, we're coming for the car.'

Now, I am generally a nice person, but I don't appreciate bad manners or ingratitude.

'No, lads, you're not. If you do we'll bury you out on our training area. It's a big old space and no one will ever find the bodies – not even big units, like you.'

I had to repeat it a few times before they understood what I meant, and that I was for real, that I wasn't joking.

So, that was Dino for you – my problem child. And now he'd gone and lost his NVG several map-stops back, and not breathed a word until now. In some ways the worst of it was that we had to pay for any kit we lost or damaged via negligence. Dino paying for a missing Pilkington's NVG set – it was about as likely as him ever keeping the BMW.

I figured I had no choice. Dino would have to be sent on a solo mission back to the point where we'd HALO'd in, to find and retrieve the missing kit. If a bear ate him en route that would be one less problem I had to deal with.

Now, trekking through a forest inhabited by large wild things with big teeth, claws and jaws as a team of five is a very different thing to doing so alone. As a patrol of five, you feel pretty much invincible. When you're a team of one, well – the phrase 'shit scared' comes to mind.

As we'd witnessed at first hand, the threat was very real. We'd just come from an exercise in the Florida Everglades, basically one large forest-swamp. We'd HALO'd in, and a Force Recon guy had landed in a flooded part of the forest. Unfortunately, a very large alligator inhabited the pool in which he'd landed, and it proceeded to chomp on his leg.

He was lucky to make it out of there alive.

One thing about Dino: he didn't seem to scare very easily. He set off back the way we'd come seemingly as happy as a lamb.

I just hoped he wasn't a lamb to the slaughter.

36

By the time we got to our end destination, I was still wondering whether I'd done the right thing. But, hell, every cloud has a silver lining. If Dino did get mauled and eaten by a bear, at least I might wangle to keep the BMW. After all, the bailiffs were hardly going to come and repossess a motor from a dead man.

My patrol was positioned in the cover of some trees looking out over a clear stretch of terrain: the proposed DZ. We'd RV'd with the Force Recon unit, and they were positioned in the forest next to us. The plan was to work together to call in the drop, and see what we could learn from each other about how best to do such things.

As the dawn brightened I told Tricky – my signaller – that we needed to send a sitrep to HQ. It would cover wind direction, wind speed and visibility – all key to making a successful drop – and it would confirm the status of the DZ, which as far as we could tell was largely free of obstructions and the enemy.

Tricky broke out the comms gear and began setting up. We needed to send a radio message from North Carolina to the Florida HQ of US Special Operations, so no more than 950 kilometres. He unrolled the antenna braid from its reel and attached one end to the radio. On the other was tied a long roll of string, and he now had the challenging task of getting the antenna hoisted high enough to enable communications – similar to what we'd done on the Belize ridgeline, when spying on Dodge.

Tricky tied his water bottle to one end of the string, and hurled it upwards, trying to snag a branch, while I surveyed the terrain below me through my binoculars. I felt a tap on my shoulder. It was the Force Recon commander.

'Hey, buddy, you gonna talk to your command?'

I glanced at where Tricky was still hurling up his water bottle on a string. 'Yeah. Trying to, mate.'

'Me too. I got to talk to my guys.'

He turned to his signaller and gave a thumbs-up. I watched in awe as the bloke grabbed hold of his Bergen, sprang open the two main straps, flipped up the top cover, reached inside and pulled out a metre-long black telescopic antenna. He hit a release switch, and hey presto – it unfurled into a helix-shaped dish, similar in appearance to the one that pipes Sky TV into your living room.

He fixed the dish to the top of the Bergen, reached inside, turned a knob – clearly, the power button – pulled out a handset and spoke into it: '*Bulldog, Bulldog – Easy One*.'

'This is *Bulldog*. Roger, *Easy One*. Wait out.'

Having raised his HQ – codename 'Bulldog'; don't you just love those Yank call-signs? – the signaller passed the handset across to his commander.

'*Bulldog, Bulldog – Easy One*. Eyes-on target, no movement, wind westerly four knots, cloud four to eight nimbus, cloud ceiling twelve thousand feet, no sign of enemy.'

'*Easy One,* this is *Bulldog* – roger, out.'

Comms done, the commander passed the handset back, his signaller collapsed the antenna and ten seconds later they were done.

Behind me, Tricky was still trying to snag a tree branch.

Partly in an effort to cover my embarrassment over the water bottle hurling fiasco, I asked: 'So, who the fuck's *Bulldog*?'

'The Divisional Commander.'

'You just spoke to the Div Command?'

'Yeah, the Div Commander. Who you guys talking to?'

'Fucking no one yet. Once he's finished throwing the water bottle into a tree . . .'

Non-Americans like to say of US forces that they have 'all the gear, no idea'. In truth, they generally have both: *gear and ideas.* In particular, their elite forces are every bit as good as our own. I'd learned as much from training alongside such outfits. These Force Recon guys would prove no different.

As Tricky continued to hurl, I concentrated on doing a visual recce of the proposed DZ. The clock was counting down and we needed to complete all of our crucial 'person-on-the-ground' tasks. We had to identify and mark two DZs, and find defendable points where a commander could rally his men if the landing proved hot.

We needed to find areas of good cover, keep constantly monitoring the weather conditions, and transmit all of this information back to HQ, so those in command could get their ducks in a row. Basically, we had to send back a constant stream of information, and if we couldn't communicate there was no point us being here at all.

In a way, your comms kit is the most important piece of gear that you carry as a patrol. If you're there and you can't communicate, you're better off not being on the ground at all, for your very presence can compromise the entire mission.

Eventually, Tricky succeeded in snagging his branch, and we got comms up and running, which meant we didn't have to ask the Force Recon guys if we could borrow their kit.

We sent a sitrep, then set about recceing a stores DZ and a PAX (passenger) DZ – the former for all the stores and heavy equipment, the latter for the paratroopers.

The two DZs would be set side by side one kilometre apart, so that they could be used simultaneously. Hercules C130s would fly in loaded either with stores (rations, ammo, etc.) and medium stress platforms (light tanks, jeeps, artillery pieces), or with PAX – forty-five hairy-arsed paratroopers packed into either side of the aircraft.

The recceing of the DZs was truly a life-and-death tasking. You need some four kilometres of open terrain to disgorge ninety paratroopers from a C130 Hercules. We'd place an Approach Marker at the start-end of the DZ – when the aircraft would be 250 metres out. At that point the pilot would need to get his C130 level and straight at a steady 120 knots – the slowest speed such an aircraft can fly at before stalling. Any faster, and the pilot would risk injuring the paratroopers as they got sucked through the aircraft's slipstream.

When you jump from an aircraft's side door you are thrown forward into its path, not backwards as you might expect, and the G-shock of doing so is severe. The other reason the pilot has to stick to 120 knots is because if he flies any faster he'll reach the end of the four kilometres before his full ninety-strong complement of jumpers has left the aircraft.

He'd run out of room.

And with 16,000 men-at-arms plus all their kit inbound, no way was any single aircraft going to do an about turn and come in for a second pass.

With eight kilometres of DZ identified, walked and checked, we now had to assure ourselves there was no other human presence anywhere nearby. We also had to assess how we could help defend the DZs until the in-load of combat power was complete, and the force could start to protect itself. Finally, we had to establish entry and exit points for vehicles, muster points and routes to reach the target.

When all of that was done, we had to agree a P Hour – Parachute Hour; the timing for the start of the drop. On the American side we had the men of the 101st Airborne Division and the 82nd Airborne flying in, and on the UK side we had the blokes of 5 Airborne Brigade.

We set P Hour for 0300 the following morning.

We then had to file a 'Wet Report' – a final assessment of any weather conditions that might render the drop undoable. For this we used a hand-held anemometer – a device like a mini windmill – to gauge wind speed, and the mark one human eyeball to assess cloud cover.

We were extremely busy bees, so much so that when Dino pitched up without the slightest scratch or tooth-mark on him – NVG safely retrieved and slung around his neck – I barely had time to tell him about the designs I'd had on his BMW.

It was a hundred and twenty minutes until P Hour, we were hunkered down in a covert OP in the woodline overlooking the PAX DZ, and we had another team overlooking the stores DZ.

At P Hour minus sixty we moved out to start the DZs marking process. We were using 'black light', so devices that emit a pulse of infrared illumination. The stores DZ would be marked differently to the PAX DZ, so that the pilots could more easily differentiate between the two.

By now, the two streams of inbound aircraft – the PAX armada and stores armada – would have reached their forming-up points, way distant from us. In the first aircraft of the PAX armada would be the ground commander, designated 'Stream Leader'. We had TACSATs – satellite communications devices, similar to civvie satellite phones – which would enable us to speak to Stream Leader, talking him down in real time.

But the TACSAT was an insecure means of voice communications, so we'd only ever use it for the last-minute talk-in.

We were P Hour minus twenty by the time the PAX DZ was fully marked. By now the aircraft would be speeding in from their forming-up point, each assuming its allotted position in the airstream, and sticking to the same altitude and airspeed. If they were flying in across the ocean, or any other 'permissive environment' – terrain devoid of known threats – they'd be dropping down to an altitude of 200 feet, to minimise their radar profile and avoid detection.

Some twenty kilometres out the paratroopers would be standing up, and their kit – Bergens, weaponry – fitted. Then they'd move into their positions by the open doors. At five kilometres distance the aircraft would climb to their drop height, which is 800 feet, at which stage they'd be visible to the enemy's radar.

Parachutes would be clipped to the jump cable inside the aircraft, which ensured each jumper's chute would open as soon as he exited. At four hundred metres out the lead aircraft would be looking for the Approach Marker, which would give it the run-in to the Alpha Marker.

Long before that moment we could hear them, of course. The roar of the approaching air armada filled the sky, as if an earthquake were rolling across the starlit heavens. We couldn't see much yet, for all of the aircraft were flying on black light, but we knew for sure they were coming.

I could just make out the shadowy forms in the distance – each a darker patch of black against the night sky. Off to our right I could see the stores armada likewise making its final approach. We had seventy-three C141 Starlifters flying in, each carrying 140 paratroopers, plus sixty-four C130s – and that was just the PAX DZ.

As soon as the lead aircraft hit the Approach Marker the red 'get ready' light in the hold would come on, telling the paratroopers to prepare to jump. When it hit the Alpha Marker the green-for-go light would blink on, and along each side of the aircraft the first men in the sticks would start to hurl themselves into the void.

Above us the lead Hercules thundered overhead, with fifteen further PAX aircraft stacked up behind it in close formation. By the time aircraft one was nearing the rear of the DZ, aircraft two, three and four were disgorging their jumpers, so they drifted earthwards in a series of 'blankets' or waves.

Blokes were landing all around us – thousands of 'em. Once down, they bundled up their chutes and hurried off the DZ, to try to clear it for the next man. Over on the stores DZ we had sixteen Starlifters chucking out gear, as the earth shook with the noise of thirty-two massive warplanes thundering past above.

Needless to say, it was an awesome spectacle. But we weren't spectators: there was work to be done. After that first wave there would be fifteen minutes to clear the DZ, before the next thirty-odd aircraft would roar in and spew out their human cargo.

It took one and a half hours to get all the paratroopers dropped, and for all that time we were at the DZ, guiding aircraft in, and directing blokes on the ground. At the end of it all there had been just one serious casualty, among 16,000 paratroopers. A bloke from 5 Brigade's Parachute Engineers had got his chute tangled with another jumper, and had hit the ground far too hard.

It's easy enough to do. With the C130's slipstream throwing the jumpers forward, the guy from the port side had gone through the guy from the starboard side's rigging, and he was left hanging beneath him. In such situations the only option was for both guys to try to get down safely under the one chute. That's what they'd done, but the lower bloke had landed hard and got injured.

The injured guy was casevac'd (casualty evacuation – by air), and we set about our next task – target acquisition and prosecution. We sent one team to get eyes-on the enemy positions, while another sorted forming-up points for the paratroopers, routes to target, plus fire-support points for the artillery.

As the main force advanced towards their lines of departure – the points from which they'd launch the ground assault – we morphed into our next role: taking out high-value targets. Using sniper rifles, we'd hit the command and control elements of the enemy – their senior officers. 'Decapitating the snake', we called it. Plus we'd call in close-air support – ground attack aircraft – to further smash them.

Purple Star culminated in a massive exercise – a simulated ground battle – and it all went swimmingly. We'd worked seamlessly with the Force Recon boys, and we'd almost persuaded them to swop one of their fancy radio kits for our bottle-on-a-string version. It had been a hard sell, even for us lot, but the Force Recon guys weren't buying it. Pity.

As luck would have it, Exercise Purple Star would be the perfect preparation for what was coming.

Though I didn't know it at the time, I was about to be air-dropped into World War Three.

37

Time passed. I'd been in the Pathfinders a good eight years when it was first mooted that I might indeed be suitable material for the dream job – that of platoon sergeant.

I'd been drawn to the position having seen how Dave Moore had handled himself in that role. With his Freddie Mercury look and deadpan delivery he'd been perfect to beast us through Selection, but he was also as fine an operator as any to hone the unit to perfection.

Together with Jon H, he'd pretty much achieved it. There was no one better trained or more capable at what we did than the men of the X Platoon. The trouble was, as always, the gear.

You've heard about the radios. Add to that an endless list of kit failures, and you'll start to get the picture. Unbelievably, we'd recently had the SA80 assault rifle foisted upon us. The M16s that Jon H had blagged had been well worn, even by the time we'd got our hands on them. Ten years of use and abuse, and we'd trashed them. But when we tried to get a replacement batch, someone decreed that we would get the SA80.

And we fucking hated it.

I'd been forced to witness an endless category of such mishaps, and none more so than within the parachuting field. By this time I was one of the most experienced military freefall parachutists in the British Army. Airborne insertion is the bread and butter of what the Pathfinders do: we train for it more exhaustively than any other unit in the armed forces.

By now I had over 1,200 jumps under my belt. I was one of only a handful of military freefall Tandem Masters in the British military, meaning I could freefall with another human being strapped to my person – say a spook – a piece of high-tech weaponry, a specially-designed canister packed with 1,000 pounds of ammo, or even a military working dog.

But with such training and experience came responsibilities. I'd been tasked to JATE a great deal, testing cutting-edge parachute insertion equipment. Numerous times I'd leapt from the edge of the Earth's atmosphere – from above the altitude that commercial airliners fly at – testing highly experimental parachute rigs. But recently the British military had decided to develop a very different kind of chute, and with disastrous consequences.

The idea of the LLP – the low-level parachute – was perfectly sound in principle. It was designed to enable paratroopers to pile out of a Hercules at well below 800 feet, and still reach the ground in one piece. In theory, it would enable a jump height of 250 feet, so keeping the aircraft just below radar-detection level.

Good idea on paper.

Troublesome in practice.

With bare seconds in which to open, the chute had to have as flat and wide a profile as possible, so as to catch the maximum air. We tested the LLP over water, where it didn't matter so much if you piled in – water being a bit softer than land. Even then we found it would need to have a rocket-assisted reserve, in case the main parachute failed.

Trouble was, the MOD decided there wasn't the budget to design, test, trial and perfect such a piece of kit. They may well have been right. The budget could well have been better spent elsewhere. But the real screw-up was this: the LLP had already gone into mass production, and it had been issued widely to British Airborne units.

The LLP's profile might have been right for ultra-low-level insertions. It wasn't right for making a standard 800-foot jump. With the previous chute, the PX4, you could land effectively in anything up to a sixteen-knot wind. With the LLP the flat profile tended to set the chute oscillating, and the pendulum swings were exacerbated by a light breeze. As a result, at anything more than five to eight knots you'd take a hard, potentially injurious landing.

In addition, the LLP was set up in such a way that it was very difficult to lower your Bergen on a release system, as you could with the PX4. With your Bergen hanging below you it would hit the ground first, taking the impact. But if you couldn't get it to drop before landing, your body – your legs first and foremost – would take the punch.

We warned our taskmasters about the LLP's shortcomings for use at that height and how the wind affected it more but unfortunately they didn't seem inclined to listen. The Yanks had an excellent chute, designated the T10. As with the SA80–M16 debacle, we could have purchased a job lot of T10s off our closest ally and for a fraction of the cost of the LLP, getting a rig that was designed for the job.

I loved serving in the Pathfinders. I cherished the unit and those who served in it, and I had a similar feeling for the PARAs and associated outfits. But the kit failures – they had me boiling up with rage. By now, of course, the British Army was everything to me. It had given me the one thing I asked for in life – a fair chance.

But how could such a fine organisation be peopled by individuals who made such utterly bone choices? This was bad decision-making by those in charge of the Army's procurement, research and development.

Of course, in truth I was in no position to question them, though whenever I got the chance I said exactly what I thought. But it left me keener than ever to work my way into a position where I could try to make a real difference. If I made Pathfinder platoon sergeant, I could at least try to police kit-procurement within our own outfit.

But in order to get my promotion I would first have to return to my parent unit – the Parachute Regiment. I was reluctant, but needs must. And so it was that in the summer of 1999 I would deploy to the war in Kosovo, as a bolt-on to the PARAs.

And that was the first step to being sent in to wage war against the Russians.

38

In the spring of 1999 the NATO powers had unearthed plans drawn up by Slobodan Milosevic, the president of the then Yugoslavia, to ethnically cleanse Kosovo. Milosevic proposed using the Yugoslav army to drive out the Kosovo Albanians, in what was codenamed Operation Horseshoe.

All that stood between Milosevic and his troops was a bunch of Kosovan rebels, plus NATO – if NATO could be persuaded to act. The Western powers appreciated that they had to tread softly-softly – the Balkans was a tinderbox, and Milosevic was backed by the Russians, Yugoslavia being an old Soviet ally. No one exactly wanted to spark World War Three.

The Balkans are defined by a centuries-old culture of ethnic hatred – but right then it boiled down to Milosevic's men forcing hundreds of thousands of men, women and children out of Kosovo, with reports of possible genocide. In March NATO launched air-strikes against Milosevic's forces, and his resistance was expected to crumble within days.

It didn't quite work out that way.

By then, I was well and truly back with the PARAs, and rumours were circulating of the 1 PARA Battle Group getting deployed into Kosovo. Milosevic proved a far tougher nut to crack than anyone had envisioned. Initially, it was predicted he might last a week under NATO bombing. He'd held out for ten, with little sign of him pulling his troops back, or of halting the mass killing.

The CO of 1 PARA was Lieutenant-Colonel Paul 'Gibbo' Gibson. He was tall, skinny and gaunt, with the physique of a long-distance runner. Over time I would develop a grudging respect for the man.

He could make gutsy, timely decisions. His calls might be right or wrong, but either way he was not a ditherer – which was about all you could ask for in a senior commander.

Gibbo knew that I was working a promotion stint before returning to the Pathfinders. He wanted me for his Patrols Platoon, a hand-picked bunch of guys who acted as his forward recce and intelligence-gathering unit.

With a Kosovo ground deployment imminent, Gibbo needed his Patrols Platoon licked into shape. He asked me to put the lads through their paces, drill down into their skill-sets, and check they had the right kind of kit for what was coming. Not that we knew what was coming.

At the same time Neil, my brother, was about to get married and I was scheduled to be his best man. I told him the simple truth: I'd be there for him come hell or high water, unless we were sent to war. As matters transpired, I didn't make the wedding, nor even his stag night – 'cause by then we were already in Macedonia, the stepping stone for battle.

The Patrols Platoon commander was Captain Alan Robbins, a tall stick of a bloke fresh in from the Royal Artillery. He was twenty-five years old, he lacked experience, and he hailed from a gunnery unit. What on earth he was doing commanding a recce and intel-gathering outfit was anyone's guess.

Gibbo gave me a clear tasking. 'Right, I'm moving you to Patrols Platoon. They will be key in Kosovo. I want a steady hand on the helm. That's you. Go over there and fire a shot across the bows. Take Captain Robbins, pull him in close and stay on him. It's going to be a very challenging time for him.'

Needless to say, I wasn't flavour of the month with Patrols Platoon. The Platoon colour sergeant was Ben Green, a lad I knew well and a Falklands veteran. He'd been told I was coming over in an 'advisory role', but he knew that I was there to kick arse.

'What are you doing here?' Ben asked, just as soon as I'd rocked up. 'Have they lost faith in us? Why's no one said anything?'

I figured there was no way to sugarcoat this. 'At the end of the day, mate, the CO's got it into his head there is an issue. I've been sent to ensure that whatever that issue is, it's corrected and corrected very quickly. Patrols Platoon is going to be the cusp of the Kosovo deployment: we have to get sparking.'

With most, it went down like a lead balloon, but Captain Alan Robbins couldn't have been happier. He wasn't feeling the love in the Platoon, and suddenly I was there as his adviser, not to mention someone who would help him take some of the flak.

Either way, there was precious little time for niceties. I had to mine down into their kit, tactics, communications, SOPs, and attitude to small unit operation behind enemy lines, plus the basic human capabilities and morale of the guys.

Were they robust and mentally strong? Were they self-contained? Were they gelled as a patrol, or were there loners and bullies? Were they wrapped up in their own self-importance? Were they round pegs in square holes?

Captain Robbins took me aside at the very start and said: 'Do what you have to do, Steve. Whatever you ask, I'll back you all the way.'

As the colour sergeant, Ben Green was the Platoon's second-in-command, so one below captain Robbins. So to add insult to injury I'd usurped him as the captain's right-hand man.

I started each day by announcing: 'This is what we're going to do today.' Then I followed it up with a long list of kick-arse action points.

When I finished up, Ben would sigh and tut. 'But why do we need to do that? I've checked all of that already.'

I'd almost forgotten what it was like. In the Pathfinders, rank is secondary to merit. That was why Andy Parson had called prayers when he'd proposed doing the CTR into Dodge, and why he would have accepted being outvoted by those he outranked. It's a meritocracy, and quite often you have patrol commanders outranked by those in their patrol. They led by dint of their experience.

Here it was utterly different. In Ben's mind rank was everything, and he outranked me by several factors.

'Ben, I'm not here to fall out,' I'd tell him. 'I'm here at the behest of the CO. If there's an issue with what I'm proposing, you need to go see the CO. I don't want to fall out with you, but at end of the day I've been given a job.'

It took a few days, but the rough and tumble soon settled down. Ben stopped the headshakes and the under-the-breath remarks, and we got on with the job in hand. I also figured that harsh reality was starting to kick in. We were clearly on the brink of going to war against a well-equipped, battle-hardened military, in the European theatre.

None of us had ever faced anything like this before. During the Falklands War, we'd pretty much steamrollered over them, at least once the ground campaign had started. In the Iraq War, we'd steamrollered over them in a hundred hours or so.

But so far, a massive NATO air campaign had failed to stop Milosevic's army, and we were talking state-of-the-art warplanes here, including stealth bombers. NATO forces had flown 38,000 sorties, but still Milosevic's boys held firm.

We needed to shape up, fast.

I got Captain Robbins to issue a couple of 'gypsy's warnings' to the worst offenders. Either they got their shit together, or they'd be removed from the Platoon. Slowly, the unit started to gel.

Gibbo told me I was getting my own four-man patrol to command in the field. I was given 'Taff' Bridges, 'Ginge' White and Peter 'Hendo' Henderson. Hendo would be my lead scout, Taff my medic and Ginge the signaller. Hendo was your typical young and keen Army-barmy private. He was cheery, wanted to do well, loved his guns and was determined to make it as a PARA.

Taff was a 6' 4", 16-stone monster of a Welshman. He was big, strong and powerful, if not the sharpest tool in the box. Everyone from Taff's valley seemed to be married to someone else in the valley, but thankfully he was no English-hater, as the Welsh sometimes tend to be. Taff was my lump. My sledgehammer. The lads had a catch phrase for him: 'Taff: nice lad, he can lift a lot.'

At 5' 8" Ginge was the patrol's short-arse. We used to start any conversation with Ginge by asking him if he was stood in a ditch. It was good to twist him. He was a typical PARA – stocky, aggressive and up for a scrap, with the ability to carry a house on his back, which he pretty much had to do with all the radio kit.

All in, it was a fine enough patrol. I had no issues with any of them, and all seemed to have what it took.

Of course, the Pathfinders were based not far from 1 PARA, so I'd hardly gone away. I was forever popping in for a coffee and a chat, and most weekends I was off freefalling with the unit. There were lots of familiar faces there still. Tricky, my signaller from Purple Star was there, plus Mark 'Jacko' Jackson – the son of General Sir Mike Jackson – was the unit's second-in-command.

I hated being out of the unit, and especially at such a time as this – when we were about to go to war.

Another Pathfinder old hand was Grahame 'Wag' Wardle, the unit's operations warrant officer. Wag was 'Gimli' – the Staff who'd beasted me through Selection – and he and I had gone on to become the best of mates.

I used to moan on about being out of the Pathfinders non-stop. 'Why do we need to leave? Why do I have to do all this time away? It's insane. I'm just marking time until I can get back.'

'I've had to do the same thing, mate,' Wag would respond, in his thick Burnley accent. 'It's the fucking price we have to pay.'

We deployed to Kosovo via the Air Mounting Centre at South Cerney, near Cirencester – the muster point for all British military operations going out by air. I headed over to the 'black hangar', a fenced-off area from which any specialist and secret units deploy. The black hangar is in isolation: once blokes go into it, they are cut off from all other forces, to prevent intel leaking out.

The Pathfinders were there, of course. But no one knew any more than the basics: we were deploying to Macedonia, the nation to the south of Kosovo, as a starting point for any ground operations. I had a chat and a laugh with the blokes, but my joviality was somewhat forced. While I had a responsibility to the Patrols Platoon, and especially my three lads, I was gutted not to be deploying with my unit.

I wandered back to my patrol, feeling down. This was by far the most significant military deployment of my career – and I wasn't doing it with the Pathfinders. How fucked up was that? This was the closest we'd come to full-scale war as a nation – *and a war in Europe* – and I wasn't with the lads of the X Platoon.

This is shit, I told myself. *They'll get all the peachy ops – all the action – and I'll be left on the sidelines.* Well, little did I know . . .

You've heard of that old saying – 'beware of what you wish for'? I was about to live it, in spadefuls.

39

We flew out to Macedonia's Skopje Airport on the RAF's ageing Tristars. On the flight, I ruminated on the state of the Patrols Platoon. Had I done enough of what Gibbo had asked for? Captain Alan Robbins was my strongest ally. He was young, capable and a listener. Not arrogant. Ready and willing to be advised.

With Ben there was still some unease and tension beneath the surface. I figured it was simmering, but workable. In short, Gibbo's order to shake down the Platoon had been executed, as far as it could have been in the time available. It was in the lap of the gods now.

We touched down at Skopje Airport just as the evening light was fading. It was a scene of utter chaos and confusion. Tristars were landing and disgorging hordes of blokes; newly-arrived Hercules were shedding their loads of vehicles and stores. Wagons were revving, horns were blaring and blokes were yelling – as 850 men-at-arms tried to get their shit sorted.

We were ordered to board some trucks and we set off into the darkness without a clue as to where we were headed. All we had were our Bergens, belt kit and personal weapons. We had no food, or more importantly, ammo.

After an hour's drive we ended up on a small country lane in the pitch black. Our truck stopped and there were screams for everyone to debus. We were ordered to move forward in single file but still we had no idea where we were or where we were going.

We tabbed through a grassy meadow, ill-lit by the moonlight, having formed a classic 'battalion snake' – 850 blokes playing follow my leader. At the end of the pasture a steep hill reared into the darkness, so up it we went. We reached the top to find a dense forest – a natural broadleaf woodland, as opposed to a plantation.

We hit, the edge of the trees and followed that for about three kilometres. For the entire trek I'd been counting my left footfalls, and keeping track of the distance covered. But without a map, or a clue as to where we had started from, there was precious little point. Old habits die hard, I guess.

Finally, we reached a point in the woodland that was our harbour area. 'Push in the woodline,' someone ordered. 'Set ponchos up. You're staying here tonight. As from this moment you're on a war footing – so stags and sentries.'

'What we gonna do, throw stones and shout at 'em?' came a voice from out of the night.

It was Ginge, the joker on my patrol. It was fair enough: we still didn't have any ammo. It's a private soldier's prerogative to winge. They're at the bottom of the food chain. No one listens to a word they say.

We pushed into the wood and strung our ponchos from the trees, basha-ing up, then settled down to God knows what. Our last meal had been a butty-box on the Tristar. Contents: a cheese sandwich, a packet of Prawn Cocktail flavour crisps, a Kit Kat and a Panda cola. We still had no ammo or food rations.

Only one thing for it: sleep.

We set a sentry rota, broke out our maggots and got our heads down.

At first light the following morning we could see the readiness for war all around us. The meadow that we'd trekked through was now choked with armour. There were thirty-six Challenger main battle tanks, plus APCs (armoured personnel carriers), Warrior Armoured Fighting Vehicles, the works. Jeeps and trucks were tearing back and forth, and on the far side of the valley was a small tented camp: Gibbo's HQ.

We still had no food, so I took a careful swig of water from what I'd brought with me in my kit. Breakfast.

It was steaming hot already – this being the Balkans in summer – and there was no sign of even a water resupply. It was midday before a British Army Bedford truck crawled along the edge of the wood, with a couple of privates hurling boxes off the rear. We were issued one 24-hour ration pack each. Still no ammo. Still, it was good to finally get a brew and a scoff on.

We lazed around in the wood all day: sleeping, writing blueys (letters home), nattering. Even now I knew the Pathfinders would be co-located with the Brigade Headquarters – so deep within Gibbo's chosen circle. They'd know exactly where we were, what was being mooted, and their input would be asked for as the plans developed – especially as they would be tasked with the most risk-laden missions.

And here I was deep in the woods doing my best mushroom impression: being kept in the dark and fed on shit. That was the big difference; that was the 'them and us'; and I'd been too long a part of 'them' to enjoy being 'us' any more.

We killed time, spending a second night in the woods. On the morning of day three the Bedford truck drove down again, dropping off piles of ammo. We were each issued 120 rounds per man for our assault rifles – the lovely SA80 no less – so four magazines of ammo per man.

I tried getting the lads motivated: *Let's do a kit check; let's get the radios up and running; let's test comms; let's break out the medical packs and check 'em over.* But any which way you tried to look at it, this was the world's greatest anti-climax. We'd thought we were rushing off to war. Instead, we'd spent two days camping in some woodland.

The third night was the same as the previous two, and the morning of day four was a repeat of those that had gone before. It was scorching hot, and I tried to busy the lads by running through what our 'lost comms' procedure should be.

It was midday when everything changed, in the blink of an eye.

Suddenly, there was a mass of screaming: 'EVERYONE OUT

OF THE WOODS! Out! Out! Out! Patrol commanders – grab your patrols! Grab your kit! Get out! NOW!'

No one had a clue what was happening.

We joined the snake of bodies moving in the opposite direction to the way we'd arrived, only this time we were running as fast as we could go. As the woods emptied, it was like ants piling out of an anthill. We streamed along the ridge heading for the flat meadow where the armour was parked up.

Everyone was asking the same question: 'What's wrong? What's wrong? What's up?'

No one knew. 'Dunno. Dunno. Just move. Everyone down.'

I told my patrol to stay with me. Stick close. It was total mayhem, but at least if I could keep the lads together we'd be better able to deal with whatever shit was coming.

We reached the flat of the meadow, and suddenly it was as if we'd been parachuted into the set of the movie, *Apocalypse Now*. Apart from the missing theme tune, the 'Ride of the Valkyries', it was like a re-enactment of the scene where the American helicopter squadron assaults the Vietnamese village.

Until now, the eastern horizon had been sun-blasted but empty. Suddenly it was a blur of dark objects, throbbing and glinting menacingly, and the air itself seemed to thunder and vibrate. As first I couldn't believe it. I had never seen so many helicopters in one patch of sky at any one time.

But as the air armada neared us, I had to take it for what it was. We had thirty-plus helicopters inbound. I counted sixteen giant, twin-rotor Chinooks, the same number of Pumas and a smattering of Lynxes.

By the time we hit the meadow, sweating like pigs and lungs heaving fit to burst, the helos were jockeying for landing position. They came down in waves, one on top of the other, all but clipping rotor blades – they were that close.

As we ran towards them a column of trucks pulled up on the road that we had travelled in on, blokes hurling off crate-loads of ammo. Figures on the ground began ripping open the crates, and literally tipping their contents onto the deck.

'GRAB YOUR BANDOLIERS! GRAB YOUR BANDOLIERS!'

A bandolier is a long green sleeve that you sling around your torso. It consists of five compartments, each of which contains thirty rounds for your SA80. At one the human wave altered course, as 850 paratroopers rushed to grab some bullets.

The guys on the next truck along chucked out bandoliers of ammo for our GPMGs – the 7.62mm general purpose machine gun. The next truck carried crate-loads of LAW-80s – a 94mm light anti-tank weapon, which is like a disposable bazooka. We were screamed at to grab as many LAWs as we could carry.

At the end of the convoy was a truck carrying a weapon I'd never even seen before: the rifle-launched grenade (RLG). Several of the RLGs were carried in a back-pack, and the weapon was designed to fit over the end of the SA80. Basically, you took aim, pulled the trigger, a round hit the RLG's percussion cap and unleashed the grenade.

It was like a poor man's M203 40mm grenade launcher. To complement our pile-of-shit assault rifles.

Blokes were grabbing anything they could lay their hands on, regardless of the weapon's lethality, in one massive free for all. Last thing I wanted in my patrol was no extra ammo and a rake load of dodgy, muzzle-loaded grenades.

'Everyone, make sure to grab two bandoliers!' I yelled.

'Taff – grab a couple of LAWs!'

'And Hendo – grab a few RLGs. What the fuck . . .'

That was it. We could barely walk under the weight.

A series of cries rang out.

'C Company – on me!'

'A Company – on me!'

And so on and so forth.

We were mustering to mount up the helos.

Whatever was happening, you didn't need the brains of a rocket scientist to work out that something had gone badly tits-up, and we were about to be sent in to try to sort it out. But I had never in my life seen 850 paratroopers scrambled and armed-up in such a crazed, chaotic fashion, nor such a massive air armada assembled to fly us in to . . . to what?

It had to be one hell of a peachy tasking, that was for sure.

Maybe to stop the end of the world?

It had that kind of feel to it, anyway.

We formed up as companies, milling about confusedly. Everyone was asking everyone else what was going on, and still no one had the faintest clue.

'My patrol – stay with me!' I yelled. 'Get ammo sorted. Get bandoliers sorted.'

A cry rang out for company commanders to go see the CO. A couple of minutes later Captain Alan Robbins returned, his face whiter than a freshly laundered sheet. Either he'd just met Gibbo's ghost, or this was not the best of news.

'Patrol commanders, on me,' he yelled. 'Close in quickly.'

We gathered, with Captain Robbins in the centre, all of us sensing that something wasn't right here.

'The Russians are coming,' he blurted out. 'Basically, a Russian tank column is making its way towards Pristina airport. We've been ordered to intercept them and deter them from Pristina airbase at any cost. And we're going now.'

Utter speechlessness all around. Pristina airport was Kosovo's main hub – the place to in-load men-at-arms and war material for any peacekeeping force that might get sent in. *But the Russians were going to take it?*

'What did you say?' someone managed.

'The fucking Russians are coming. Get with it. We're going in against the Russians.'

'We're going against the fucking Russians?'

Captain Robbins nodded, his face like death. 'Yeah, and we're going now. So go back and brief your patrols.'

I turned and headed for my lads. How was I going to put this, I wondered? We'd just gone from facing Milosevic's boys, to this: us, against the might of the Russian Red Army. At best, we had LAW-80s, and they would bounce off the side of the T90, the Russian main battle tank, like peashooters.

The T90 is encased with explosive reactive armour (ERA). Even MILAN anti-tank missiles – a superlative NATO weapon – won't dent that. LAW-80s – we might as well be going in with NERF guns.

I gathered my patrol. 'Close in.' A deep breath. 'Guys, we are gonna move by helo to take and secure Pristina airport. Intel reports a Russian tank column moving to take the airport. They cannot be allowed to take it. We gotta get there first.'

Eyes bulged.

Predictably, it was Ginge who spoke first. 'We're going in to fight the fucking Russians? You're fucking joking. Tell me you're fucking joking.'

In the back of my mind I was thinking: *How in the name of God has it come to this? This is a Third World War in the making.*

Before I could answer Ginge, Captain Robbins yelled out orders. 'Let's go!' He jabbed a finger towards the nearest Chinook, the rotors of which were turning and burning. 'Mount up! LET'S FUCKING GO!'

We started to run for the Chinook's open ramp.

'Guys, no matter what happens when we get off that helo, we stay together,' I yelled at my lot. 'You follow me. You take my lead. Do not get separated! If the shooting starts find something to shoot at, but stay together.'

'Yeah. Okay. Yeah,' came the breathless replies.

But no matter how the lads responded, their body language said it all. As we ran, I could read it in their faces. The blood had drained away. They knew their weaponry well enough to realise that nothing we had on us could halt a T90 in full charge.

This was futile.

A suicide mission.

We were going to get massacred.

We knelt before the open ramp, sweat-soaked and panting in the burning heat. To left and right I could see the pilots in their cockpits hunched over their maps, trying to work out the best route in. Loadies were crouched by the doors of the Pumas, ready to shovel the paratroopers aboard.

As we waited, my mind was a whirl. *This is it: World War Three,* I was thinking. *We're going to mallet a few Ruskies, but mostly we're going to get fucked.* I had visions of us unleashing LAWs and the rockets bouncing harmlessly off, as the T90s swung around their massive, gaping 125mm gun barrels. I saw Chinooks coming in to land, and getting raked with 12.7mm heavy machine gun fire.

My mind was still full of visions of mayhem, fire and blood, even as the order came to mount up the helos.

'Inside! Inside!' the loadie yelled, as he shovelled blokes aboard.

The thirty odd men of Patrols Platoon tore up the helo's open ramp. I glanced across at the Chinook next to us, and who should I see moving up the ramp but Dan Miller, my old mucker. We raised one hand to each other – a last farewell – before each of us was swallowed up by the helo's empty shadows.

Inside the Chinook the air was thick with burning avgas fumes. To either side of the helo's open ramp waves of blokes were charging past, rushing to get to the helicopters in front. It was sheer madness.

I was gagging with tension and, I have to admit – fear. My combats were soaked with sweat. I had a thirst to die for, and in all the chaos and confusion I realised we'd not managed to get a water resupply. It went without saying that we had no food, but a soldier can soldier on for a good while on an empty belly. Water – in this heat – was an entirely different matter. Still, I didn't figure we were going to live long enough for dehydration to kick in.

So why worry?

40

The turbines screamed above us, the noise precluding all possible talk. Each of us was entombed in our own thoughts – saying, I guess, our last goodbyes.

I glanced out through the Chinook's open ramp into the blinding daylight. I had visions of Armageddon flitting through my head. I saw the TV news full of images of dead PARAs strewn around Pristina airport. I saw the streets of Middlesbrough on fire, as Russian warheads slammed into them. London likewise.

There wasn't an American soldier on the ground in the Balkans yet. This was all UK Plc, and Britain would thus bear the brunt of the Russian retaliation. I thought about my mum and dad. I didn't figure they'd seen this coming, when they let me take the train to Junior PARA – that I was going to be in the unit that started the War To End Human Kind.

We were riding to our death.

We were just gonna get slaughtered.

I didn't have the slightest problem with being sent in to fight the Russians per se. Bring it on. But it had to be on a slightly more even playing field – not four mags and two bandoliers of ammo, versus the T90s.

We were sat there for fifteen minutes – 900 seconds in which every bloke aboard the Chinook doubtless had his life flashing through his mind. I know mine was – dodgy milk-float thieving and all. For all that time I was secretly thinking: *I hope to fuck someone somewhere sees sense and changes their minds.*

We were sat in the best position to exit, so all facing the rear – which meant I saw the loadie's expression as he climbed up the ramp. He had a look on his face as if Al Qaeda had just unzipped his orange jumpsuit and told him he was a free man.

'EVERYONE OFF THE HELO! OFF THE HELO! EVERYONE OFF!'

We got to our feet and moved down the ramp. For a moment I wondered if our Chinook had had a malfunction, and we were about to board another, but to left and right I could see it was the same picture – blokes piling off the helos. It looked as if it was a force-wide order. Like we were being stood down.

We joined the general flow, which was back towards the trucks that had delivered the extra ammo and weaponry. As we walked away the rearmost helos started to take to the air, flying up and over the top of us, then executing a wide turn to head back the way they had come.

We reached the road.

'I'll go and see what's happening,' Captain Robbins suggested.

I parked my arse on my Bergen and said the world's biggest thank you to whoever is up there. A temporary thank you, that is. We all sensed this was a postponement, not a cancellation.

I'd been there for five minutes when the distinctive forms of two American Black Hawk helicopters appeared overhead, and touched down right next to where we were sitting. They were thirty yards to my left, near some kind of old, dilapidated barn.

On my right, two hard-skin Army Land Rovers pulled in off the road, and parked up next to where we were sitting. The doors opened and instantly I recognised the figure who jumped out. It was General Mike Jackson. With his son being second-in-command of the Pathfinders, he was forever popping in for a beer and a chat. He'd chuck his beret on the table, light up a ciggie and chill.

I liked him. A lot. He was a soldier's general. Tall, skinny and cadaverous, he had a well lived-in skin. He had real presence, and he nurtured a great affection for the Parachute Regiment, plus airborne forces in general. Right now he was a lieutenant-general, so the British force commander on the ground. But he was known to us all, affectionately, as 'The Prince of Darkness'.

Needless to say, my eyes were glued to what unfolded next.

The side door of the nearest unmarked Black Hawk slid open. A group of senior commanders in combat fatigues dismounted, and moved across to The Prince of Darkness's Land Rovers. I saw them shake hands with him. They moved to the front of the nearest wagon, and with all the noise of the remaining helos taking off and leaving, they had to scream to make themselves heard.

I sidled closer, so I was just about able to get the gist of what they were saying. The long and short of it was this. A Russian column consisting of thirty armoured vehicles was heading for Pristina airport – the only one in Kosovo capable of taking military transport aircraft. The Russians intended to take it and in-load combat power – with their end-plan still to be determined.

US General Wesley Clark – NATO's Supreme Allied Commander Europe (SACEUR) – had ordered us to take the airport ahead of the Russians, hence the panic and chaos of the last thirty minutes. But in the meantime, the obvious issues with doing so had begun to raise their ugly heads.

First off, Milosevic had agreed to a ceasefire and the withdrawal of his forces from Kosovo, but only if NATO ground troops remained out until they were gone. If we thundered in, the terms of the fragile ceasefire would be broken, and he still had three hundred tanks of his own in the region. Second, going into a shitfight with the Russians would very likely trigger World War Three.

Our key NATO partners were supposed to provide support as we were airlifted in at the tip of a very unsharpened spear. The French had promised a battalion of airborne troops, plus Puma helos as transport, but they had just been withdrawn. Probably rightly, the French didn't want to be the ones to light the touchpaper.

The Americans were supposed to provide six Apache gunships – state-of-the-art tank-busters – but they were poised to withdraw them, for fear of sparking a Third World War.

As we'd sat on the helos senior commanders had argued the toss, General Clark insisting that Apaches or no Apaches, French or no French, we would go in as intended. Well, that was mighty nice of him. At least that way, no Yanks or Frogs would have to put their lives on the line.

General Jackson had thrown his rank slides onto the HQ table, and offered to resign on the spot. He'd made it clear that this was madness, that he could not follow his orders and would oppose them publicly, should our mission go ahead. And so, eventually, after a bit more argy-bargy, we were stood down.

The chat between General Jackson and the American commanders seemed to end with some degree of difference, if not outright animosity. The Americans did an about turn and went to re-mount their helos, their gait pumped up and punchy, their body language not exactly suggesting they'd got their own way.

As the Black Hawks took to the skies again, General Jackson climbed aboard his wagon and the two Land Rovers set off the way they had come. I didn't know the whole story, but it looked to me as if The Prince of Darkness had just won us our deliverance.

I figured there were two possible outcomes. Option one: they were going to come up with some sort of better plan to insert us by helo to take the airport. Option two: Jacko had made them see sense, and the assault had been called off, at least until we could get properly manned, armed and planned.

It was around 1630 by now. We were told to muster at the point where the meadow met the rise to the woodland, and remain in a holding pattern, pending further orders.

In other words – limbo.

We'd just got a brew on, when Captain Robbins came over. Apparently the CO wanted to have words. We headed over to his tent.

'The move to take Pristina is still going to happen,' Gibbo announced, 'but in a more subdued manner, one less likely to cause World War Three. There's now an urgent need to report on movement by the Russians into Pristina. If we end up in a shooting match we need to know where they are.' The CO jabbed a finger at his map. 'The only way anyone can get through is via here – the Kacanic Defile.'

The name meant nothing to me, because prior to this moment I hadn't been party to any of the briefings or even been issued with a map.

'The KD is a MSR that cuts through this gorge. Pristina is ringed by impassable mountains, and it's the only way in.'

MSR stands for main supply route – basically, any major highway – Pristina being the capital city of Kosovo.

The CO glanced in my direction. 'Sergeant Heaney, I want your patrol to insert ahead of the Battle Group, to a position high above the Kacanic Defile. I want you to report on any movements of Russian or Serb troops, vehicles or tanks. And if necessary, you're there to put a stop to them.

'You will not be able to rely on any fire support from the Battalion mortars, 'cause you'll be well out of range. However, Seven RHA have their one-oh-five millimetre guns and you will be in range of them – just. Plus you'll have the ability to call for airstrikes. You'll be flown across border to a drop-off point, and under your own steam you're to move to your choice of OP.'

Seven RHA stood for the 7th Parachute Regiment Royal Horse Artillery – as fine a gunnery regiment as ever there was. The maximum range of their L118 howitzers is 17.2 kilometres, which meant that I now had a good idea of how far we were going in: that kind of distance, just under.

I had not said a word, but in my mind I was thinking: *So why the fuck not use the Pathfinders?* This was a classic X Platoon mission. I was thinking: *I have a young, inexperienced patrol. They're fine lads; paratroopers at their best; but they are very raw at this kind of work.* Even for Pathfinders this would be a real premier tasking.

The CO eyed me, and it was as if he'd read my mind. 'Steve, you're getting this because you are a Pathfinder. The four of you will be going in alone. But you have to understand the risk of fratricide. The Kacanic Defile is the only route via which Kosovan refugees are getting out of the country, so it's jammed solid.'

He paused. 'So, to be clear, yours will be the Battle Group's most-forward asset, and from when you are inserted you will be out on a limb. One independent patrol. You alone. That's it. And the Seven RHA Battery Commander – he'll only put down fire if called in by you, personally, 'cause he knows your background.'

Captain Robbins was sat beside me, silent as a ghost. I'd still not said a word.

'Wheels up at zero four hundred,' the CO rounded off. 'Liaise with the Company signaller and get all of Seven RHA frequencies and call-signs, plus those of air support, so you can call in fire. Any questions?'

I shook my head. 'Nope. You've pretty much covered it. Wheels up at zero four hundred.'

'Yep. And I want you in position as soon as you can thereafter.'

We left, Captain Alan Robbins and me walking back through the gathering dusk towards the blokes.

'That's pretty fucking way out-there, to be fair, Steve . . .' remarked the captain, but I was only half listening. I was mapping out a plan of action in my mind.

The sun was sinking fast. I had eight or nine hours of darkness in which to prepare my patrol. I'd work to the one-third, two-thirds rule: one-third of the time for mission planning, two-thirds for briefing and prepping the blokes. I worked backwards from L-Hour, our lift-off time from here – which was 0400.

We'd need a good thirty minutes to walk to the helicopter, so we'd have to be on our way by 0330. The lads needed sleep, but I wanted them up and having a brew and a kit check by 0220, so reveille would be 0200. I wanted them to have six hours' kip minimum, for I had no idea when we'd next get any sleep – which meant they needed to hit the hay by 2000 hours, less than two hours away.

And that meant I had them to myself for the next hour and a half max. In that time I needed Ginge to talk to 7 RHA, plus the Tactical Air Control Party (TACP), whose job it was to control all air-assets assigned to us, sorting call-signs and frequencies. I needed the rest of the blokes to sort kit, weaponry and ammo, imposing some order and sense on the weapons free-for-all we'd experienced that afternoon. Plus I needed all of us to do a shed-load of map orientation.

In the Pathfinders every bloke carries a map, keeps track of location and knows exactly where he is and where he's going. In regular units only the more senior ranks tend to. But we were being sent in as honorary Pathfinders, and that being the case I was going to run things according to our credo.

'Alan, give me an hour with the blokes,' I remarked to Captain Robbins. I'd heard not a word of what he'd been saying. 'I'll come and back brief you on my intentions.'

I dumped Alan and headed for my patrol. 'Close in lads; got a task.'

I sat on my Bergen, opened the map at my feet and Ginge, Taff and Hendo gathered around. 'We're on a helo at zero four hundred, going in isolated, as one patrol. This is our task.' I outlined the mission and finished with this. 'Make sure you're carrying as many full water bottles as you can. I want you to square your kit away, check your batteries, clean and prep your weapons. You're then on enforced rest from twenty hundred hours to zero two twenty.'

'I don't care what's happening around you,' I continued, 'who's trying to talk to you – I want you in your maggots fast asleep by twenty hundred. Reveille is zero two hundred: final kit checks – brew and a hot scoff inside you, and be ready to move from this location by zero three thirty.'

I paused, taking a moment to look around my team. None was older than twenty-two. I was thirty, which made me the old, grizzled bastard in their midst. Even in the fading light I could tell that the pasty-faced look they'd had earlier was coming back.

I let out a bit of a chuckle. 'Look at it this way, lads: if it all goes Pete Tong at least we can call in a grand finale from the guns. Questions?'

'So, let's get this right,' Ginge ventured. 'We're on a helo zero four hundred tomorrow morning?'

'Yeah.'

'And we're flying across the border . . .'

'Yeah.'

'On our own . . .'

'Yeah.'

'No one else . . .'

'No.'

'Just the four of us . . .'

'Yeah. Look guys, come on – time to get sparking.'

'To look for the Russians?'

'Yep. The Russians. And don't forget the Serbs.' I tried a winning smile. 'Lads, if it makes you feel any better you can each write a bluey home . . . We'll leave 'em with the admin guy.'

Ginge snorted. 'Oh, well that's all good then. Best we get scribbling.'

'That's the spirit,' I confirmed. 'Right, crack on with your admin and I'll go and find us some scoff.'

I headed off to dig out some ration packs. I figured the lads had to be thinking: *Fuck me, did we draw the short straw when we got Heaney as our patrol commander, or what?* As for me, I wasn't in the Pathfinders right now, I'd suffered months of rules and rank crap – and yet I'd managed to land this.

Bingo.

Christmas had just come very fucking early. How many British soldiers ever got to spy on the Russians, or if we were lucky, to rain down shock and awe upon them?

Needless to say, I went to search out the rations with a real spring in my step.

41

As luck would have it I managed to get Ben Green – my biggest critic – to root out the rations, because strictly speaking he was in charge of the Platoon's stores, and I was busy. He came back with one box – 24 hours – per man. I chucked one to each of the lads.

'That's all you've got: use it wisely.'

Ben hung around, clearly itching to know what was happening. 'How's it going, mate? You happy with the plan? I hear you might have to call in the fucking arty?'

'Yeah. Once we get in position I'll send our OP location as a free fire area, so the gun line know what's what.'

'A free fire area?'

'Yeah. So the gunners know our position and can fire into it, dropping pretty much danger-close all around.'

Translated, that meant the 7 RHA commander would have a ten-figure grid of our exact location. Everywhere outside of that grid would be fair game. Because 105mm high-explosive rounds have a lethality range of 250 metres from the point of impact, they could drop that close to our co-ordinates, leaving a 500-metre no fire zone straddling us. We could call in fire in relative safety, leaving everything else to be flattened.

I explained as much to Ben.

'Oh, right – yeah, yeah, yeah.'

I figured it would be good having a liaison back at base – someone who knew something of what we were up to. Ben was going to be that man.

I got him to commandeer a Land Rover and we drove across to the Brigade HQ, so we could liaise with the Pathfinders. It was good to see that Wag was there. Tricky, my signaller from exercise Purple bloody Dinosaur, or whatever it was called, was also present. Or was it Dino the Purple Dinosaur?

Whatever. It gets confusing.

'Lads, there's a chance we're going across the border before you, and we'll be on one of your flanks,' I told them. 'Fancy giving us your call-signs and comms plans, just so we can deconflict, and maybe support each other should it come to that?'

'No problem,' said Tricky. He glanced at Ben. 'But you know the protocol, mate – only you get these.'

We chatted for a short time, but there wasn't much to report from their side: the Pathfinders were yet to get a tasking. It was bizarre. Why on earth were they sending us four across the border, and leaving these guys sat here twiddling their thumbs? Still, I rated Gibbo highly as a commander and he was sure to have a cunning plan.

Visit to the Pathfinders done, we drove back to our position, and I got a much-needed scoff-on and a brew.

There was something I noticed, as I hunched over my scoff pot, which was warming over a tiny Hexi stove set between my legs. The three lads of my patrol were gathered together heating up their own nosh. They'd been in the Patrols Platoon for a year, the PARAs for longer, and they shared a certain bond. I was a man apart.

I was left to my own thoughts. I stared into the flames, my arms folded across my knees, running through it all in my head. And I have to admit, a part of me did wonder: *Shall I write a bluey to Mum and Dad?*

Last thing before getting some kip, Ginge gave me our call-sign: *Delta Two One*. I liked it. It sounded suitably warlike, but covert.

Then I crawled into my maggot, reminding myself to have a chat with the helo's aircrew before we got airborne, so we could decide on a route in and a suitable LS to put the four of us lucky lads down on.

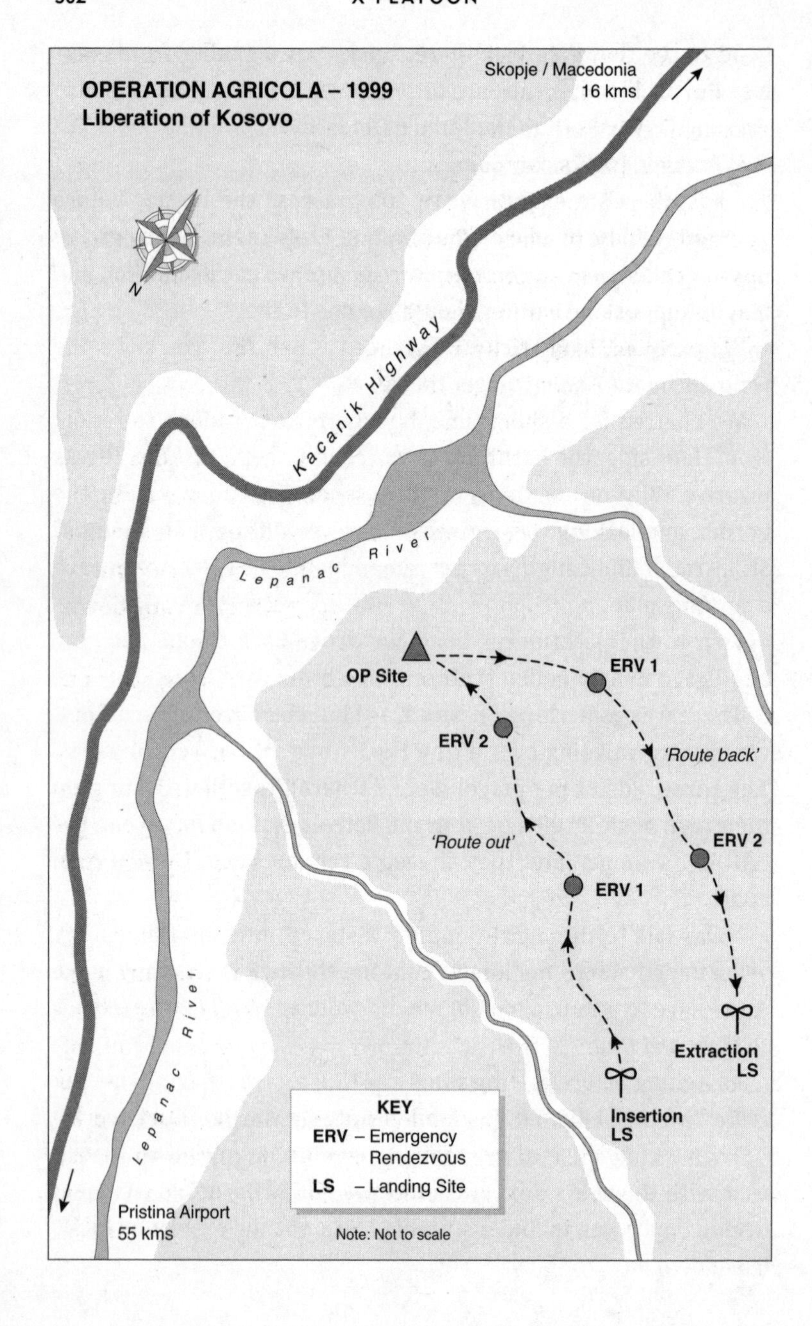
OPERATION AGRICOLA – 1999
Liberation of Kosovo
Skopje / Macedonia
16 kms
N
Kacanik Highway
Lepanac River
OP Site
ERV 1
ERV 2
'Route back'
'Route out'
ERV 2
ERV 1
Extraction LS
Insertion LS
Lepanac River
KEY
ERV – Emergency Rendezvous
LS – Landing Site
Pristina Airport
55 kms
Note: Not to scale

I woke in the pitch dark, to the distant noise of a lone Puma flying in. The others were awake already, brewing up. I got a quick drink down me, then we hoisted our Bergens and weaponry and set off. We made our way out to where we'd mounted up the Chinook, the previous afternoon.

I went forward to chat to the RAF pilot. He looked at the LS I'd chosen off the map – somewhere that put us high in the mountains, but on a slope running away from the Kacanic Defile, so our landing was less likely to be observed.

'No problem,' he confirmed. 'We'll get you as close to that point as we can.'

Following a steep climb above the LS there would be a place for our OP, one set high above the plunging ravines and scree-slopes of the Defile. The position should offer us a clear view of the road north – providing ample time to spot a column of T90s, fix their co-ordinates, and dial up 7 RHA to rain down fire.

The pilot confirmed he was good to go, and we'd be 'wheels up in ten'.

I returned to the lads. 'Kit on, guys.'

They loaded their Bergens aboard the Puma, folded out the canvas seats and plonked down their arses. It was dark in the helo, and it would stay that way: the pilots would be flying in on NVGs and showing no lights.

No one was saying much.

The Puma's starter motor whined, the twin turbines fired up and she spooled up the speed. We took off, banked hard and the pilot set a course northwest, climbing over the forested hills of Macedonia towards the border.

The loadie passed me the intercom headphones. I listened in to an echoing void of static. For a moment I thought the intercom must be knackered, then I realised that no one was saying a word in the cockpit. Clearly, it wasn't only the four of us who were tense as hell.

Five minutes in the pilot uttered his first phrase: 'We're approaching the border.'

I don't know what alerted me – maybe some kind of sixth sense – but I glanced out of the Puma's porthole-like window and saw a ghostly apparition on our starboard side. It was the dark form of a blacked-out US Cobra gunship. I glanced to our port, and sure enough there was a Cobra silhouetted there too. We were flanked by them – our escorts into God only knew what.

'That's us,' the pilot's voice broke in. 'We've crossed the border – now in Kosovo.'

The moment we were over the border the Puma seemed to drop like a stone. I figured the pilot was hugging the contours, to avoid getting picked up by any Yugoslav or Russian radar and being targeted by a SAM (surface-to-air-missile).

Several NATO warplanes had been shot down over the Balkans, including most recently a US F-117 Stealth Bomber. The threat was very real.

It was so dark in the Puma's hold I couldn't see the lads' faces. I wondered what they were thinking. We climbed and dropped over a series of ridges – the ranges that separated the two countries – before diving into a deep valley, after which the Puma proceeded to weave and slalom its way through.

We were thirty minutes in the air when the pilot announced, tensely. 'Five minutes out.'

I turned to my guys and flashed five fingers. They nodded and shuffled uneasily in their seats.

'Two minutes,' the pilot announced. I felt the Puma start to lose air speed and altitude. 'Thirty seconds.'

Moments later the arse-end of the helo dropped, and there was a thud as it made contact with Kosovan soil. I grabbed my weapon and jumped out of the side door, going down on one knee facing the hold. One at a time the lads threw their Bergens out to me, then followed. I darted fifteen metres to one side and got down low, the others following suit.

For a moment I was aware of the pair of Cobra gunships, no more than twenty-five feet off the ground and just off the Puma's tail fin, twitching to their left and right as they searched for the enemy. Then I flashed a thumbs-up to the loadie, he returned it, and the helos were gone.

The noise of the three aircraft faded fast. It was 0515 hours. Below us was a curtain of low-lying mist, white and gossamer-like in the valley. Above us, the sky to the east was just starting to lighten to a salmon pink with the first rays of dawn.

We were on the ground in Kosovo, and as far as I knew we were first-in. The helo had put down on a flat patch of thin pasture, lying at the base of a long climb. I took out my compass and map, orientated myself, and gave the bearing.

'Lads, east up that feature on to the top. Off we go.'

We started off across the pasture. It was already light enough to see to walk. We hit the start of the climb, and began to zig-zag across the gradient, as all the while I scanned the terrain to either side. It was utterly deserted; clear of human habitation, of domestic animals, of tracks or roads. We reached the summit by 0630, just as the sun rose right into our eyes.

We dropped our Bergens for a breather and a water break. I glanced back the way we'd come. The low-lying mist had cleared and I could see the vast curve of the valley sweeping west. Here and there in the far distance were two or three red-tiled houses, clustered together, interspersed with pastureland and thick forest.

It was eerily quiet, even serene. I found it hard to believe the country was riven by war, mass killings and horrific bloodshed.

We traversed a small plateau – the high-point – walking into the rising sun. We came to the lip of what had to be the Kacanic Defile. Approaching on all fours we peered over. Some thousand metres below lay the road. Even at this hour it was clogged with traffic: civvie vehicles and crowds of people on foot, all moving south towards Macedonia and what they hoped would be safety.

I left Taff and Ginge on lookout, and scouted along the ridge with Hendo, looking for where to site the OP. We came upon a patch of natural woodland. The trees were low and stunted, the cover was thick, and it offered us a cracking view of the road below in both directions. We could set up the radio here and remain unobserved, while keeping watch on all traffic.

We fetched the others, entered the bush from the rear-side, pushed in a good seventy metres and set up camp just off the forward edge. It was 0830 hours and we were in position, just as Gibbo had asked.

'Hendo, drop your kit and start observing. Ginge, get the radio set up. I want to send a sitrep asap. And Taff, sit on your Bergen, face back the way we came – you're rear sentry, mate.'

It wasn't long before Ginge had the radio up and running. '*Zero, Delta Two One:* Sitrep. Location grid one one three four six seven eight nine three three. In position, observing target area. No movement spotted.'

'Roger. Out.'

That grid would now be passed to the gun line, as per my brief. It was now the Anchor Grid, from which all bearings and distances would be computed so they could get their gun line to the target. I set a standard routine; two observing the Defile, one on rear sentry, one getting some rest.

The only niggle in my mind right now was food. We each had a breakfast and a lunch remaining, but that was it. With all that had happened the day before it had been another on-the-bus-off-the-bus kind of thing, and we'd been given no task duration. Gibbo had just told us to get it done.

Still, there wasn't much I could do about that now.

At around 1100 I sent Hendo back to get some rest. I wanted some time alone to think. Something was bugging me, but I couldn't quite work out what it was. Finally, I called Ginge forwards to have words.

'Mate, let's set up the radio on listening watch. I've just got this feeling they're gonna want to talk to us today . . . Man it twenty-four seven, okay?'

Ginge did as I'd asked. Normally, you'd only have your radio up and running when sending your two daily sitreps, so morning and evening. But I just had this uncanny feeling Gibbo was going to want to talk to us sometime soon.

All through the blistering heat of the day no call came in. In fact, the entire scene was deceptively peaceful. If you didn't know the Defile was clogged with refugees fleeing a genocide, you'd think it was a bunch of people making a summer break for the seaside.

At 1630 that afternoon I sent my second sitrep. 'Nothing to report. Heavy civilian movement south down the Defile. Patrol status good.'

'Roger. Out.'

With sunset the temperature quickly dropped. It was chilly and exposed up on the ridge, but down below us the mass exodus continued – one that was now only visible by car headlights.

Finally, deep in the night, the message came in from Gibbo. 'Move immediately. Make for the pick-up LS.'

It came from out of the blue, Gibbo giving us a grid to head for, but not a hint as to why we were being pulled out. Still, ours was not to reason why.

We crawled out of our maggots, collapsed the position, and began the trek down the hillside. By the time we were at the new pick-up grid it was well light. We sat off in the cover of some shrubs, watching the LS. We'd been there for thirty minutes when we heard the distinctive *thwoop-thwoop-thwoop* of an inbound Chinook.

I walked out to the centre of the LS, held up my AMP and the helo came straight in to land. Then I called to the blokes: 'Right, let's go!'

We thundered up the ramp, and there we found twelve of the Patrols Platoon, Bergens and weapons at the ready. This looked interesting. I had a brief conversation with one of the patrol commanders, a bloke I knew reasonably well.

'Where've you just come from, mate?'

'From the field you lot mounted from – first time in. How did it go with you lot?'

'All good. Loads of refugees piling south but no Russian or Serbian armour that we could see. Where we going?'

He shrugged. 'Rumour is straight into Pristina.'

We took off. The top half of the Chinook's ramp remained open, and I could see other helos – Chinooks and a Puma – to either side of us, and likewise dipping and diving through the terrain. I guessed this was a rerun of the previous attempt at an air invasion, only with a bit more firepower and strategy behind it.

Our Chinook flared out and touched down. I had absolutely no idea where we had landed, but there were other airframes to left and right putting down. The ramp lowered and the loadie roared: 'OFF!'

We piled off into an all-around defence, and I could see we'd landed in a sun-bleached meadow. There were twenty or more helos disgorging paratroopers all around, and below lay a city that had to be Pristina. I recognised it from all the reports I'd seen on the TV news.

We hefted our Bergens, formed up in human snakes and began to double-time it into the city. The tarmac road was utterly deserted. To either side lay bombed-out buildings, the doors and windows to the houses lying smashed and broken, like empty eye-sockets.

So this was Pristina: question was, where were the Russians?

42

Slowly, almost imperceptibly, the first human beings started to show themselves. Very quickly the trickle became a flood.

Old men in frayed jackets; old women in long skirts and head-scarves – what looked like typical gypsy clothing. Young women carrying babies. Kids running wild.

Civvies, obviously.

The citizens of Pristina.

And everywhere, people started cheering.

We'd heard lots and lots of stories of beatings, mass rapes and worse. Our build-up training had stressed to us what horrors Milosevic's forces were perpetrating here. These, then, were the victims; the survivors. It was like a scene from some Second World War movie as Allied troops liberated French cities. It was hugely moving.

It was the closest I'd ever come to feeling like a hero.

Zero to hero: *there you go.*

To be welcomed as liberators and showered with flowers, as opposed to going up against a squadron of T90 main battle tanks: it wasn't quite what I'd been expecting.

There were a couple of sporadic exchanges of fire as we pushed further in, but it was all way off target and nothing came close to us. Milosevic's forces – plus the Russians, presumably – had clearly decided war was not the answer.

We pushed right into the heart of the devastated city.

We passed entire tower blocks with all their windows blown out; shopping malls half collapsed; massive craters in the middle of a road. I noticed buildings everywhere scrawled with graffiti. I couldn't read it. It was all in Cyrillic – Russian – script. Presumably it was the language of ethnic cleansing daubed on the walls of this benighted city.

By the time we hit downtown Pristina the streets were clogged with vehicles: people were beeping horns, shouting and yelling with joy. We pulled to a halt by what had to be the city's tallest building. It looked to be thirty floors high, and every single window had been blown out. Curtains flapped in the summer heat. Blinds swung to and fro in the faint breeze blowing off the mountains.

Captain Alan Robbins came up to me. 'Sergeant Heaney, you're to take up position in this skyscraper. To secure it.'

He addressed me as 'Sergeant Heaney' whenever there were other soldiers within earshot. If it was just the two of us I was 'Steve'. In the Pathfinders, as you've probably noticed, it's all done on first name terms, regardless of rank. It's a meritocracy. This was green army mentality.

The tall building turned out to be a German bank. Presumably, its vaults had been well-looted. But as I dropped my Bergen and signalled for the lads to do likewise, don't think for one moment that the thought hadn't crossed my mind. *A deserted bank? In the midst of a war-zone? Come on, let's take a butchers!*

Opposite the bank was a big yellow building – the city's Ministry of Justice. That was where Gibbo had decided to establish his headquarters. Captain Robbins went to get a briefing with the CO. He came back and drew me to one side.

'Steve, the CO wants an elevated view of the city. He wants eyes-on twenty-four seven. He wants you to take up residence in the bank, and see if you can get onto the roof. He wants an obs post up there, as soon as. He doesn't care how you do it. Break down doors if you have to.'

'Right, mate, no problem with that. But Alan, can you chase up some scoff? We've not had anything for twenty-four hours.'

Alan said he'd rustle us up some food pronto.

I took a good look at the bank. The damage was mostly superficial. A building behind it had been targeted by what I figured was a NATO air-strike. It had been sliced in half. The blast from the bomb had blown out the windows in all of the neighbouring buildings, the German bank included.

Gaining entry wasn't an issue. We just stepped in through the broken windows and door. The foyer was smashed to smithereens. Whatever had been dropped on the building next door, it must have been big. The bomb blast had punched right through.

There was no power, and as we went further in all was in shadow. Glass scrunched underfoot. I signalled my three lads to find the staircase, for there would be no taking the lift to the 32nd floor. We passed through an office area. Chairs and tables had been crushed and overturned, drawers had been upended and paper was strewn everywhere.

No bank notes, sadly.

Or not ones that I could see.

'Lads, scout around. Try to find the safe; the vault.'

I figured we had a duty to secure it, in addition to setting up our rooftop OP. And like any good Pathfinder, I was going to seize the initiative.

They found the bank vault. Its doors had been blown off their hinges and there was nothing of any obvious interest left inside. In fact, as we would discover, the entire city had been comprehensively looted. The banks had been targeted first, after which anything else of value had been fair game. The Pristina Art Museum had also been cleaned out, not a painting left hanging on its walls.

We started to climb the stairs. The higher we got the more the wind whistled through the empty windows. After thirty-odd flights we reached the top floor, and found the door leading up to the roof. I got Taff – our resident lump – to boot it off its hinges.

Outside, a metal ladder was bolted to the final stretch – twenty feet straight up to the high-point.

I turned to the lads. 'Ginge, Taff: stay here with the Bergens. Hendo – let's take a butchers.'

The view from the roof was stunning. Or rather, shocking more like. We were stood on the highest point of Pristina, which offered a 360-degree view of the city. I broke out my binoculars. In all directions were thick palls of smoke, abandoned cars, shattered streets and wrecked buildings.

No doubt about it: if Gibbo wanted eyes-on 24/7, this was the place from where to deliver it.

Hendo followed me back down the ladder. 'Right, lads,' I said, 'find yourself somewhere to billet yourselves on this floor. Clear up and tidy as best you can. I want two guys on roof-watch, one guy resting, plus one guy doing permanent watch on the stairwell. Get a chair, put it at the top of the stairs. No one can get to us unless they get up the stairs. I want that chair manned at all times.'

There were nods and murmurs of assent.

I went back to the roof with Hendo. The sun was starting to set across the city. Here and there I could see columns of PARAs moving through the streets. The CO was setting out his stall. He was sending a clear message: *The PARAs are here. The streets are secure now. We own the city.*

We'd been up there for less than an hour when there was a shout from below. 'Steve! Platoon commander's here!'

I went down to find that Captain Robbins had allocated me four extra blokes. I now had an eight-man shift to man my bank-watch. I put together a stag-roster and mapped out in which of the bank offices the guys would be billeted. I found myself an empty office, dumped my Bergen, kicked as much of the glass to one side as I could, and laid my maggot on the carpet.

Home sweet home.

There was a shout for me out in the corridor. It was Ben Green. 'Right, Steve, rations and water at the entrance.'

I glanced at him. 'You didn't carry any up yourself? Right mate, I'll sort it.'

I allocated some of the new lads to water and food carrying duties, and cornered Ben for a chat. 'Right, Ben, what do you know, and what're the rumours, mate?'

'CO and HQ element are in the building opposite. Me and the boss are co-located with them. We're getting foot patrols out across the city. The CO's still concerned, as there are elements of Yugoslav and Serb forces still around.'

'And what about the Russians?'

'No idea, mate.'

'Okay – how does he want us reporting what we see?'

'Log book, mate. Any Serb or Yugo forces you see – log everywhere they come from and go to, numbers, arms; you know the score. And get it across to us on the double.'

By now the guys had hefted up the jerry-cans of water and the ration packs. Ben left, and I told the lads of my patrol to get some scoff on. We were all ravenous.

'But if you're cooking up make sure you do so on a solid, tiled surface,' I warned them. 'Last thing we want is the building on fire with us on the top floor.'

I headed for my room, broke out a Hexi stove plus a boil-in-the-bag meal and took it all into the toilet, which led off like an en-suite. I sat myself on the shitter, seat down, with the Hexi stove on the tiled floor. I sparked up the tiny fuel blocks, got my metal pot heating, and glanced out of the open door into the bomb-wrecked office, the night wind howling through the smashed window.

Nice.

Doesn't get any better.

Brewing up in the rest room.

Thirty-six hours earlier we'd been flying into war against the Russians. Now I was sat in a Pristina bank on the crapper, getting a scoff on. Moments that make you go . . . *hmmmmm*.

The night felt chilly. I could feel a cold wind swirling around the toilet. It was eerie. Spooky. Ghostly, almost.

But it wasn't a touch on the darkness that was coming.

43

It wasn't long before we were pulled off bank-watch and retasked. We were two days in when Captain Robbins paid a visit, along with Colonel Gibson.

'Right,' said Gibbo, 'I'm pulling you back from here. I'm pushing out a patrol presence to the north of the city and I need you to be a response team to incidents.'

'Incidents?' I queried. 'What kind of incidents?'

'Steve, the grace period for Serb forces to leave the city has just come to an end. People are drifting back from the hills where they've been hiding. As they move back in they're starting to find dead bodies, and they're itching for revenge. There's been fighting. Murders. That's what your patrol will be responding to.'

'Right. Okay.'

'People are stopping our patrols and dragging blokes into houses, to show them what horrors have been perpetrated. It's tense. Incendiary. I need a Quick Reaction Force. You're it.'

'Right. Okay.'

We went about collapsing our position on the bank roof. When we were halfway done I got a warning from Captain Robbins to hold on. General Mike Jackson was flying in to the bank, to pay a visit personally. I didn't have a clue what was going on, but moments later a Lynx appeared in the sky above us, and proceeded to land on the flat roof of the bank.

Out stepped General Jackson.

He strode across to me, a military photographer snapping away as he went, and thrust out a hand. 'Congratulations, Steve,' he announced. Then he proceeded to pin my sergeant's stripes onto my uniform. 'There. Now you've got your stripes. From what I hear, you've more than earned them.'

I was speechless.

'So, what's it for you now?' he asked.

'Well, sir, once we're done here I figure I'll be off back to the Pathfinders.'

He beamed. 'Right. See you there soon, then.'

With that he turned and mounted up the helo, which then did one of those James Bond stunt acts, looking as if it had simply dropped off the edge of the building. Moments later it powered back into view again and thundered across the city skies.

Captain Robbins told me we were being allocated a translator to help with our new role as the Quick Reaction Force. An appeal had gone out for locals who could speak English, to work as interpreters for NATO. When our 'terp' – slang for interpreter – rocked up, it wasn't quite what I'd been expecting.

She was a young Kosovan Albanian, she'd been a university student before the war broke out, and she was to die for. She had long sandy-blonde hair, huge brown eyes and the perfect figure. Plus she was funny, chatty and cute as hell. Everyone's tongue was hanging out just at the sight of her, 'Captain Alan's' included.

We nicknamed her J. Lo, for obvious reasons, plus her real name was far too difficult to pronounce.

We couldn't exactly act as Gibbo's Quick Reaction Force from the thirty-second floor of a bank with no lift. So we were shown to a house in downtown Pristina where we could billet ourselves. The place was deserted, but it hadn't been trashed by looters, and no one had a clue as to the whereabouts of its rightful owners.

There were still family photos on the mantelpiece. They showed a young couple with two small kids. Upstairs, there was a girl's room and a boy's room, plus what had been the parents' master bedroom. But other than that we didn't know if it was a Serb house, a Kosovo Albanian house, or what.

I took the mum and dad's room. Taff, Hendo and Ginge were split between the boys and girl's bedrooms. And J. Lo – I put her in the converted attic room, well out of reach of the lads. Billets sorted, I gave the boys a bit of a stern talking to.

'Right, as you all know – *she's up there*. Nobody goes near her. Lads, I know you've been away a while, and you think you're well travelled, suave and sophisticated. But no way. No one goes up there.'

They started laughing and joking. But I let them know I was serious. J. Lo's floor – it was strictly out of bounds.

I dumped my Bergen in the bedroom. The parents' clothes were still in the wardrobe; toiletries in the bathroom; shoes under the bed. It looked as if they had run so quickly, or been dragged away, that they'd not had time to take anything personal with them. But there was no obvious sign of any struggle, either.

It was all very twilight zone.

There was running water, the loos all flushed, the electric cooker in the kitchen worked, and the big TV bolted to the wall was hooked up to some kind of satellite system, which included MTV. Even the phone was still connected. We called HQ, gave them the number, and told them they could call in any jobs to us that way.

We killed time patrolling the city in the Land Rover we'd been given, with J. Lo as our guide.

'Right, J. Lo,' I said, 'show us around the different districts. Take us down the main roads, the short cuts, the dead ends. Show us where the hospital is, plus anything else that may be important.'

J. Lo knew her nickname by now, and it was clear that she loved it. But she wasn't your typical 'girly' girl. There was something of the Lara Croft about her. Tough and confident, she climbed in and out of a British Army Land Rover as easily as if she'd always done it.

She also knew the city like the back of her hand. We were directed to the first major landmark – a long, grey building four floors high. Even before she told us, there was something about it that was somehow darkly sinister and evil.

J. Lo eyed the place, her eyes black with fear. 'Steve, that place – that was the MUP HQ.'

'Okay. Who's the MUP?'

'Serb secret police. Very bad people. They who would come to a house and take men, take women, take children even. They'd be here, they'd be drinking, then they'd go and take the girls . . .'

'Right, okay.'

We continued to familiarise ourselves with the city, before returning to the house that evening to cook an all-in with the ration packs. It turned out J. Lo's favourite was meatballs in pasta, so that's what we had.

I warned her: 'J. Lo, get yours first – as there won't be anything left if you go last.'

I like low-maintenance women and J. Lo scored highly on that scale. Meatballs in pasta really seemed to light her candle – for this was the evening that J. Lo decided to dance. We were sat in the living room watching MTV, one ear tuned to the phone in case an incident was called in. J. Lo was upstairs powdering her nose.

All of a sudden, the real Jennifer Lopez came on MTV, singing one of her first ever songs: 'If you had my love'. We were sat glued to the screen, when her namesake flounced into the room. She was wearing a figure-hugging skirt, a tight T-shirt and bright pink trainers, and she looked good enough to eat.

She walked into the centre and began to move. This was no traditional Albanian folk dance, either. This was real nightclub, hip-thrusting, hair-swishing stuff. The four of us gawped at her, our chins on the floor. Jennifer Lopez finished singing, J. Lo gave a little bow-cum-curtsy, and we stared at her in silent . . . well, let's admit it, steaming-mad-stir-crazy animal lust.

I suggested to J. Lo she might like a cup of tea. I took her to the kitchen. 'Look, that dancing thing. I mean, don't get me wrong – it was . . . fantastic. But please – don't. I have three young private soldiers I am trying to keep under control here. They're young, dumb and full of . . . Well, you get the idea. And you're whipping them up into a frenzy . . .'

J. Lo smiled. 'I understand. No more dancing, no?'

'No more dancing,' I confirmed.

The following morning we readied ourselves for our early morning patrol.

'Has anyone given J. Lo a shout?' someone asked. We mustered at the bottom of the stairs and started yelling. 'Right, J. Lo! Come on! Get ready!'

I turned to the lads. 'Typical woman – always ten minutes late.'

As we waited for J. Lo, I half expected Captain Alan to put in an appearance. Ever since she'd been parachuted into our patrol, he'd seemed keen to spend as much time as possible with us. In fact, he was like a love-sick puppy. I'd started twisting him about it.

'Alan, you know J. Lo's been asking about you?'

Captain Alan's face would blush red. 'Really? *Really*?'

'Yeah, mate. She's asking all the time.'

We sat out in the Land Rover, tooting the horn until J. Lo got her shit together and joined us. We took off, Taff driving, me in the vehicle commander's – the front passenger – seat, and J. Lo sandwiched between Hendo and Ginge in the rear. We'd not been out long when we got the radio call.

'*Delta Two One*; *Zero*.' Zero was the HQ call-sign.

'*Delta Two One*. Send, over.'

'Can you respond to a domestic in the Kadjiki area; reports of disturbance in one of the buildings.'

HQ passed us the exact street address.

'*Delta Two One*. Roger, out.' I glanced in the back. 'J. Lo, where's this place?'

She leaned between the seats and began to direct us. I could smell her. I had her hot breath on my neck. *Get a grip, man.*

J. Lo directed us to a grim-looking tower block. Out front we could see a punch-up in full swing. There were five guys doing a lacklustre impression of knocking seven bales of shit out of each other. They were surrounded by a gaggle of women who were shouting and screaming abuse in all directions.

We got out. 'J. Lo, go ask the women what's what.'

J. Lo went to speak with the nearest local. She was back shortly with an answer. 'They are fighting because two of those men were breaking into an apartment. But no one who lives in the building recognises them.'

The brawlers were backing off by now, seeing the four of us had rocked up. There was still the odd, half-hearted punch being thrown, but it was cooling down to nothing.

'Let's go take a butchers,' I suggested. 'Taff and Hendo, stay on the entrance keeping watch. I'll take Ginge and J. Lo with me.'

We climbed a bare concrete stairwell to the first floor, where a front door had been kicked in. As I approached it the first thing that hit me was the smell. It was the sweet, sickly, gagging smell of decay. I pushed what remained of the door ajar, which opened onto a living room. It was a total mess. Drawers, papers and nick-nacks were strewn across the floor.

'Ginge, go have a look that way,' I told him, pointing to what had to be the bedroom.

For some reason I was drawn in the opposite direction, to the kitchen. It had a small window set above the sink looking out over a similar block of flats. The rubbish bin had been emptied onto the floor, which accounted in part for the stench. I glanced around the place and noticed a small white fridge set about shoulder height.

I do not know why I did this, but I reached out and opened it. The fridge was full of half-rotten food. Wilted vegetables. Mouldering cheese. A carton of milk long turned sour. Nothing so remarkable there. I was about to close it, when I stopped dead.

On the central shelf was a white dinner plate, and on the plate were lying four human hands.

44

The hands were placed with the fingers towards the rear of the fridge – so cut ends towards me. The cuts weren't clean. It looked as if the wrists had been sawn through.

The hands on the bottom were clearly male. Laid over them with the fingers crossed was a pair of female hands, complete with reddish-brown nail varnish.

'Fuck.'

I felt J. Lo's presence on my shoulder. I closed the fridge rapidly, turned, took her by the shoulders and steered her back into the lounge.

'Ginge!' I called. He popped his head out of the bedroom. 'Do us a favour mate – take J. Lo back downstairs, will you?'

'Yeah, mate. Why, what is it?'

'Laters. Just take her down.'

As soon as they were gone I got on my hand-held radio. '*Zero – Delta Two One*.'

'Send.'

'I've responded to that call. I've found two pairs of severed hands in the fridge. No bodies, just hands. The flat's clear.'

'Roger. Wait out.'

I was now stood in the flat looking out of the window, but my mind was in a very different place. I couldn't imagine what in the name of God could have happened to result in two pairs of severed hands being put in the fridge. There was no blood anywhere. There were no bodies. So how did the hands end up in the refrigerator?

I stared out over the dark city, thinking: *What the fuck has gone on here? What the fuck?*

Five minutes later I got a radio call confirming they were sending out a team of 'body collectors' to retrieve the hands.

I walked downstairs. There was still the odd bit of scuffling going on, but the scrap was most definitely at an end.

'Right, lads, get in the fucking wagon. Leave 'em to it.'

Everyone got in.

'Let's go,' I told Taff. 'Let's just have a drive around for a bit.'

I was quite angry and the lads could feel it.

When we got back to our billet, Ginge popped the question. 'Steve, what was it with the flat, mate?'

I'd told the guys that when there was no one else around they were free to call me simply 'Steve'. If we had other military types about, they'd have to address me as 'Sergeant Heaney'. The Regular Army has this big thing about rank, and I wasn't about to mess with it.

J. Lo was upstairs, so I figured we could talk. 'I opened up the fridge and found a couple of sets of chopped hands lying on a plate.'

'*What?*'

'Yeah, two pairs of hands. Lying on a dinner plate. Don't say anything to J. Lo, obviously.'

The colour had drained from Ginge's face. 'Right,' he muttered. 'Okay.'

The reports started to come in thick and fast now. Bodies, body parts – there was stuff being found all across the city. The RMPs had jetted in a specialist HAZMAT – hazardous materials – team. They came equipped with full body suits, gloves and masks, plus body bags for zipping up the dead.

I was given their call-sign: *Romeo Three Zero*. At least someone still seemed to have a sense of humour.

I lay on the bed in the house we'd commandeered, but I couldn't seem to get that image out of my head. *Fucking hell, I hope they shot them first before sawing off their hands.* The hands must have been cut off somewhere else, for there was no blood. They must have bagged them up, carried them home, opened a kitchen cupboard, found a dinner plate, and laid them carefully on it, before popping them in the fridge.

But why take them home?

Were they some kind of sick trophy?

Or were they a depraved kind of a warning? *Revenge*?

Maybe the flat belonged to the former 'owners' of the hands? Maybe whoever had sawn them off popped them in the fridge, so whenever their relatives came to investigate they'd discover them lying there? *Imagine it.* Imagine getting your loved ones' hands back, but nothing else? It would torture you for the rest of your days.

I just couldn't get this shit out of my head.

Hands.

In the fridge.

On a dinner plate.

Fortunately, we got called out again pretty quickly. If I kept busy, maybe I could stop seeing those carefully crossed-over fingers in my mind.

The next job concerned a report from a couple who had been out walking their dog. *Go figure.* Life goes on, I guess. They'd come across a man leaning against an obelisk – a carved stone memorial situated on the outskirts of the city. Trouble was, they weren't sure if he was asleep or if he was dead.

I asked J. Lo where the obelisk was and how we got there. She said we needed to take the M9 to the northeast of Pristina, then head a kilometre or so into the hills. So off we went.

We'd been driving for twenty minutes or so when a report was radioed in from another patrol. They'd come across a body, but the locals had warned them that the Serbs had booby-trapped it. If they tried to move it or bag it up, they'd get blown to pieces. The warning was going out not to touch any of the dead, at least not before we'd checked they weren't a set-up, designed to blow our patrols to smithereens.

We arrived at a parking area overlooking the city. A point of 'scenic natural beauty' you'd call it. A path led up from there to a large stone monument, set on a rock plinth. The path took you into the rear of the monument, and I couldn't see anybody propped up against it.

I moved around to the front. A figure was slumped against the plinth. He looked about forty years old, he was wearing a brown tweedy jacket and slacks, and he was dead. It was weird. Otherworldly. Sick. He'd clearly been set where his dead eyes could look out over the city.

I got the guys to pull back. We put a call out for the HAZMAT team and settled down to wait. There had been no way that I could hide the existence of the body from J. Lo. It was very quiet in the Land Rover.

I got out and mooched about, wondering why they had placed the dead guy in that position. I could only imagine they'd set him there, telling him he could look out over the city they had 'cleansed', and that would be the last thing he would ever see.

My God, the hatred.

I couldn't see how they had killed him. There were no gunshot wounds on the body. No pools of blood, either. He'd been dead quite a while, though. His eyes were shut, his head was hanging down, and his skin was shrivelling up as his body started to dry out.

The HAZMAT team turned up. There were four guys, and they took a good look at the corpse. They clearly weren't very happy. 'Dunno. Looks risky.'

'Yeah. I know. Don't worry, we haven't touched it.'

'Looks like he's been set there . . .'

'Yeah. Booby-trapped.' I glanced at our Land Rover. 'Tell you what. Got some rope in the wagon. We'll clip the rope to the body with a carabiner, and drag it for a while, just to see what's what.'

The HAZMAT guys shrugged. Bomb disposal wasn't their baby. 'If you're good with that . . .'

'I'm good.' I turned to Ginge. 'Go get the rope, mate. The rest of you – back in the wagon.'

I figured I'd have to make the walk. Never ask your blokes to do what you're not willing to do yourself. Ginge passed me the rope with the carabiner – a D-shaped metal clip – attached to it. Slinging my weapon, I walked up the gravel path towards the body.

I approached closer. He was sat on the stone steps, his back against the plinth. I knelt in front of him, still not touching a thing. It's easy enough to booby trap a corpse. You grab a grenade, remove the retaining pin, hold the spring-loaded detonating lever down, and place the grenade beneath the body, so that the weight of it keeps the lever in place. The person moving the body releases the lever, the grenade detonates and . . .

I did a careful visual inspection, checking over the corpse as best I could. Then I reached forward, threaded the rope around the back and brought it around to the chest area, clipping the carabiner to the rope again. It was now looped around its torso.

That done I walked back down the gravel path, playing out the rope as I went. Problem. The rope ran out. I hadn't factored in how much we'd need to loop around the body and fasten it. There wasn't enough to reach the Land Rover's tow-hitch.

The answer was The Lump. 'Taff! Come and help me pull!'

Taff lumbered over.

'Get hold of the end of the rope,' I told him. 'Rather than a clean and jerk we'll do a steady pull, and back up ten steps.'

Taff nodded.

'You ready?'

Taff braced his back and shoulders. 'Yeah.'

'Start backing up; gradual, steady pull . . .'

We heaved and tugged. The body slumped forward. I tensed for a blast. We kept pulling, the corpse falling off the plinth onto its back. The body was surprisingly heavy. We had the rope twisted around our forearms, and we were using all our strength to haul it down the gravel path.

Fifteen seconds passed and still no explosion. No kaboom.

'Right, okay, Taff – that's enough.'

We stopped pulling. I turned to the HAZMAT guys. 'He's all yours.'

They walked past, knelt with a black body bag, zipped up the corpse and loaded it aboard their vehicle.

For us, it was a long, heavy drive back to the city.

We were getting a sense of the depths of depravity and evil that had descended on this place. It was hellish dark. Far worse than any of the TV reports had ever suggested. But at least we were getting an idea of the savagery that had been unleashed across this city; across this land.

Or so we thought.

In truth, we hadn't seen anything yet.

In truth, we hadn't even scratched the surface.

45

The next morning we were told to head for a patch of waste ground that ran between some blocks of flats. Gibbo wanted the area – a stretch of derelict bush, scattered with piles of rubble, abandoned fridges and burned-out cars – checked over.

We didn't know why exactly, but we approached the place with a real sense of foreboding. After we'd parked up, I left Ginge and Taff with the wagon, and walked between two low-lying tower blocks towards the open ground, with Hendo and J. Lo in tow.

I paused at the fringe of the wasteland. 'Let's just stand here for a second and see what we can see.' There were some paths running through, where people had made their way back and forth between the blocks of flats. I pointed to what appeared to be the main highway. 'Let's make our way down that path.'

I led off, J. Lo behind me and Hendo taking up the rear. The path twisted this way and that as it ran through waist-high grass. Over to my left was a cleared area, about ten yards by ten yards square. I saw the body more or less immediately, lying with its head and shoulders facing the path.

'Whoa, whoa, whoa – stop,' I announced. 'J. Lo, you wait here with Hendo while I go take a look.'

They did as instructed. I walked ahead and did a slow 360 all around the body. It was a young guy in his mid-twenties, dressed in a sports jacket, jeans and trainers. He looked like he'd once been a university student. He could even have been one of J. Lo's college friends.

His eyes and mouth had been taped shut with black gaffer tape. His feet and hands had been bound, before his legs and arms were pulled back so far that he ended up in a reverse foetal position. The right leg of his jeans was sliced open from his groin to his knee and it was soaked in dried blood. A huge amount of blood was pooled all around him, mixed with the grass.

I could see what they had done. They had cut his right femoral artery, and left him here to bleed to death. It takes around three minutes to bleed out and fall unconscious, after which death quickly follows. For all of that time he'd lain here in this bastard wasteland, knowing that he was dying, that no one was coming to help him, and that there was nothing that he could do.

I studied the body carefully to check for booby-traps. It took me maybe ten minutes to satisfy myself that he was most likely 'clean'. For all of that time I could hear kids' voices drifting across to me from the flats. I could hear laughter, people chatting and birdsong.

Getting to my feet, I returned to the others. 'Yeah, it's a young guy who's been killed. Let's walk back up to the wagon and I'll call it through.'

We headed back in silence. I radioed headquarters and they promised to have the HAZMAT team with us as soon as possible. I sent Ginge and Taff halfway down the track to stand guard. I didn't think anyone would be pitching up to steal the guy's body, but what else was I supposed to do?

As we waited, I had images flashing through my head of what they had done to him. They'd tied him with what looked like piano wire, or maybe really strong fishing line. He'd wriggled and writhed so much it had all but sliced through his wrists and his ankles. It was so deeply buried in his flesh that in places I couldn't even see it.

I had a taste of bile in my throat now. I'd had it first with the hands in the fridge, and now I had to fight back the urge to vomit. My first instinct was to hold the lads and J. Lo back from the worst, because they were young. They didn't need to see this. Plus with J. Lo I figured she might have known him.

Pristina wasn't a large city. He might have been her friend.

Fuck, for all I knew he could even be her brother.

She'd told us nothing about herself. Her family. We hadn't pried, because we didn't know what skeletons were lurking in her cupboard.

The HAZMAT guys pitched up, but again they were worried the corpse might be booby-trapped. Taff and I had to rope up and drag this one, too. Trouble was, the longer I studied the body, the less I was able to work out how to attach the rope. There was nowhere to tie it to.

Eventually, I had to loop it around his right arm, where it was tied behind his back. I was trying to offer the guy some form of dignity, even in his death, but it just wasn't possible. I explained to Taff that I only wanted to pull him a bit, and that we needed to be gentle. If we weren't, we'd rip his arm out of its socket.

We dragged him a few slow yards. That done, I called the HAZMAT guys over. I glanced at their body bag. 'Lads, you won't get him in there. Not unless you cut the wires.'

Reaching into my belt pouch I pulled out my Leatherman. 'Here.' I opened it up to the pair of pliers.

One of the HAZMAT guys took it, knelt by the corpse and sliced through the bindings. It took an age for him to do so. Then they forced him out straight and bagged him up.

He handed back the Leatherman. 'Thanks, mate. We're done. We'll get him to the morgue.'

'Where is it, exactly?' I asked.

'City Hospital.' He glanced at me. There was a haunted look in his eyes. 'You've got to see it. You won't believe it 'til you've seen it.'

We pulled in behind the HAZMAT guys' wagon and tailed them to the morgue. It was set far out on the city's western outskirts.

'Where are we going?' Ginge asked.

'We're following them to the hospital, to see where all the bodies are being put.'

Twenty minutes' drive.

Silence.

The City Hospital was a massive, slate-grey edifice, which didn't seem to have suffered the slightest bomb damage. It was an ancient, Soviet-style monstrosity of a place towering six stories high. The car park was choked with vehicles, and people were moving back and forth: hospital staff, trying to get the place up and running again.

We parked up alongside the HAZMAT vehicle at some orange steel shipping containers. They were rusty and dented and they had big metal shutters for doors. One of the HAZMAT guys got out and unlatched the nearest door. It creaked open. Inside was a plastic inner door. They got the body bag, slid it through the plastic door and disappeared inside.

The smell hit me first. *Oh my God.*

It was dark. Unrefrigerated.

It took a good few seconds for my eyes to adjust to the gloom. The interior of the shipping container was racked out with wooden shelves. They were piled high with body bags. But right near the door was a stack of wooden fruit boxes, like the kind grapes and bananas are delivered in.

Each contained a severed head.

Plus hands.

'Fuck . . .' I felt my senses reeling. 'Fuck . . . Whoa, lads, fucking hell.'

The nearest HAZMAT guy shook his head. 'Yeah. I know. I know.'

'I'm gonna have to go stand outside.'

I stepped out into the light. The lads and J. Lo were still in the wagon, thank God. Each body bag had a label tied to it, and each had a unique number.

'Bag zero two three. Twenty-five-year-old white male. Unidentified. Found in X area.'

It was the same with the hands and the heads.

I stood in the fresh air breathing deeply. The HAZMAT guys finished labelling up the corpse we'd just delivered, shut up the shipping container and came and joined me.

'What's with the heads and hands?' I asked. 'Why heads and hands?'

The nearest guy shrugged. 'That's what we're finding now. Lots of heads. Lots of hands. Headless bodies, plus hands and heads in other places.'

'Looks like they're trying to make the bodies unidentifiable,' another of the HAZMAT guys said. 'If you chop the hands and heads off, how will we ever ID them? There are no DNA records, plus the hospital staff say all their dental records have been burned and destroyed. So there's no way we can work out who's who.'

I shook my head. 'Fucking hell. That's . . .'

I felt a presence beside me. It was Ginge. 'Is that where the bodies are?'

'Yeah, but it's just a storeroom. You don't need to see anything in there.'

'Oh, right, okay.'

I turned back to the HAZMAT guys. 'Why're you storing them outside? Why in *shipping containers*?'

'The hospital mortuary's full. *Full.* If you want to go have a look, go have a look.'

There was just something about the way in which he said it. 'What is it about the mortuary?'

'Go have a look,' he repeated, slowly.

I don't know why I went. Was it morbid curiosity? Looking back on it, I don't think so. I just felt this driving need to work out their MO – the method to this sick, crazed madness. What would I gain? I'd know what we were up against. *Know your enemy.* It was a key lesson from my time in the Pathfinders.

Know your enemy.

The HAZMAT guy pointed to the massive hospital building. 'There's the mortuary – down on the basement level.'

I set off.

'You'll go down some stairs,' the guy called after me. 'But leave the door open, 'cause you'll need the light. And trust me, you'll need the air.'

I had forty yards to walk. It was a hot and sunny day and it was unusually breezy and airy for Pristina. As I neared the building the smell came to me on the wind. I went down some concrete steps and came to a door. It was solid metal with no windows.

I pushed down the handle and swung it back. The instant I did so the stench nearly knocked me off my feet. The air was torpid and gluey with putrid death. It was thickly sweet-sour in my bile-retching throat. I dragged my smock up over my face, bunching up the sweaty material to filter the air, but even so I had to fight the urge to vomit.

I started down the concrete steps. I couldn't bear this any more. I pressed my hand into my face as hard as I could, closing my nostrils and forcing the breath in through my mouth. Somehow I made the last few steps, and I could go no further.

The light was streaming in through the open doorway behind me, illuminating the windowless morgue. In front of me it was jammed wall to wall with hospital trolleys. On the bare metal of the trolleys were laid the corpses. Beyond those, there was just this huge heap of bodies, stacked one on top of the other.

The place was alive with maggots, larvae and flies.

It was a vision of utter hell.

I turned, stumbled up the steps and slammed the door behind me.

Ripping my face out of the smock I dragged in these massive gasps of air. Fresh air. Pretty much. *Life.*

I glanced at the Land Rovers. The HAZMAT guys were there, leaning over their bonnet and filling out some forms. My lads were there with J. Lo, killing time. No one had seen me come out yet. I stood there for a good five minutes, breathing hard and deep and trying to get a grip on myself.

Finally, I walked back to the vehicles. 'Come on, lads, let's go.'

'Is that . . .?' Ginge began.

'Yeah, the morgue. You don't need to go in there either. It's pretty unpleasant.'

We mounted up the wagon and drove back to our ghost house.

The days passed. We settled into some kind of a rhythm, retrieving bodies and body parts and breaking up fights. The fighting was becoming intense, as more and more people flooded back to the city intent on revenge. And all the while we kept our noses to the ground, trying to sniff out the bad guys. The perpetrators.

The KLA – the Kosovo Liberation Army, those who had fought against Milosevic's forces – were moving back en masse. They started taking over public buildings. Flying their flags from them. Walking about with KLA armbands in full view. Most were in some kind of uniform, and most were armed.

And no doubt about it, they'd come looking for revenge.

As luck would have it, my time on the 'Body Patrol' was pretty much done now. I was told to move to A Company's headquarters, for they needed a Senior NCO to run their operations room. This was it, then: time to say goodbye to my patrol.

I found J. Lo, Taff, Hendo and Ginge in the ghost house, having a brew. 'Right, lads, I'm getting posted to A Company,' I told them. 'You'll need to go speak to Captain Robbins, 'cause you'll be getting a new patrol commander and a new tasking. J. Lo – you'll most likely stay with the guys for now.'

Long faces all around.

'Lads, it's been great. You're a fantastic bunch, I enjoyed working with you, and you worked hard for me in tough conditions.' I glanced around the three of them. 'You should consider going for Pathfinder Selection, all of you.'

'Thanks, Steve.'

'Good stuff.'

'Yeah, cheers.'

I turned to the lady amongst us. 'J. Lo – good luck. It's been fabulous, and thank you most of all for the dancing. You have now got your city back. I hope it all works out. And you know something – whatever else you do, keep dancing.'

There were tears in J. Lo's eyes. There were in mine too.

It had been a tough few days. Emotional.

I didn't see them again until we all flew out at the end of July. J. Lo had been working for the HQ patrol as their translator.

I spent the rest of my time in Pristina running A Company Operations Room trying to keep the lid on an increasingly fractious city, and trying to nail the bad guys. When we pulled out I was proud of what we had achieved. Milosevic's killers were gone. We'd nabbed a good few of 'em. A semi-legitimate government was back in power.

In short, the British Army – the PARAs – had been first-in, and we'd won the prize.

There was nothing much left to do now. The Dutch and the Americans had arrived in force, as peacekeepers. We'd been there long enough for Captain Robbins to fall head over heels for J. Lo, and it was starting to feel like a force of occupation. We were dog tired, we'd been under weeks of unbelievable stress, and we needed to get ourselves gone.

The KLA were in the habit of driving around the streets in cars packed with pretty girls, leaning out of sunroofs and firing off their AKs and their Makarov pistols. All it would have taken was for one of our blokes to snap, and return fire, and we'd have completely spoiled a job well done.

It was our time to leave.

46

It was November 1999 – so four months on from Kosovo – when I returned to the Pathfinders as platoon sergeant. By now the unit had moved to a special facility reserved purely for the X Platoon, based at one end of Wattisham Airfield, in Norfolk, which also houses the Army Air Corps Apache Attack Helicopter (AH) Squadron.

We had our own highly secure, fenced-off area, complete with vehicle hangars, classrooms, Interest Room – the works. It was good to reconnect with all the old faces. Wag was there as the Platoon's operations warrant officer. The two of us were thick as thieves. And Jacko was there as our second-in-command.

We'd managed to grow the ranks to some forty-plus men, and I was looking forward to really gripping and shaping the unit.

Jacko and I shot the shit for a while about Kosovo, and what his father – the general – had got up to. I recounted the scene I'd witnessed, when General Jackson had fronted up to the American commanders, as they dismounted from their Black Hawks.

'What's the truth to the rumour your old man pretty much said we're not gonna go start World War Three with the Russians?' I asked.

Jacko smiled. 'That's it, pretty much. In a nutshell.'

'Is it? Shi–ite.'

We all knew the general had received a direct order from the Americans: *Get your force on those helos and stop the Russians, who are headed for Pristina airport. Stop and overpower them.* That's when General Jackson had responded: 'I will not be responsible for starting World War Three.'

I whistled. 'Good fucking call. All of us lot, plus seventy-odd RAF aircrew, would have died that day. And there were no Yanks going with us.'

Thank God for General Jackson.

First thing on my books as platoon sergeant was to organise some Arctic training, together with some rival elite forces' units, plus the Swedish Special Forces. We'd been asked to raise a four-man team and I decided to lead it.

I picked Tricky – my former Purple Dinosaur mucker – as patrol signaller. I chose Steve Brown – 'Steve B', a cracking bloke who was super-fit and very robust mentally – as my lead scout. Brian 'Bri' Budd – the soldier who would go on to be awarded the posthumous Victoria Cross, in Afghanistan – was patrol medic.

We deployed by C130 to Sweden, ending up in Karlsborg – a small town to the south of the country. From there we flew to the far north and parachuted on to a frozen lake. We pitched camp in the snows nearby, and proceeded to do a three-week 'skills package', which basically meant – at least it did for Tricky and me – learning how to ski.

Bri Budd and Steve B were real Franz Klammers, but I had never skied and neither had Tricky. I'd never spent so much time face-down in my life. By contrast, the Swedish SF guys had been born on skis. Each day we donned our Arctic camo-whites and set off into the snow, returning in the evenings to cook up some scoff and fall into an exhausted sleep.

At the end of the skills package we set off on the major Arctic exercise. We packed up the entire camp, placed our gear onto a 'pulk' – a hardened plastic sled on skis – and set off into the bleak whiteness. The pulk was operated by two skiers at the front pulling with ropes, and two guys behind steering. We had to carry all of our food, fuel and kit with us, so the contents of the sled weighed 175 pounds, which made it quite a haul.

When we reached the 'survival area' we RV'd with some Sami – the reindeer-herding tribe that inhabits Scandinavia's frozen north. The Sami killed some reindeer, and we jointed up the meat and packed it on the pulk – for that would be our main source of food for whatever was coming.

Next the Swedish SF guys cut a man-sized hole in the ice with a chainsaw. We had to ski into it as if by accident, with all our gear on – then remove skis and Bergens and clamber out, all before we froze to death. The only way to manage it was to throw your Bergen onto the ice, then drive your ski-poles into the ice vertically beside the hole, and use those as anchors via which to drag yourself free.

Once you were out you had to roll around in the snow, so it would 'soak up' the excess water, then start a fire as fast as humanly possible. Without a fire to dry yourself over, you'd freeze to death in no time. In the pulk we carried an iron-mesh wood burner, plus logs. Fire duly started, you'd change into some dry clothes and try to regain your core body heat.

You can see why I preferred the jungle.

The Final Exercise involved several four-man teams – Swedish SF, the rival elite forces' unit, plus us Pathfinders – getting inserted by helicopter into a giant snow-bound fjord. From there we had to ski ten kilometres west into an observation point, where we could get eyes-on a giant, frozen hydroelectric dam. We had to pitch a white tent, cover it in white camo netting, and obscure our ski and sled tracks – so that with the first dusting of snow we would be utterly invisible from the air.

After spending three days observing and logging activity at the dam, we were ordered to return to the original helicopter drop-off point. There we were picked up by the same Huey that had delivered us. But twenty minutes into the return flight the helo's alarm started blaring, and the aircrew went into a – simulated – crash-landing.

Once on the snow again the loadie passed us a slip of paper. 'Ski to that grid.'

We skied for five kilometres across a frozen lake, where we were met by another Swedish SF guy. He told us we needed to extract 'out of the country' for fifty kilometres on skis, for we were now on the run in hostile terrain. En route we had to RV with a series of 'agents', who would give us our next grid to head for.

We set off. My patrol had been the last of all to be pulled out of their obs position by the Huey. The first patrol had a good eight hours' start on us, and all the others were in front by an hour or more. We had five agents to RV with, each set ten klicks apart. By the time we reached the second agent – so twenty klicks in – we'd overtaken all seven of the rival four-man patrols.

We reached the final RV – an old and deserted school. We were told to clean and service our kit, get a rest and a brew on and get our heads down. We'd been asleep for ten hours, when the last four-man patrol finally made it in.

That last group got a right bollocking. 'They are the Pathfinders, and it's their example that you should be setting your sights on,' they were warned. I know this because the Swedish SF commander told me. He took me to one side at the end of the entire training programme. 'Steve,' he said, 'we really need to forge some links with you guys. You we do need to cross-train with.'

He gave me his card, and I said we'd be in touch and get it sorted. They were class operators, and in terms of Arctic skills they had everything to teach us.

For some reason there was no aircraft available to fly us back to Blighty, apart from the Royal Flight – the airliner the Queen and her entourage usually travel on. So they sent that over. I managed to have a butchers in the Queen's bedroom, and take a quick squirt of Prince Philip's aftershave.

I tell this Arctic training story simply to indicate the quality of guys we had in the X Platoon. We boasted some of the finest blokes in elite forces soldiering the world had to offer.

And for the operation that was coming, we were sure going to need them.

47

No operation would ever encapsulate the maverick, can-do spirit of the Pathfinders better than Sierra Leone. In May 2000 twenty-six Pathfinders deployed alongside 1 PARA, tasked to carry out an NEO – a non-combatant evacuation operation – in that war-torn West African nation.

The murderous rebels known as the Revolutionary United Front (RUF) were advancing on the capital city, Freetown, threatening to overrun it and unleash unimaginable brutality and savagery upon its long-suffering inhabitants. For good reason the RUF had been nicknamed 'Africa's Khmer Rouge': their signature was amputating the hands and feet of innocent villagers; of men, women and children.

But in contrast to Kosovo, they did not do so to disguise the identity of their victims. Their aim was purely to spread terror, for they adhered to some perverse kind of ideology that suggested via fear and force of arms alone they could seize control of an entire country and subjugate an entire people. They had plunged Sierra Leone into a ten-year civil war of sickening barbarity, and they were now poised to take the nation's capital.

The 1 PARA Battle Group was airlifted into the country to evacuate all 'entitled persons' – British passport holders and allied nationals. But in order to do so they needed to secure Freetown's main airport. Colonel Gibson was in command of the Battle Group, and Brigadier David Richards – the future Chief of the Defence Staff – was in overall command of the Sierra Leone deployment.

Both men figured the only way to secure the airport and get our people out was to put a stop to the rebel advance, and well before they reached the evacuation points. For their part, the RUF had vowed to 'do a Somalia' on the British – a reference to the 1993 rout of American elite forces in Mogadishu, the war-torn capital of Somalia. In other words, they were intent on driving us out of the country in sheer humiliation.

Battle was clearly going to have to be joined.

Brigadier Richards decided he needed to lure the rebels into a decisive firefight, one in which they could be given a right bloody nose. He needed a force to insert deep into the jungle, to deliberately lure the RUF onto their guns. That force would have no air support, little backup and no obvious escape routes, other than a major E & E through uncharted terrain.

We were chosen to be that force.

A unit of twenty-six Pathfinders facing 2,000-plus heavily-armed rebels.

We were inserted into the jungle way ahead of the main British force – the 800 men of 1 PARA. Typically, we had no heavy weapons, no body armour, no grenades, a fraction of the food rations we needed, no HE mortar ammuntion, bugger all ammo and the useless and much despised SA80 assault rifle.

We were also massively outnumbered and outgunned.

We reacted to the shittiest of situations by improvising as never before – a story as told in my first book, *Operation Mayhem*. We survived on stews made of giant African land snails and jungle fungi, and we launched a hearts-and-minds initiative with the local villagers to bring them onside. Without their help – their eyes and ears; their intel; their fighting spirit – we knew the coming battle could never be won.

With the locals' help we sowed the jungle with killer traps – ones that would wound, injure, incapacitate and ensnare the approaching RUF rebels. Again with the villagers' assistance, we manufactured our own DIY weapons out of old tins, wood, rusty nails, gravel and sharpened fragments of bamboo. As a result, when the rebels finally hit us they advanced into one shit storm of a death trap.

We survived that epic mission, fought off the rebels in a pitched battle, often at close quarters, and turned the tide of the war. In doing so I undertook one night-time mission that involved crawling ahead of our most-forward troops onto the enemy guns, to put up illume – flare rounds – via our man-portable mortar. The light above the rebels enabled us to see, target and kill them in their droves.

It was a crucial battle-winner.

That operation – which we nicknamed 'Operation Mayhem' – would became one of the most highly-decorated single missions undertaken by the British Army since the Second World War. In short, Sierra Leone was exactly the kind of mission that we in the X Platoon lived and breathed for.

I managed to blag myself a seat on one of the first post-mission flights heading back to the UK. I had special reasons. My brother, Neil, was playing in a crucial footie match, one that would pretty much decide whether his team got promotion or not. I'd missed his wedding. I'd missed a lot of other crucial family times. All the Heaney clan were going and I was desperate to make that match.

I flew out of Sierra Leone on the night of 25 May, and by mid-morning on the 26th my weapons and kit had been checked in at our Wattisham base. Kick-off at Wembley was 7.45 p.m. I could just make it. After grabbing a shower and a change of clothes, I caught a cab to the local station, and made the 2.54 train from Stowmarket to London, direct.

I sat on the train thinking: *Thirty-six hours ago I was in the African jungle, in the fight of our lives. And at least this time we've defeated those who believe that chopping off people's hands is a right and proper way to behave in this world.*

When I arrived in London, I took a cab across the city, and got to the Hilton Hotel adjacent to the stadium with an hour to spare.

I walked into the bar and surveyed the clientele, searching for my mum and dad and my sister-in-law, Isobel. It was my mum's voice that drew my eye.

I caught her saying; 'Cor blimey, doesn't that bloke look like our Steve?'

I wandered over. 'Hi Mum. Hi Dad. Hi Isobel. Hugs 'n' kisses, then.'

Mum promptly burst into tears. She cries at the change of the wind, these days.

'When did you get back?' Mum sobbed. 'Why didn't you call us? Where . . .'

'Whoa . . .' I silenced her. 'No questions. Let's just enjoy the day.'

'Beer, son?' Dad asked.

I smiled. 'Does a bear shit in the woods?'

As Dad ordered me a pint of lager, Mum was still trying to ask me all these questions.

'Look, love, he'll tell you when he's good and ready,' Dad told her.

It was a short walk to the stadium. We got seats over the tunnel where the players run out.

I spotted Neil, and yelled out: 'Oi! 'Eaney! You little shit!'

Well, I had drunk a few beers by then.

Neil glanced around. I could see this expression on his face: *You look just like my brother.* He obviously could not compute that I was here. They had all thought me off in deepest darkest Africa, soldiering for Queen and country. Which I had been, until a few hours ago.

'Mate, score one for me!' I yelled.

He knew it was me then. His face was a picture.

They played a blinder of a match and dominated the game, but a lucky goal from their opponents cost them their promotion. We made up for it with a skinful of beer in the Hilton afterwards.

And thereby ends a story.

*

I had a week's leave, and I was back to work at our Wattisham base early Monday morning. Captain Grant Harris, the Pathfinders' 2iC, pulled me to one side. Grant had been forced to take command in Sierra Leone, when we'd lost the unit's OC. He had done a blinding job of it, too.

'Just for your information, Steve, you and Nathe have been put forward for gallantry awards.'

Amongst many of the lads who had distinguished themselves in the Sierra Leone jungle, Nathe Bell, my foremost patrol commander, had done us all proud.

I was shocked at Grant's news. 'Oh. Okay, mate. Me and Nathe . . . Who by?'

'Myself, Jacko and Chris James wrote up the citations, and got 'em endorsed by Gibbo.'

Chris James was the 1 PARA adjutant.

'Oh. Well, thank you, mate, great.' I paused for a moment. 'Can't we just write everybody up? Every man on the op deserves something, your good self included, mate.'

Grant shook his head. 'No, mate. Gibbo said it needs to be selective, or else it'll get a blanket rejection. If we write everyone up, we'll likely get nothing. That's just how it is.'

I didn't think a great deal more about it. The pace of work – training, exercises, keeping the lads on a permanent roster of Ready Status in case of threats to UK or international security – kept me more than busy.

Several weeks later I was at home, in nearby Ipswich, on a few days' leave. It was 8 a.m. when the phone trilled.

'Who is it?' I mumbled. What I really meant was: *Who is calling this bloody early?*

'Steve, it's Lenny. You awake?'

'I am now, mate. But I'm in me scratcher.'

Lenny Croyden was our new OC at the Pathfinders, and a better man to command the unit you could never have wished for. He was a total diamond geezer.

'Mate, I've been to a meeting at Brigade in Colchester. I'm on my way back and I'm gonna stop by.'

I rubbed the sleep out of my eyes. 'Oh, really? Anything to worry about?'

'No, no, no. I'll be there in twenty.'

'Oh right, better get dressed, then.'

I pulled on some shorts and a vest, brewed a cup of tea and flicked on the news. A few minutes later a diesel Land Rover bumped up onto the kerb in front of the house. Lenny slid out of the driver's seat, in full uniform, two massive magnums of champers clutched in his hands.

I was standing there in my shorts and vest, mug of tea in hand, thinking: *What the fuck?*

Ding-dong! Ding-dong!

I opened the door. Lenny was married, so I was expecting him to announce: *I'm gonna be a dad!*

I'd taken Lenny through Pathfinder Selection, when I'd been his 'Staff'. We'd soldiered in the same patrol together and we were great mates.

'Are you gonna invite me in, or what?' he asked.

'Yeah, suppose so. Come on in.'

He followed me into the lounge and put the champers on the coffee table. I still had my brew in my hand. Then he undid his smock and pulled out a thin white envelope, with 'Sgt Heaney' handwritten on it. He handed it to me.

'You're gonna have to read that,' he said.

Straight faced. Not giving anything away.

I had no idea what it was, but I figured the champers meant I wasn't going to jail. I put the tea down next to the bottles, so now there were two magnums plus my big white brew mug sitting next to each other. I ripped open the envelope. Inside was a handwritten note on a 16 Air Assault Brigade letterhead, from Brigadier Wall, the overall Brigade commander.

> Dear Sgt Heaney, I have the great honour to inform you that you have been awarded the Military Cross in this year's Honours and Awards.
>
> Congratulations. Well done. The honour is justifiably earned.

I looked up from the page. 'Fucking hell, mate.'

Lenny cracked a smile from ear to ear. 'Right, let's get drunk.' He grabbed the first magnum and began ripping off the gold foil around the top. 'Oh, and by the way, Nathe got an MID.'

'Oh, right – fantastic.'

I was still in shock.

'Nathe already knows, but I wanted to tell you in person.'

'Oh, right – brilliant.'

Lenny was just about to pop the first bottle, when he stopped himself. 'Tell you what – I've got a better idea. The Platoon's got the day off. Let's take the champers, drive back to Wattisham, get the blokes and . . . *then* let's get drunk.'

'I tell you what mate, let's do it. But first – two phone-calls. Mam and Dad, then Neil.'

I phoned home and told Mum.

'Oh, brilliant,' she said. 'An MC, you say. So what's that then?'

I explained as best I could, and I could hear both her and Dad cheering on the end of the phone. 'I'm just gonna give Neil a quick tinkle, and then go get drunk with the blokes.'

I called Neil. My little brother was over the moon with the news.

I went upstairs and got dressed, then we jumped in Lenny's wagon and drove to Wattisham, heading direct to the Pathfinder Interest Room. By the time we got there, the entire Platoon had gathered. There were cheers and grins and pats on the back as we walked in.

The Interest Room is where the heart of the Pathfinders beats strongest. It's a long thin room, easy chairs and sofas slung around it, with a kitchen down one end. The walls are adorned with all the paraphernalia associated with a unit such as ours; war souvenirs from the four corners of the earth; shots of the blokes skydiving over the Mojave Desert.

There are plaques from just about every unit the world of the military elite has to offer; statues; gifts; empty shell cases; ammo tins; a US Ranger's decommissioned assault rifle; several ceremonial swords. Plus the glory wall – the photos of those injured or killed in the line of duty.

Lest we forget.

Down one end are two big fridges shoved in the corner and stacked full of beer.

Everyone got on the drink.

We figured, as Pathfinders, we'd earned it.

The End

INDEX